ELEMENTS
OF BIBLICAL
EXEGESIS

ELEMENTS
OF BIBLICAL
EXEGESIS

REVISED AND EXPANDED EDITION

A Basic
Guide for
Students and
Ministers

MICHAEL J. GORMAN

HENDRICKSON
PUBLISHERS

Elements of Biblical Exegesis: A Basic Guide for Students and Ministers, Revised and Expanded Edition
Hendrickson Publishers, Inc.
P.O. Box 3473
Peabody, Massachusetts 01961-3473
Copyright © 2009 Michael J. Gorman

ISBN 978-1-59856-311-5

Elements of Biblical Exegesis, Revised and Expanded Edition, is a revised edition of *Elements of Biblical Exegesis,* © 2001, which was a revised edition of *Texts and Contexts,* © 1994, 1998 Michael J. Gorman.

Printed in the United States of America

Second printing — November 2009

Library of Congress Cataloging-in-Publication Data

Gorman, Michael J., 1955–
    Elements of biblical exegesis : a basic guide for students and ministers / Michael J. Gorman.—Rev. and expanded ed.
        p. cm.
    Includes bibliographical references and index.
    ISBN 978-1-59856-311-5 (alk. paper)
    1. Bible—Criticism, interpretation, etc. I. Title.
    BS511.3.G67 2008
    220.601—dc22

                                                            2008029346

To my teachers and my students

The revised and expanded edition is dedicated especially to the memory of
Bruce Manning Metzger (1914–2007)
and to my daughter Amy, performer of Scripture

Table of Contents

Acknowledgments
Revised and Expanded Edition

As the second edition of this book goes to press, I of course wish to repeat the expressions of gratitude I made in the Acknowledgments for the first edition. In re-reading them, I am saddened to note the passing of my mentor, Bruce Manning Metzger, in early 2007. Until the end of his long and fruitful life, he was an active scholar (publishing his last book in late 2006) and a revered Christian gentleman. I dedicate this edition especially to his memory.

I dedicate it also to my daughter Amy, who is by any account a theological interpreter and a performer of Scripture. I love and admire her greatly.

Since *Elements of Biblical Exegesis* first appeared, in 2001, it has apparently filled a void in introductory biblical studies at both college and seminary levels, and even in certain courses in church settings. Used throughout the United States and in other countries as well (including Korea, where it has been translated into Korean), *Elements* seems to provide just the right combination of exegetical method and basic hermeneutics (interpretive theory), at least according to its users. For this edition, therefore, I add my deep gratitude to the students and their instructors who have utilized the first edition, found it to be helpful, and conveyed to me both their positive feedback and their recommendations for improvement. Among the professors who have helped to make the book better are my colleagues Tim Cargal, Dennis Edwards, and Ed Hostetter; my former colleague Paul Zilonka; and faculty members at other institutions, including especially J. Richard Middleton (Roberts Wesleyan College) and Fr. Michael Byrnes (Sacred Heart Major Seminary).

In 2005, Hendrickson issued a companion volume to this book, which I edited, entitled *Scripture: An Ecumenical Introduction to the Bible and Its Interpretation*. I am grateful to my current and former colleagues in the Ecumenical Institute of Theology at St. Mary's

Seminary & University in Baltimore for their contributions to that book and for the privilege of working together with them in theological education and interpretation.

I wish also to express again my gratitude to the many keen readers of Scripture I am privileged to know as colleagues and friends. I note for special recognition three who have led the way in the much-needed return to the theological interpretation of Scripture: Steve Fowl of Loyola College in Maryland, Richard Hays of Duke Divinity School, and Joel Green of Fuller Theological Seminary. I am grateful in particular to Joel for reading the revision of chapter 8 and making several insightful recommendations.

I also wish to thank my students, who have reacted to the book with both appreciation and suggestions. Terrye Ashby reminded me that my practice of doing exegesis in the context of prayer needed to be stated explicitly in the book. My current research assistant, Lenore Turner, contributed much to this edition by reading and commenting on the entire revised manuscript, with special attention to chapter 8, and by verifying and updating all print and electronic resources as well as the index. To both of them I say a special "thank you."

For this edition, I am grateful to Amanda Hanselman, a student of Richard Middleton, for allowing me to include her exegesis paper, and to Richard for suggesting the inclusion of an Old Testament paper and for connecting me with Amanda.

Finally, I once again express deep gratitude to my editor (and now, after all these years of working together, friend) at Hendrickson, Shirley Decker-Lucke. As I said in 2001, her belief in the project and astute suggestions have contributed immensely to its completion (now twice) and its success.

Acknowledgments
First Edition

I willingly acknowledge the input of others, especially my own teachers, in the development of the method described in this book. Among those who were especially formative were John Herzog, Gordon Fee, David Adams, Paul Meyer, and Bruce Metzger. Special thanks are due to the late Professor J. Christiaan Beker of Princeton Theological Seminary, whose clear procedure was surpassed only by the depth of the results obtained when he employed it. I am grateful to my former colleagues at the Council for Religion in Independent Schools who read the earliest manuscript and made helpful suggestions: Catherine Sands, the late Nancy Davis, and Daniel Heischman. I am also grateful to two friends from graduate school and teaching days at Princeton Seminary: Bart Ehrman, now of the University of North Carolina at Chapel Hill, and Duane Watson, of Malone College, each of whom reacted favorably to earlier versions of this book.

Likewise, I thank colleagues at St. Mary's Seminary and University who appreciated and made use of earlier forms of this book: Peter Culman of the homiletics department; Sr. Sarah Sharkey and Fr. Pat Madden, both formerly of the Scripture department; and Fr. Paul Zilonka and Steve McNeely, my current colleagues in New Testament. I owe a special debt of gratitude to Paul Zilonka, who carefully read every word of the manuscript in draft form and made many helpful suggestions. In addition, I am grateful to my colleagues in Hebrew Bible/Old Testament, Fr. Michael Barré, Ed Hostetter, and David Leiter, who provided assistance in preparing the bibliography.

I am also grateful to my friends and colleagues at other institutions who constantly force me to think carefully about both how and why I read the Bible, and whose interpretive abilities, in many cases, are extraordinary. I acknowledge particularly Steve Fowl (Loyola College in Maryland) and Greg Jones (Duke Divinity School), both of whom have been colleagues with me in the

Ecumenical Institute of Theology; Richard Hays and Stanley Hauerwas, both of Duke; Jim Brownson of Western Theological Seminary; and Frances Taylor Gench of Union Theological Seminary in Virginia. I of course do not hold them, or any of the other people mentioned in this book, responsible for my perspectives or for the execution of them in print or in the classroom. (Nor do I, of course, concur with each or any of them at every point along the way.)

I am especially grateful to my students at Princeton Theological Seminary and at St. Mary's Seminary and University (both the School of Theology and the Ecumenical Institute of Theology) for what they have taught me. Extra thanks goes to one of my students, Bill Garrison, who served as my research assistant throughout the writing of this book. He helped particularly with the bibliographical sections of the book and made a thorough critique of several drafts. His invaluable suggestions have improved both the content and the format. Seminarian George Gannon, my new research assistant, helped with the proofreading and indexing. Last but not least, very special thanks are due Annette Chappell and Bryan Lowe, two excellent students who both used early versions of the book and contributed their fine exegetical work to the final product.

Finally, I express gratitude to my editor at Hendrickson, Shirley Decker-Lucke. Her belief in the project and astute suggestions have contributed immensely to its completion.

Introduction
Revised and Expanded Edition

Much has happened in the field of biblical studies since the original publication of this book. There have been archaeological discoveries and rumors of archaeological discoveries (ossuaries and tombs being among the most notable). There have been new skirmishes in the Bible wars, especially over the interpretation of certain ethical issues. Some new translations have appeared, and some methodologies of biblical study have been revamped or fine-tuned.

However, arguably the most important development in the field of biblical studies since the turn of the twenty-first century has been the turn (or, rather, return) to the *theological* interpretation of Scripture. This development expresses a deep desire on the part of many biblical scholars and theologians to explore and articulate ways of biblical interpretation that attend to the biblical text primarily as theological text, as vehicle of divine revelation and address. To many outside the theological guild but inside the church (and perhaps even outside it), such a focus is altogether self-evident and natural. To many inside the guild, however, years of exposure to nontheological interpretation have made reading the Bible as Scripture seem almost abnormal, and those of us who wish to change this bias are aware of the challenges before us as we attempt to move forward in the appropriately theological task of biblical interpretation.[1]

Already discussed and embraced in the first edition of *Elements* (especially in chapters 1 and 8), theological interpretation receives much more attention in this edition, accounting for the most significant change: the considerable expansion and renaming of chapter 8. That chapter is now called, not merely "Reflection," but "Reflection: Theological Interpretation." Three points about these changes need to be made here.

---

[1] This paragraph is drawn, with minor modifications, from the opening paragraph of my article "A 'Seamless Garment' Approach to Biblical Interpretation." *Journal of Theological Interpretation* 1 (2007): 117–28.

First, theological interpretation does not own a particular exegetical method or methodology. Its practitioners can, and do, make use of a variety of methods. My own approach (expressed in this book) is still rather eclectic but largely synchronic, as discussed in chapter 1.

Second, the revised chapter 8 is longer and more theoretical than most of the other chapters, and deliberately so because of the subject matter. The chapter still makes practical suggestions, but it does so within a more fully developed framework than a purely "nuts-and-bolts" approach would do.

Third, despite the location of the extended discussion of theological interpretation near the end of the book, readers should not conclude that theological interpretation is an afterthought, or that it takes place only after all the "real work" of critical or scientific (historical and literary) exegesis is finished. Rather, theological interpretation involves an attitude, a modus operandi, and a goal (*telos*) that permeate the entire process. In sum, theological interpretation means reading the scriptural text as closely and carefully as possible, employing the best methodologies available, because theological interpreters believe that during and after that process they can hear God speak in and through the text.

This increased emphasis on theological interpretation does not in any way negate the basic historical and literary aspects of sound exegesis that any interpreter of the Bible needs to consider. In fact, interpreters who are not committed to a theological reading of the biblical texts will still profit from the basic approach and method advocated in this book. That is to say, whether one considers theological interpretation the main course or an unnecessary dessert, there are certain staples of an exegetical meal that are common to all careful readers of the Bible, and those staples constitute the building blocks both of this book and of any good exegetical method.

Another major addition to this edition is the inclusion of a much-needed sample exegesis paper on a text from the Old Testament/ Hebrew Bible. Other alterations to this edition are relatively minor but significant: changes to a few exercises, clarification and/or elaboration on several matters, and especially the addition of new resources. The purpose of the book, and its intended audience, remain the same: *Elements* provides students and ministers with an unapologetically practical approach to exegesis that is built on a strong theoretical foundation.

Introduction
First Edition

Father Robert Leavitt, the president-rector [until 2007] of the institution I serve, is an avid golfer with a three handicap. After he returned from a summer golf school at the famous Pebble Beach golf course in California, he surprised me by saying that his class included students of all abilities, from beginners to near-pros like himself. When asked how the instructors could meet the needs of such a diverse class membership, he responded, "They taught the basics." In fact, he said, that's what they do when PGA pros return to Pebble Beach for off-season instruction: they go back to the basics.

Preventing Exegetical Illiteracy

This book is about basics, about fundamentals. Designed for students, teachers, pastors, and others wishing to think and write about the Bible carefully, it began as a guide for seminary students learning to do careful analysis of the New Testament for classes, ordination exams, and preaching. First presented to classes and to study groups preparing for ordination exams in the Presbyterian Church (some of whom had failed their first attempt at the exam, usually because they lacked a clear method!), the material proved to be a simple-to-learn and helpful tool. It was then put down in writing as a brief hands-on guide to biblical exegesis.

In 1990 the Council for Religion in Independent Schools published a form of the guide as *Texts and Contexts: A Guide to Careful Thinking and Writing about the Bible,* which served many students in various settings. A revised edition, published first at St. Mary's Seminary and then by Wipf & Stock Publishers, served hundreds of students at St. Mary's Seminary and University, with much success.

This book is a thoroughly revised work, though the basic principles of the method have remained the same even as I have tried to incorporate new insights from the never-static field of biblical interpretation. I am told that students are still failing exegesis exams, and I know from personal experience that much of today's preaching still reveals ignorance of the basic principles of exegesis.

This book is offered, therefore, for use at several levels and in several ways. The concepts and method are understandable to beginning Bible students in colleges, universities, pretheology programs, and seminaries. For these students, both the discussion of the method and the practice exercises at the end of each chapter are recommended. The book is useful as introductory or collateral reading in a course on the Bible or on any part of the Bible, or it can be given to students for independent reading and reference. Its use does not require, nor does it preclude, knowledge of the Bible's original languages.

For more experienced students and for ordained preachers, the discussion of a clear, logical method for studying the Bible may give them something they have not found elsewhere. Most biblical scholars use something like the method presented in this book in their own thinking, writing, and teaching, but I am afraid that this strategy is often not communicated methodically to students. My experience with pastors as well as seminary students has confirmed this hunch. Furthermore, many of the exegetical handbooks in print are too detailed and complex for most students and preachers to use on a regular basis. This book suggests how to read the biblical text carefully, whether one is preparing to discuss a passage in class, write an exegetical paper, or venture into the pulpit. It can thus be used as a reference in classes or seminars in biblical studies, exegesis, or homiletics. For seasoned preachers, this book will not so much provide tips on how to preach the text as it will offer advice (or reminders) about how to read the text more responsibly.

Cautions

Three words of caution may be in order before we begin. First, although the elements or steps are simple, mastering this process is not easy. It requires hard work and trial and error—but the hard work will pay off.

Second, I do not want to create the impression that I believe the method presented in this book is the only way to think and write about the Bible. There are many other ways that can be used by the modern interpreter. The method presented here is for the basic but careful historical, literary, and theological analysis of a relatively short text, though its principles can apply to reading Scripture (and almost anything else) in general. The method presented here is chosen as the starting place by a wide variety of readers; it can also be useful to those who wish to supplement it with other interpretive strategies.

Third, therefore, this book is not intended to replace more detailed books on interpretation of the Bible, on specific literary genres, or on hermeneutics. I am convinced, however, that the already difficult task of biblical exegesis and interpretation is becoming so complex, with the unending array of new methods and methodologies (not to mention new historical discoveries), that many students and preachers are tempted to abandon any hope of being "scholarly" or even careful in their reading and use of the Bible. When that happens, students and preachers—not to mention the houses of worship and the general public—will (and do) suffer immense losses. This book is *deliberately* basic, not to curtail further study but to stimulate it and, in the meantime, to prevent disaster in the classroom and the pulpit. My agenda, therefore, is quite simple and straightforward: to help prevent exegetical illiteracy among everyday readers, teachers, and preachers of biblical texts.

Readers will notice that the length of the chapters varies considerably in proportion to the nature of the topic under consideration. The chapter "Detailed Analysis," for example, is much longer than the very short chapter "Survey." Readers will also notice that both sample exegesis papers, written by two of my students, are based on New Testament texts. That is solely because New Testament is the area in which I teach. [An Old Testament paper has been added for the revised and expanded edition.]

Suggestions for Teachers

1. It is beneficial to have students work through the entire text, both readings and exercises.

2. The book can be used in an introductory unit in a biblical studies course. Perhaps assign one section of the method, including at least one of the suggested exercises and the

appropriate section on resources for expanding and refining that step, per class. This results in a base unit of about eight classes for the students to work through the method. Then allow ample time for writing a draft and final copy of an exegetical paper, perhaps in conjunction with the main biblical books read in the course. Alternatively, the book can also be spaced out over a longer period of time, integrated with the course content.

3. Encourage students to think for themselves as they read the Bible. Emphasize the fact that all students, no matter what their background, can make a valuable contribution to the group's understanding of the Bible. One way to stress this is to assign a nonbiblical text, such as a newspaper editorial or excerpt from a historical document, for individual or class "exegesis" before beginning the study of the Bible.

4. Devote extra time to any section of this book that especially perplexes your students and, of course, to any section that *you* deem particularly important for your students. In my own view, the material on historical and literary contexts and on form, structure, and movement are the most crucial for students to grasp.

5. In class, you may wish to have students discuss, and even defend, their answers to the exercises. If time permits, do additional exercises together in class. The more students practice, the better their exegetical work will be.

6. Have students read the sections of the sample exegesis papers that correspond to each assignment, but only *after* reading the "theory" and doing the exercises themselves.

7. When assigning exegetical papers, start small, with perhaps an essay of three to four pages (750–1,000 words). Students may eventually be encouraged to write a substantial paper of 2,000–3,000 words or more, depending on the level of the course.

Orientation

CHAPTER ONE

The Task

Take up and read, take up and read.
—*A child at play, overheard by Augustine,
according to the* Confessions *8.12*

And now the end has come. So listen to my piece of
advice: exegesis, exegesis, and yet more exegesis!
—*Karl Barth, in his farewell to his students
before his 1935 expulsion from Germany*

What is exegesis?

Whether you are reading the Bible for the first time or you have
been reading it since early childhood, there will be passages that
seem nearly impossible to understand. There will also be passages
that you *think* you understand but that your instructors, class-
mates, fellow church members, or parishioners interpret quite
differently. These kinds of experiences occur when people read
any kind of literature, but we become particularly aware of them
when we read *religious* literature—literature that makes claims on
us. As we know, the Bible is the all-time best seller, a book read,
interpreted, and quoted by millions of people in countless ways.
It would be easy to abandon any hope of understanding the Bible
with some degree of confidence.

Such despair, however, is unnecessary. Although there are many
approaches to the Bible, there is also a fair amount of common
ground among responsible readers of the Bible. The purpose of
this small book is to help you read, think about, and write about
the Bible carefully and systematically using some of these common strategies. Although it is useful for the study of a portion of
the Bible of any size, it is designed primarily for intense, precise
study of a small section—a brief narrative, psalm, lament, prophetic oracle, speech, parable, miracle story, vision, or chapter-
length argument, etc.—most of which consist of no more than

several closely connected paragraphs. The technical term for such careful analysis of a biblical text is *exegesis,* from the Greek verb *exēgeisthai,* meaning "to lead out" (*ex,* "out" + *hēgeisthai,* "to lead"). In this chapter we consider the task of exegesis and survey the method proposed in this book.

Exegesis as Investigation, Conversation, and Art

Exegesis may be defined as the careful historical, literary, and theological analysis of a text. Some would call it "scholarly reading" and describe it as reading in a way that "ascertains the sense of the text through the most complete, systematic recording possible of the phenomena of the text and grappling with the reasons that speak for or against a specific understanding of it."[1] Another appropriate description of exegesis is "close reading," a term borrowed from the study of literature. "Close" reading means the deliberate, word-by-word and phrase-by-phrase consideration of all the parts of a text in order to understand it as a whole. Those who engage in the process of exegesis are called exegetes.[2]

Many people over the years have understood the goal of exegesis to be the discovery of the biblical writer's purpose in writing, or what is called the "authorial intention." While a laudable goal, this is often difficult to achieve. Many interpreters today reject authorial intention as the goal of exegesis. It can be hard enough to grasp our own intentions in writing something, let alone those of another person from another time and culture.[3] A more modest and appropriate primary goal would be to achieve a credible and coherent understanding of the text on its own terms and in its own context. Even that goal is a difficult one. This primary objective is often, though not always, pursued with a larger (and ultimately more important) existential goal—that somehow the text in its context may speak to us in our different-yet-similar context.

---

[1] Wilhelm Egger, *How to Read the New Testament: An Introduction to Linguistic and Historical-Critical Methodology* (ed. Hendrikus Boers; trans. Peter Heinegg; Peabody, Mass.: Hendrickson, 1996), 3.

[2] However, exegetes should resist the temptation to create a new verb "to exegete," as in "to exegete a text."

[3] Though always difficult, the pursuit of authorial intention may be wiser, easier, and more appropriate in certain situations. For instance, the task may be a bit easier in reading, say, part of a letter known to be from Paul than in considering a passage (say in 2 Kings) whose author is unknown.

Exegesis is therefore an *investigation*. It is an investigation of the many dimensions, or textures, of a particular text. It is a process of asking questions of a text, questions that are often provoked by the text itself. As one of my professors in seminary used to put it, the basic question we are always asking is, "What's going on here?" In some ways, that question is enough, but it will be helpful to "flesh it out," to give this basic question some greater form and substance. Exegetes must learn to love to ask questions.

To engage in exegesis is to ask historical questions of a text, such as "What situation seems to have been the occasion for the writing of this text?" Exegesis also means asking literary questions of the text, such as "What kind of literature is this text, and what are its literary aims?" Furthermore, exegesis means asking questions about the religious, or theological, dimensions of the text, such as "What great theological question or issue does this text engage, and what claims on its readers does it make?" Exegesis means not being afraid of difficult questions, such as "Why does this text seem to contradict that one?" Finally, exegesis means not fearing discovery of something new or puzzlement over something apparently insoluble. Sometimes doing exegesis means learning to ask the right questions, even if the questions are not immediately resolved. In fact, exegesis may lead to greater ambiguity in our understanding of the text itself, of its meaning for us, or both.

It would be a mistake, however, to think that we are the first or the only people to raise these questions of the biblical text as we seek to analyze and engage it carefully. Exegesis may also be defined as a *conversation*. It is a conversation with readers living and dead, more learned and less learned, absent and present. It is a conversation about texts and their contexts, about sacred words and their claims—and the claims others have made about them. As conversation, exegesis entails listening to others, even others with whom we disagree. It is a process best carried out in the company of other people through reading and talking with them—carefully, critically, and creatively—about texts. The isolated reader is not the ideal biblical exegete.

Nevertheless, we often read the Bible alone, whether by choice or by virtue of our "profession." Students are normally required to write exegesis papers on their own. Pastors or other ministers usually prepare and preach sermons or homilies, grounded in careful study of the text (we hope), on their own. Whatever outside resources students or ministers may or may not consult, they need a method for the careful study of their chosen or assigned text. They need a way to enter the ongoing conversation about this or that text with confidence and competence, so that they too may contribute to the conversation. Hence the need for an exegetical method.

The word *method,* however, should not be equated precisely with "scientific method" or "historical method." Good reading—like good conversation or any sort of good investigation—is an art more than it is a science. Exegesis, as we will see throughout this book, is therefore an *art.* To be sure, there are certain principles and steps to follow, but knowing what to ask of a text, what to think about a text, and what to say about a text can never be accomplished with complete certainty or done with method alone. Rather, an exegete needs not only principles, rules, hard work, and research skills, but also intuition, imagination, sensitivity, and even a bit of serendipity on occasion. The task of exegesis requires, therefore, enormous intellectual and even spiritual energy.

Exegesis, then, is investigation, conversation, and art. As conversation and art, exegesis requires an openness to others and to the text that method alone cannot provide. However, without a method, exegesis is no longer an investigation. Thus the principal focus of this book is on developing an exegetical method.

Choosing an Approach to the Task

Handbooks on "studying the Bible" and on "exegetical method" are plentiful. Some are simplistic, others incredibly complex. The method of exegesis presented in the following pages is neither. It may be similar to methods you have learned for reading and writing explications of poetry or other literature. For example, as a student of French in high school and college, I learned how to examine French literature closely, just as students in France do. The process and result was called an *explication de texte.* As noted above, this way of careful reading of a small portion of literature is sometimes known as "close reading." If you have never learned such a method, this book will also help you to be a more careful reader of literature in general.

The approach to exegesis advocated in this book is grounded in the conviction that we can read a text responsibly only if we attempt to understand the unique setting (historical context) in which it was produced and in which it is situated (literary context).

Furthermore, we can understand a text only if we pay careful attention to both the whole and the parts (details), the proverbial forest as well as the trees. Before considering in detail the approach to exegesis proposed in this book, we need to understand something about the options available. In order to do that, we must become familiar with some rather technical terms.

Exegesis can be, in fact, a very technical field of inquiry. Interpreters of the Bible employ a variety of general approaches and specific methods to understand and engage the text. Some of these methods are called *criticisms*. The use of the term *criticism*, as in *redaction criticism*, does not necessarily imply negative judgment; the primary meaning of the term is *analysis*, though it may also mean judgment—whether negative, positive, or both—about the historical, literary, or theological value of a text.

There are perhaps three basic approaches to exegesis today. We will call them *synchronic, diachronic,* and *existential.*

The Synchronic Approach

One approach to exegesis is called *synchronic* (meaning "with[in] time," i.e., "same time"; cf. "synchronize"). It may be compared to a cross section of a plant's stem depicted in a biology textbook. This approach looks only at the final form of the text, the text as it stands in the Bible as we have it. It is not interested in the "long view" or "prehistory" of the text—any oral traditions, earlier versions, or possible written sources (such as the hypothetical sources called J, E, D, and P in the Pentateuch or Q in the gospels[4]). Rather, the synchronic approach uses methods designed to analyze the text itself and the text in relation to the world in which it first existed as a text. The most common labels for this approach are narrative-critical, social-scientific, and socio-rhetorical. (Rhetoric is the art of effective communication.) Socio-rhetorical criticism, for example, may be defined as an approach that "integrates the ways people use language with the ways they live in the world."[5]

---

[4] On these matters, consult any introductory OT or NT text, or see "The Character and Composition of the Books of the Old Testament" by David Leiter and "The Character and Composition of the Books of the New Testament" by Michael J. Gorman, in Michael J. Gorman, ed., *Scripture: An Ecumenical Introduction to the Bible and Its Interpretation* (Peabody, Mass.: Hendrickson, 2005), 45–70, 71–90.

[5] Vernon K. Robbins, *Exploring the Texture of Texts: A Guide to Socio-Rhetorical Interpretation* (Valley Forge, Pa.: Trinity, 1996), 1.

This book will devote significant attention to synchronic methods of exegesis, but without a lot of the technical language that sometimes accompanies the discussion of these methods. They include:[6]

- **literary criticism**—the quest to understand the text as literature by employing either traditional or more recent models of literary criticism that are employed in the study of literature generally; corollaries of literary criticism are **genre and form analysis,** the quests to classify a text as to its type

- **narrative criticism**—as a subset of literary criticism, the quest to understand the formal and material features of narrative texts (stories) or other texts that have an implicit or underlying narrative within or behind them

- **rhetorical criticism**—the quest to understand the devices, strategies, and structures employed in the text to persuade and/or otherwise affect the reader, as well as the overall goals or effects of those rhetorical elements

- **lexical, grammatical, and syntactical analysis**—the quest to understand words, idioms, grammatical forms, and the relationships among these items according to the norms of usage at the time the text was produced

- **semantic or discourse analysis**—the quest to understand the ways in which a text conveys meaning according to modern principles and theories of linguistics

- **social-scientific criticism**—the quest for the social identity, perceptions of the world, and cultural characteristics of the writers, readers/hearers, and communities suggested by the text; usually divided into two distinct subdisciplines, **social description** and **social-scientific analysis**[7]

If these terms and the methods to which they refer seem at first foreign or complex, readers should bear in mind that they have probably already been introduced to them in the study of litera-

---

[6]For a more inclusive overview of the various criticisms and the questions they seek to answer, see the table in Appendix A.

[7]The questions asked and/or methods used in this type of biblical criticism are often those of the social sciences, such as sociology and anthropology. Some scholars would suggest that social-scientific criticism is not truly a synchronic method but is rather a new approach to traditional questions of historical criticism (described below as a diachronic method), which has been concerned broadly with the historical genesis and context ("background") of biblical documents. For our purposes, we may say that the primary difference between the two criticisms is one of emphasis, whether on describing and analyzing the social setting contemporary with the biblical text (social-scientific criticism) or on reconstructing the historical developments that led to the production of the biblical text (historical criticism).

ture. The synchronic approach to the text is quite similar to the way in which literary critics analyze a poem or other short text. Literary critics, when explicating a poem, for example, may consider the following features of it:

- **genre and implied situation**—the type of literature the text is, and the life situation implied by the text

- **intellectual core**—the topic and theme ("slant") of the text

- **structure and unity**—the arrangement of the text

- **literary** (e.g., poetic) **texture**—the details of the text

- **artistry**—the beauty of the text[8]

As we will see, these are all very similar to the elements of exegesis presented in this book. Many advocates of a primarily synchronic approach to texts also incorporate some of the methods of diachronic exegesis discussed below.

A synchronic approach to the Sermon on the Mount (Matthew 5–7) might ask questions such as the following:

- What are the various sections of the Sermon, and how do they fit together to make a literary whole?

- What does the narrator of this gospel communicate by indicating the setting of the Sermon, the composition of the audience before and after the Sermon, and the audience's reaction to it?

- What is the function of the Sermon in the gospel's portrayal of Jesus and of discipleship?

- How would a first-century reader/hearer understand and be affected by this Sermon?

The Diachronic Approach (The Historical-Critical Method)

The second approach to exegesis is the *diachronic* (meaning "across time") approach, and it focuses on the origin and development of a text, employing methods designed to uncover these aspects of it. It takes the "long view" of a text and may be compared to a longitudinal perspective on a plant stem in a biology text. As a constellation of methods, this approach is often referred to as the *historical-critical method,* and it was the approach of choice by many, if not most, biblical scholars of the twentieth century.

---

[8]Adapted from Leland Ryken, *Words of Delight: A Literary Introduction to the Bible* (2d ed.; Grand Rapids: Baker, 1992), 207–11. Similarly, the basic standard parts of an *explication de texte* in French literature are situation, form, subject, analysis, and conclusion.

This book will give some, but limited, attention to the so-called historical-critical methods of exegesis. They include:[9]

- **textual criticism**—the quest for the original wording of the text (and the ways later scribes altered it)

- **historical linguistics**—the quest to understand words, idioms, grammatical forms, and the relationships among these items, often with attention to their historical development within a language

- **form criticism**—the quest for the original type of oral or written tradition reflected in the text, and for the sort of situation in the life of Israel or the early church out of which such a tradition might have developed[10]

- **tradition criticism**—the quest for understanding the growth of a tradition over time from its original form to its incorporation in the final text

- **source criticism**—the quest for the written sources used in the text

- **redaction criticism**—the quest for perceiving the ways in which the final author of the text purposefully adopted and adapted sources

- **historical criticism**—the quest for the events that surrounded the production of the text, including the purported events narrated by the text itself[11]

A diachronic approach to the Sermon on the Mount might ask questions such as the following:

- What written or oral sources did the evangelist (gospel-writer) adopt, adapt, and combine to compose this "Sermon"?

- What are the various components of the Sermon (beatitudes, prayers, parables, pithy sayings, etc.), and what is their origin and development in Jewish tradition, the career of the earthly Jesus, and/or the life of the early church?

- What does the evangelist's use of sources reveal about his theological interests?

- To what degree do these teachings represent the words or ideas of the historical Jesus?

---

[9]For an overview of the various criticisms and the questions they seek to answer, see the table in Appendix A.

[10]The technical term for this phenomenon (the "situation"), though it is now less widely used, is the German phrase *Sitz im Leben* ("setting in life").

[11]I am using the term "historical criticism" in a rather general way to encompass the investigation of what has often been called the "occasion" of a document's writing as well as any other historical events related to the genesis, development, production, and background of the text under investigation. In this sense, as indicated in an earlier note, "historical criticism" and "social-scientific criticism" are closely related but differ in emphasis.

There are some critics of the diachronic method who want to retain its historical emphasis but find the presuppositions of some of its practitioners (e.g., those who deny the possibility of miracles or the role of God's Spirit in the production of the Bible) inappropriate for the study of Scripture. They might propose a modified historical-critical method, one that accepts some of the goals of the method but not its "alien" aspects. One such scholar has proposed using the term "historical biblical criticism."[12]

Practitioners of the diachronic approach are also interested in some of the questions raised by advocates of a more synchronic approach to the text. They may, for example, combine rhetorical criticism with more traditional historical-critical methods. Indeed, few exegetes today are "pure" practitioners of a diachronic approach.

The focus of investigation in both the diachronic and the synchronic approaches to the text is twofold: the world *of* or *within* the text and the world *behind* the text. That is, exegetes who investigate the text with these methods are literary and historical critics—analysts of the historical and literary features of the text. There is clearly some overlap in the two approaches. For example, practitioners of both approaches are interested in the historical or sociopolitical contexts in which texts come to life and in the kind of literature texts are. But these are not the only possible focal points of investigation of a text. Some readers want to focus on the world *in front of* the text, the world that the text "creates."

The Existential Approach

A third approach, which has no commonly used name, may perhaps be labeled *existential*. Since it is an increasingly common but also occasionally criticized approach to exegesis,[13] we will consider

---

[12]Karl P. Donfried, "Alien Hermeneutics and the Misappropriation of Scripture," in *Reclaiming the Bible for the Church* (ed. Carl E. Braaten and Robert W. Jenson; Grand Rapids: Eerdmans, 1995), 19–46, esp. 22–25.

[13]Choosing an appropriate label for this approach is extraordinarily difficult, and none is completely satisfactory. Other options, all of which have problems of their own, include *hermeneutical, instrumental, transformative, self-involving, pragmatic,* and *interactive.* (As we will see, the main "existential" approach is *theological,* and though it is tempting to use that label here, theological interpretation is actually part of a wider approach to reading texts.) Two points of clarification about the term used, and the concept it represents, are in order. (1) By using the term existential, I do not mean to make any connection to existentialism as a

it now in more detail than the others noted above, which are thoroughly discussed in many handbooks[14] and which will be considered as part of the exegetical procedure outlined in subsequent chapters.

Proponents of the existential approach to reading the Bible are primarily interested not in the text per se—whether understood in terms of its formation (diachronically) or its final form (synchronically)—but in the text as something to be engaged. Existential methods are therefore "instrumental" methods: they allow the text to be read as a means to an end, not as an end in itself. The end, or goal, of this kind of reading is often an encounter with a reality beyond the text to which the text bears witness. This "something beyond" may be a set of relations among people, a "spiritual" truth beyond the "literal" truth, God, and so on. The exegete may desire either to embrace or to resist the reality, depending on the nature of the reality perceived and encountered. Those who approach the text fundamentally to encounter God through the mediation of the text may refer to this approach as *theological* and *transformative*.

More generally, we may describe this approach to exegesis as *self-involving;*[15] readers do not treat the text as a historical or literary artifact but as something to engage experientially—something that could or should affect their lives. The text is taken seriously

---

philosophy or to identify this approach exclusively with the specific existentialist interpretation of the Bible associated with the name of Rudolf Bultmann. I especially differentiate this approach to exegesis from the very individualistic emphasis found in Bultmann. (2) Some practitioners of exegesis more narrowly understood would argue that existential exegesis is not exegesis at all but *interpretation*, or *hermeneutics* (the technical term for interpretation). This argument often incorrectly assumes that diachronic (and perhaps also synchronic) approaches are objective or scientific while existential readings are biased. In fact, however, all reading is biased, and the methods chosen affect both what is observed and which conclusions are drawn. Moreover, this third approach to exegesis has likely been the main one used by the majority of Bible readers throughout history, with the possible exception of some professional biblical scholars of the last two centuries or so. Its legitimacy is, nonetheless, still questioned by some professional theologians and biblical scholars, while others advocate it vigorously.

[14] See chapter 11, section 1, pp. 182–89, "Resources for Understanding the Task."

[15] For a use of this concept that rescues it from the privatistic inclinations of existentialism, see Anthony C. Thiselton, *New Horizons in Hermeneutics: The Theory and Practice of Transforming Biblical Reading* (Grand Rapids: Zondervan, 1992), 272–307, 564–66, 615–18.

with respect to human existence now, both individual existence and life in community (the private self and the corporate self). The reader wants to engage not merely the world behind the text or the world of the text but the world *before* the text. Powerful texts in general, and religious texts in particular, have the ability to create an alternative world and to invite their readers to engage it.

By using methods that allow their own participation in the exegesis, existential readers enlarge the contexts within which the biblical text is read:[16]

- **theological exegesis, missional interpretation, and spiritual (or sacred) reading *(lectio divina)*—**exegesis is done in the context of a specific religious tradition and for religious purposes.

- **canonical criticism—**exegesis is done in the context of the Bible as a whole.

- **embodiment or actualization—**exegesis is done in the context of attempting to appropriate and embody the text in the world.

- **ideological criticism (including postcolonial criticism), advocacy criticism, and liberationist exegesis—**exegesis is done in the context of the struggle *against* unequal power relations and injustice and *for* justice or liberation.

These contexts significantly affect the methods, goals, and results of exegesis.

The existential approach to reading texts also challenges the ideologies of education and knowledge that have been pervasive in the West since the Enlightenment. Such ideologies tend to equate knowledge and education with the acquisition of information. Existential, transformative approaches to knowledge and education are at least equally interested in the formation of a certain kind of people. This kind of knowing is sometimes called "embodied knowing." It will ring true to those who have theological interests in "studying" the Bible.

The existential approach to the text might ask the following kinds of questions of the Sermon on the Mount:

- To what kind of contemporary faith and practice does the Sermon call contemporary readers?

- How might the text about "turning the other cheek" be a potential source of difficulty or even oppression for the politically or socially downtrodden?

---

[16] For an overview of some existential methods, see the table in Appendix A.

- Does love of enemies rule out the use of resistance or violence in every situation? What does it mean *practically* to embody the teachings about nonviolence in the Sermon?

- What spiritual practices are necessary for individuals and churches to live the message of the Sermon in the contemporary world?

Readers who approach the text in this way use diverse methods and have a wide variety of goals or agendas. Both diachronic and synchronic methods can be appropriated, and others may be introduced as well. Practitioners of existential exegesis judge the adequacy of any specific method on the basis of its ability to assist in achieving the overall goal of exegesis—its *telos.* This goal may be described as something rather general, such as transformation or spiritual formation, or as something more specific, such as liberation or an encounter with God.[17]

Excursus: Some Types of Existential Exegesis

Existential approaches to the biblical text can be divided into two basic types, those that operate with a fundamental trust in or consent to the text, and those that operate with a basic suspicion of the text. Theological exegesis, *lectio divina,* missional interpretation, canonical criticism, and embodiment are types of existential approaches listed above that are approaches marked fundamentally by trust/consent. Ideological criticism, advocacy criticism, and liberationist exegesis are approaches marked by suspicion.

Trust/Consent

The most ancient existential approach is that of *theological exegesis* or *theological interpretation,* which is currently undergoing a great revival.[18] Practitioners of theological exegesis read the text primarily as a reliable vehicle of, source of, or witness to God's revelation and will, which are discerned especially in communal reading and conversation. These interpreters read the Bible as a means of religious formation, both attitudinal and behavioral, experiencing the exegetical process, in some sense, as an encounter with God. This approach may make use of any or all of the diachronic and synchronic methods, but it also often involves expanding both the contexts within which the text is read and the kinds of methods used. This is because the biblical text is under-

---

[17] For further discussion, see Stephen Fowl, "Theological and Ideological Strategies of Biblical Interpretation," in *Scripture* (ed. Gorman), 163–76.

[18] A fuller discussion of theological interpretation may be found in chapter 8.

stood as more than a historical artifact or literary work; it is viewed as sacred text, as Scripture.

Theological exegetes may also take into account the perceived purposes of God—the divine mission *(missio Dei)*—in salvation history, the incarnation, or the paschal mystery (the death and resurrection of Jesus) as contexts for interpretation. Practitioners of *missional interpretation* specifically read the biblical text as witness to God's purposes in the world and as invitation to participate in that divine activity.

Theological exegetes often practice some form of *canonical criticism* by taking into account the canonical context—the place of the text in the entire Bible as the religious community's book—whereas a purely diachronic or historical-critical approach would find that anachronistic (since the entire Bible did not exist as one book when a particular biblical document was composed). They may also appeal to tradition or "the rule of faith" (i.e., the confessional framework of orthodox belief, such as the Nicene Creed) as the context for and guide to appropriate exegesis. In each case, theological interpretation enlarges the context of biblical interpretation beyond a text's immediate historical and literary context to include the church's canon and/or confession.

Further, advocates of theological exegesis sometimes appeal to *premodern* or *precritical* ways of Jewish and Christian reading of the Bible that allow for a variety of meanings in the text. The additional ways, which may include allegorical reading, yield meanings that are sometimes referred to as spiritual or figurative rather than literal meanings.[19] The current revival of interest in the "fourfold sense of Scripture" is especially important. This medieval way of reading the Bible insisted that scriptural texts had (normally three) meanings in addition to the "literal" or "plain" sense. Although the methods currently used differ from their medieval counterparts, the questions asked by the methods are the same: What are we to believe (faith), to expect (hope), and to do (love)?[20]

---

[19]It should be noted that some contemporary theological exegetes zealously advocate the overthrow of most modern or critical, especially historical-critical, approaches to the Bible (those developed largely since the Enlightenment) in favor of premodern or precritical (pre- Enlightenment) exegesis. Such ancient methods (including, for example, allegorical reading of the text) had their appropriate pride of place in their day, and they still have much to teach us. It is unlikely, however, that we can or should simply return to premodern ways of reading and ignore the contributions of modern scholarship. Ironically, some advocates of precritical approaches employ very modern philosophical understandings of language and meaning to justify their rejection of modern critical methods.

[20]These correspond to the medieval interpretations usually labeled allegorical (concerning doctrine), anagogical (concerning the future hope), and tropological (concerning behavior). For an introductory

A less academic variation of theological exegesis is the ancient and re-vered practice of spiritual reading, or *lectio divina* (literally, divine or sacred reading). In some circles this term may be unfamiliar, but similar practices may be called devotional reading. *Lectio divina* is an approach to reading the Bible that uses contemplation and meditation in the context of prayer to encounter God and God's word to the individual or community. Since the goal of spiritual reading is contemplation and formation (spiritual growth), not information or analysis, exegetical methods might seem superfluous. But they are not. Meditation on a text means "chewing on it"[21] and requires asking questions of the text that are similar to the ones asked by exegetes who use synchronic, and even some diachronic, methods.

Finally, many recent approaches to the Bible stress that, since the ul-timate goal of biblical exegesis is not information but transformation, true exegesis is accomplished only when individuals and communities engage in the *embodiment* or *actualization* of the text. The reading community, we might say, is to become a "living exegesis" of the text. (We will have more to say about all of this in chapter 8.)

Suspicion

A quite different, and much more recent, existential approach is known as *ideological criticism*. Practitioners of ideological criticism see the text as a witness to relations of power that can be harmful, especially to cer-tain groups of marginalized people. Often using recently developed social-scientific methods, they seek to uncover and eventually to dis-arm the relations of oppressive power that the text both signifies and sanctions. The text is read and then "un-read" as a means of naming and being freed from oppression.

Postcolonial criticism, a type of ideological criticism, is the analysis of texts by those who have been affected by, or sensitized to the effects of, colonization. It focuses especially on the presence of both affirmations and criticisms of empire and colonization in the Bible, and on ways in which the Bible has been read (or is currently read) to underwrite vari-ous forms of empire and colonization. Postcolonial criticism includes the critique of powerful colonizers' interpretation of biblical texts.

Somewhere between theological and ideological exegesis, but usu-ally embodying a spirit of suspicion, lie *advocacy criticism* and its most common manifestation, *liberationist exegesis*. This type of exegesis is often theological in that it may bring an ethical or theological goal and criterion to the process of reading: the thing advocated or the libera-

---

discussion, see Carole C. Burnett, "The Interpretation of the Bible be-fore the Modern Period," in *Scripture* (ed. Gorman), 133–45.

[21]See, for example, M. Robert Mulholland Jr., *Invitation to a Jour-ney: A Road Map for Spiritual Formation* (Downers Grove, Ill.: InterVarsity, 1993), 114.

tion sought is often, though not always, understood as God's purpose in self-revelation. Texts are judged by their perceived ability to liberate (or to be used more generally for advocacy) or not. Like ideological criticism, liberationist exegesis often draws on social-scientific methods and models and is concerned to name and address oppression. Similarly, some forms of postcolonial criticism engage in advocacy and do so for explicitly theological reasons.

The Approach of This Book

At this point, what can the average careful reader of the Bible do? The range of options can seem overwhelming. What we need is a model of exegesis that takes account of all these approaches but does not require a Ph.D. in biblical studies (or in history, sociology, and linguistics) to execute. We need a model that recognizes the common features of biblical texts as ordinary devices of human communication while also recognizing the importance of distinctly "sacred" features of biblical texts.

The approach advocated in this book is somewhat of an eclectic and yet integrated one, drawing on the insights and methods of all of the three basic approaches mentioned above, but maintaining that there is no one "right" way. In fact, the approach of this book is compatible with all three clusters of methods in use today and can serve as a foundation for more detailed or sophisticated work that does stress one approach over the others.[22]

Nonetheless, of the three approaches, the first, or synchronic one, is predominant in this book, especially vis-à-vis the diachronic, or historical-critical, approach. There are several reasons for this emphasis. The most important reason is that all exegetes, whether beginners or professionals, deal directly with the final form of the text. It is this text that readers read, preachers preach, and hearers hear. Another reason is that the other two approaches may require technical historical and linguistic skills or sophisticated theological perspectives that not all readers possess. Furthermore,

---

[22]For a comprehensive theoretical approach to interpretation that seeks to integrate all three of the basic approaches discussed here, see Sandra M. Schneiders, *The Revelatory Text: Interpreting the New Testament As Sacred Scripture* (2d ed.; Collegeville, Minn.: Liturgical, 1999), esp. 97–179. A similar holistic approach, with a more hands-on format, may be found in W. Randolph Tate, *Biblical Interpretation: An Integrated Approach* (3d ed.; Peabody, Mass.: Hendrickson, 2008).

the value (and even the possibility) of a purely historical-critical method has been questioned by many in recent years. Finally, even those whose primary goal in reading the text of Scripture is spiritual formation, the establishment of doctrine and practice, or human liberation must read in a way that is attentive to the form and substance of the words and images of the text. Indeed, existentialist approaches generally use many of the synchronic methods of biblical exegesis.

Having said all that, I would be remiss if I did not acknowledge that, as much as I enjoy careful textual analysis as a task in itself, my own ultimate aim in reading Scripture is theological—and I suspect that it is as well for many readers of this book. In my experience, an eclectic but largely synchronic approach best serves this existential *telos*.

The guidelines presented in this book rest on several assumptions. Chief among these is the assumption that the Bible must be read in its various contexts—those things that accompany, or go "with" (Latin *con*), the text itself. This assumption, and the method of interpretation it produces, attempts to take many factors into account:

- that the Bible is the work of many people, written over a period of more than one thousand years in many different specific historical situations (the historical, social, and cultural contexts)

- that every biblical passage is located within a larger work and that it contributes to the aims of that work (the literary and rhetorical contexts)

- that the Bible, like other sacred texts, gives expression to humanity's thirst for meaning and value in life (the human context)

- that for Christians and Jews the Bible is a unique and authoritative revelation of and/or witness to God's activity in history (the biblical/canonical and religious contexts)

- that all readers of the Bible, no matter how novice or sophisticated, interpret the Bible from within their own social situations and worldviews, and these social and intellectual locations affect the ways in which they understand the Bible (the contemporary context)

Each of these contexts has significant impact on the interpretation of biblical texts, and the careful reader must be aware of all of them.

A corollary to the last assumption ought also to be noted here: because of each reader's own unique experiences and "location," he or she will have insight into the Bible that no one else will have. Each reader can learn to bring together literary and historical perspectives as well as personal experience to understand a written text in a way that is unique to that individual and that contributes to the ongoing conversation about the text. Although the isolated individual is not the ideal interpreter of Scripture, there can be no conversation without unique individuals contributing to the discussion.

At the same time, however, there are necessary safeguards to ensure that one's *ex*egesis of the Bible is not really *eis*egesis—reading *into* the text (the Greek *eis* meaning "into").[23] A sound exegetical method is one such safeguard. Other safeguards include both the basic tools of biblical knowledge and research (Bible dictionaries, maps, concordances, etc.) and the fruits of research and reflection produced by biblical scholars and other interpreters of the Bible (in commentaries, journal articles, etc.). These publications can answer basic questions (who? what? when? where?) during the initial exegetical process. For example, they will provide answers to such basic inquiries as "Who was Josiah?" or "What is a denarius?" More important, scholarly resources also verify, sharpen, and correct your work after you have done your own exegesis. Thus one important aspect of the exegetical process is the confirmation and correction of your own discoveries and insights, the refinement and expansion of your ideas through conversation and research.

An Overview of the Method

Thus far we have examined rationale and theory. The remainder of this book is largely devoted to the nuts and bolts of exegesis—the careful reading of and writing about the Bible. A close, careful reading or exegesis of a biblical passage requires a process. The process proposed in this book has seven basic elements. These are briefly outlined here and will be developed in more detail in subsequent chapters.

For purposes of *reading* a biblical text, the elements in this process cannot and should not always be followed slavishly; these steps are, rather, the necessary *elements* of a careful reading, or exegesis. (Thus the title of this book is *Elements of Biblical Exegesis*.) The actual process of reading and interpretation is more like a circle than an outline, as you move back and forth from part to whole,

---

[23]Some would argue that *all* exegesis is really eisegesis. This view may be understandable but is unnecessarily cynical.

text to context, original meaning to contemporary relevance, and so on. This process is sometimes referred to as a "hermeneutical circle," hermeneutics being the art of interpretation. Interpretation is indeed more like a circular than a linear process; it has been aptly described as a process of "going forward by circling around."[24] The image of a circle is not, therefore, meant to suggest lack of progress, as in a vicious or endless circle from which there is no escape. (Some interpreters have suggested that a better image is that of a spiral, the action of which is tighter and tighter.)[25] Another helpful analogy is that of weaving: exegesis is the weaving together of unique but interrelated strands or elements of a careful reading of the text. Nevertheless, it will be extremely beneficial to think carefully through each of the discrete elements of, or steps in, the method.

For purposes of *writing* about a biblical text (e.g., an exegetical paper), the following method can be successfully used as it stands to yield high-quality written interpretations. It can also be altered according to the needs and wishes of individual students and instructors.

The seven elements of the method are:

- **survey**—preparation and overview, or introduction
- **contextual analysis**—consideration of the historical and literary contexts of the text
- **formal analysis**—of the form, structure, and movement of the text
- **detailed analysis**—of the various parts of the text
- **synthesis**—of the text as a whole
- **reflection**—on the text today
- **expansion and refinement**—of the initial exegesis[26]

---

[24] Frederick C. Tiffany and Sharon H. Ringe, *Biblical Interpretation: A Roadmap* (Nashville: Abingdon, 1996), 68–69.

[25] See Grant R. Osborne, *The Hermeneutical Spiral: A Comprehensive Introduction to Biblical Interpretation* (rev. ed.; Downers Grove, Ill.: Inter-Varsity, 2006). Osborne believes that careful study of genre, text, etc. will get us closer and closer to the biblical author's intended meaning and its significance for us, and thus the spiral becomes "tighter and tighter."

[26] Though the order of presentation may be different, the main elements of exegesis are very similar to the elements of close reading done by literary critics, as listed above: *genre and implied situation,* or what we have called analysis of *form* and consideration of the *historical and literary contexts; intellectual core,* or what we have called *synthesis; structure and unity,* or what we have called *structure* and *movement; literary* or poetic *texture,* or what we have called *detailed analysis; and artistry,* or something

It is important to note that some exegetes would consider the element of reflection to be something supplemental to exegesis itself. They might suggest that any notion of personal or theological reflection on a text is unscientific at best and an invitation to eisegesis at worst. However, as Rudolf Bultmann, the great German biblical scholar of the first half of the twentieth century, said, there is no exegesis without presuppositions.[27] We all come to the text with interests in it, maybe even an agenda. Biblical texts compel us to ask not only "What?" but "So what?" Historical and literary critics we may be, or wish to become, but we are also human beings seeking an encounter with truths and realities to which sacred texts point.

Refusing to consider responsible reflection on and with the text as an aspect of exegesis is shortsighted and unnecessary. Most exegetes have their eyes on "two horizons"—the horizon, or world, of the biblical text itself, and the horizon, or world, of their own personal and corporate experience. This is both normal and appropriate, though there are ways of engaging these two horizons that are more responsible than others. Exegetes who have no interest in the contemporary significance of biblical texts are, of course, free to refrain from reflection on them. Most people, however, even if they do not consider themselves religious, find it difficult to avoid reflecting on great literature, religious or otherwise. We do not have to be committed spiritual readers or liberation theologians to have this legitimate interest, but neither do we have to hide our religious commitments when we approach the text even in an academic setting. (Although it is of course easier and generally considered more appropriate to be explicit about such commitments in a religiously affiliated institution, there is no reason, especially in a postmodern context, that those in secular institutions must refrain from expressing their own interests and commitments, as long as they do so with intellectual humility and with respect for the views of others.)

---

like our *reflection*. For a process similar to the one proposed in this book, though presented in a somewhat less technical way and in a different sequence, see Tiffany and Ringe, *Biblical Interpretation*.

[27] Rudolf Bultmann, "Is Exegesis without Presuppositions Possible?" in *Existence and Faith: Shorter Writings of Rudolf Bultmann* (trans. Schubert Ogden; New York: Meridian, 1960), 342–51. It has been pointed out by Anthony Thiselton (*New Horizons in Hermeneutics*, 45) that by "presupposition" Bultmann was referring to a "pre-understanding" as a relation in life to the subject matter of the texts, not merely to beliefs, and especially not to fixed beliefs or doctrines that allow for no alteration.

Some Observations on the Process

Three observations about executing this method as a whole are now in order. First, readers may enter the process of exegesis at any of the first six steps (except, by definition, synthesis), including reflection on the contemporary context, but the process is not complete until all elements have been considered and all strands woven together. In an exegesis paper, these elements are carefully interconnected and systematically presented.

Second, the elements outlined here are fundamentally the same as those used by the majority of professional biblical scholars (although some hesitate to include element six, reflection) as well as literary critics. Although the work of biblical scholars and literary critics is more technical, as are the terms used to describe it (see Appendix A), scholars are basically asking the very questions about texts and their contexts that are raised by these seven elements.

Third, the reader of biblical texts who follows the basic process presented in this book can both contribute to the ongoing conversation about the Bible and benefit from that conversation. This last point implies something about the way in which students, preachers, and others proceed as they engage a text exegetically. The great temptation is to turn an exegesis paper into a research report that merely lays out for the reader the major points of view on this or that passage, verse, or key word. Students who succumb to this temptation are often intimidated by the vast quantity and technical nature of biblical scholarship, especially in comparison to their own paucity of knowledge and skill. Then they make the mistake of thinking that, if they just read all the important commentaries and articles, they will finally understand the passage. Unfortunately, some instructors reinforce this notion.

It is much, much better for all readers—students, preachers, and other serious readers—to learn the habit of first reading the text largely on their own. Even the most sophisticated advocates and practitioners of the most complex historical-critical methods emphasize this:

> Before reaching for the secondary sources, such as the commentaries, one should try to formulate a provisional analysis of the text.[28]

---

[28] Hans Conzelmann and Andreas Lindemann, *Interpreting the New Testament: An Introduction to the Principles and Methods of N.T. Exegesis* (trans. Siegfried S. Schatzmann; Peabody, Mass.: Hendrickson, 1988), 38.

By working through a text on your own, guided by a careful exegetical method, you will learn to engage the text itself, and not merely the interpreters or interpretations of the text. You will also be prepared to handle the biblical text responsibly in the absence of secondary sources. You will use secondary resources to expand, correct, and refine your own initial exegesis in a way that will enable you to learn from and contribute to the conversation about the text in your own unique ways more efficiently than those who begin with the interpretations of the text rather than with the biblical text itself.

For this reason, the last step in the exegetical process is called "Expansion and Refinement of the Exegesis." Although this is a discrete step in the exegetical process, *it does not translate into a separate section of an exegesis paper.* Rather, a paper should constantly, throughout each section of the paper, weave together one's own insights with the insights and corrective influences of others. Thus expansion and refinement of one's exegesis must occur for every element of the process.

In writing an exegesis paper that follows the elements of this process, a student must write precisely and concisely, for the process of investigation and conversation will uncover a lot of information about, and perspectives on, the text. Sometimes students are tempted to spend nearly half of their paper on contextual analysis, or on contextual and formal analysis, to the neglect of detailed analysis. While context and form are very important, they cannot replace careful, in-depth examination. The following general page-count guidelines for a 15-page (approximately 4,000 words) exegesis paper, as well as their approximate equivalents in percentage of the entire paper, may therefore be helpful:

- **survey/introduction**—1 page or less, or about 250 words (approximately 5% of the paper)

- **contextual analysis/historical and literary contexts**—2–3 pages, or about 500–800 words (approximately 10–20% of the paper)

- **formal analysis/form, structure, and movement**—1–2 pages, or about 250–600 words (approximately 5–15% of the paper)

- **detailed analysis**—8–10 pages, or about 2,000–2,750 words (approximately 50–65% of the paper)

- **synthesis**—1 page or less, or about 250 words (approximately 5% of the paper)

- **reflection**—0–3 pages, or as much as 750 words (if included, up to 20% of the paper)

This is another way of saying that generally about one-half to two-thirds of the paper will be devoted to detailed analysis. Another way to imagine the paper is in three main parts: a "prelude" to the detailed analysis (steps 1–3), the detailed analysis itself, and a "postlude" (steps 5–6). Step 7 (expansion and refinement) is intertwined throughout the paper.

Variations on this rule of thumb are inevitable. Appropriate adjustments must be made if the passage presents peculiar problems in one area, if reflection is omitted or expanded, and so on. The division of space for shorter or longer papers may be calculated proportionately following these guidelines.

In addition to deciding how to allocate space in your exegesis paper, you will need to decide how precisely to approach the research and writing task itself. The primary goal of this book is to explain and illustrate the various elements of the exegetical process. Much of this process involves significant time spent in reading, thinking, taking notes, and "playing with" the text—much like any other paper. Some hints about how to do that are offered throughout the book. Additionally, Appendix B, "Practical Guidelines for Writing a Research Exegesis Paper," presents a step-by-step outline of five phases in the preparation of such a paper. This appendix serves as a useful summary of the entire book.

Moving Forward

Chapters 3–9 of this book each introduce a particular element of exegesis. Theoretically, once one of these chapters is mastered, a reader could execute that aspect of the exegetical process on a desert island. Readers who learn the entire exegetical process qualify as desert-island exegetes. Some final hints on the process are offered in chapter 10. Chapter 11 deals with expanding and refining each particular element of the exegetical process by using other resources and tools. In other words, chapter 11 is for those who have returned to civilization from the desert island and once again have a library, computer, fellow readers, and other resources at their disposal. At the end of the book are appendixes that contain supplemental summary information as well as three sample exegesis papers.

Now that we have briefly examined the task of exegesis, we are prepared to study each of the steps more carefully. Before we can do that, however, we must consider the text that is the focus of our exegesis, namely, the Bible itself. That is the subject of the next chapter.

We conclude this introductory chapter with a quote from a literary critic. We may substitute the words "exegete" and "exegesis" for "explicator" and "explication":

> An explicator is a tour guide or traveling companion. The goal is to help a reader see what is really present in the [text]. A good explication is a lens that brings the text into focus.[29]

Review & Study

Chapter Summary

- Exegesis, a word deriving from the Greek verb "to lead out," is the careful historical, literary, and theological analysis of a text.
- Exegesis is investigation, conversation, and art.
- There are three basic approaches to exegesis: synchronic, diachronic ("historical-critical"), and existential (which includes both theological and ideological perspectives).
- The method advocated in this book is eclectic and integrated but gives priority to the synchronic approach, with an ultimately theological goal. It emphasizes the importance of contexts.
- The seven elements of exegesis, and the steps in writing an exegesis paper, are: (1) survey (preparation for reading, or introduction); (2) contextual analysis (of the text's historical and literary contexts); (3) formal analysis (of the text's form, structure, and movement); (4) detailed analysis; (5) synthesis; (6) reflection; and (7) expansion and refinement of the exegesis.
- Wise exegetes prepare a careful initial exegesis of the text on their own before consulting the experts.

Practical Hints

1. I have always found it beneficial and have often required students to print out or photocopy biblical passages

---

[29] Ryken, *Words of Delight*, 208.

for exegesis in order to "play with the text" or "think on paper." This means placing the text on a sheet of paper, with wide margins, and marking it up—underlining key phrases, circling recurrent terms, drawing lines between items, recording observations in the margins, and noting questions to be pursued. If you have access to electronic versions of the original languages or translations, you can download and rearrange your text however you like. (I suggest double-spacing the text at 12 points in a 3-inch centered column.)

2. Remember, as you begin the process of exegesis, that there is much that can be and has been said about the Bible, some insightful and helpful, some of dubious value or extraneous. At first, observe and record whatever comes to mind. As you move through the hermeneutical circle, or weave the various strands of the exegetical process together, you will begin to sift the wheat from the chaff and begin looking for what really expresses the careful reading of the text that you are doing. Eventually, you will do the same as you read and take notes on what other interpreters have said. In the end, if you write an exegesis paper, you will have to decide what is and is not worth including from both your own thoughts and those of others. What you can present will be like the proverbial tip of the iceberg in relation to all that you have discovered. You will want to ask yourself, "Of all that I could say about this text in this paper, what truly expresses and supports the overall interpretation of the text that is emerging and that I find compelling?"

3. When you begin writing an exegesis paper, do not attempt to execute methods that are beyond your ability. A beginning student should not attempt to do, say, tradition criticism without the skills to do it, or to discuss the intricacies of Hebrew grammar and vocabulary on the basis of an interlinear Bible. Rather, play to your strengths. Develop and use the skills any careful reader needs to have: observing, questioning, making connections, recognizing patterns, and so on. These will take you a long way.

For Further Insight and Practice

1. Attempt a close reading of an editorial or a political cartoon (preferably a multi-paneled one) in a newspaper or online. What is its topic? What prompted the editorial or

cartoon? How is it structured? What key words, images, and themes appear in it? What sources or authorities, if any, does it quote? What is its main point? Is it effective? How and why? How do you react to it? Does it make you want to think or act differently?

2. Review chapter 11, section 1, pp. 182–89, "Resources for Understanding the Task," and peruse at least one of the books listed.

CHAPTER TWO

The Text

> A real translation is in the main an interpretation.
> —*James Moffatt, Bible translator (1870–1944)*

How is a text selected for exegesis?

Which translations and editions of the Bible are best for exegesis?

In the previous chapter we considered the task of exegesis generally. Before we examine the various elements or steps of the exegetical process more carefully, we must consider the biblical text that will be the subject of our exegesis. This chapter begins with a discussion of how to choose a passage for exegesis. There follows a brief note on the Bible in the original languages and "interlinear Bibles." Since many exegetes work with a translation, even if they know some Hebrew or Greek, the bulk of the chapter considers what makes a good translation for purposes of exegesis and examines several Bible translations in English. Also included is a discussion of editions of the Bible in English (study Bibles).[1]

Choosing a Biblical Text for Exegesis

One of the most difficult and important decisions exegetes make is which biblical passage will be the focus of any particular exegetical investigation. For some people, of course, there is no decision to be made. A professor may assign a particular text to a student, or a religious tradition may assign a text to a preacher

---

[1] Readers who know the biblical languages or are anxious to move on to the exegetical method itself may wish to skip the discussion of English editions for now and proceed to chapter 3 after reading the opening section of this chapter.

(normally by means of a lectionary, or calendar of readings). Most exegetes, however, especially those writing exegesis papers, have some choice. Even Christian preachers whose churches assign texts via a lectionary must choose which of the assigned readings to use as the basis of their preaching and whether to attempt to connect the readings together.[2]

There is no agreed-upon, generic technical term for the text that is studied in the exegetical process. The term *pericope* (Greek for *section,* related to the verb "to cut") is generally restricted to a segment of narrative biblical literature. Some linguistically minded scholars have introduced the terms *discourse* and *discourse unit,* but these terms have not yet gained general acceptance. The terms *text* and *passage,* both sufficiently generic and widely used, are appropriate for most purposes, with the term *pericope* being appropriate for a narrative text from books like Kings, Chronicles, the gospels, and Acts.

It is wise for beginning students to choose a text that interests them, but they should probably avoid "swimming in the deep water," that is, jumping into an extraordinarily difficult or controversial text.[3] More experienced students may wish to explore a text that either excites them or confuses them, angers them or moves them. It may be a passage that has deep personal or ecclesial meaning or one upon which a complex doctrine or particular practice is grounded. It may be a text that seems to capture, or to violate, the spirit of a particular biblical writer or religious community. It may be a text that offends the potential exegete, so that he or she rejects its perceived claims or perspective. The more difficult or controversial the text, however, the more important it is for exegetes to acknowledge their biases—to themselves and perhaps even to their readers—upon undertaking the exegesis.

In any case, exegetes should be prepared to live with their texts for some period of time. Students, in particular, should ask, "Is this a text in which I want to invest a significant amount of my time, energy, and self?" "Am I interested in what others have said

---

[2] Those from churches that use or adapt the Revised Common Lectionary (RCL) should note that the first (Old Testament) and third (gospel) readings for each Sunday are chosen for their thematic or other relationship to each other, while the second (generally the epistle) reading is completely independent of the other two, except on certain special days. The same is true for the Roman Catholic Lectionary, on which the RCL was modeled.

[3] I owe this very appropriate analogy to my student Bill Garrison.

about this text?" (And, practically speaking, "Am I willing to stake a significant portion of my course grade on a project related to this text?")

An exegesis paper considers a passage that is a complete unit of manageable size. In general, the passage should not be a single phrase or verse, nor should it be a complete chapter, much less an entire biblical book. A good rule of thumb for exegesis papers is somewhere between five and twenty-five verses, depending on the length and depth of the paper, the expectations of the professor, the character of the passage to be examined, and the biblical book in which the passage is located. In a ten-to-fifteen-page exegesis paper, a passage of about eight to twelve verses allows for about a page of discussion (or a little less) per verse, after the other aspects of exegesis are addressed. It is possible, of course, to write a shorter paper on a longer passage or a much longer paper on a much shorter passage. Beginning exegetes should always consult with their instructors.

Equally important is the question of beginning and ending points. It must first be remembered that almost every text appears in the middle of a larger text, so that it is not really an entity unto itself. Nonetheless, one of the basic units of human thought and expression seems to be something like the paragraph or stanza. These units, as well as longer units of thought and expression consisting of paragraphs and stanzas linked together, often begin and end with markers that indicate a difference or shift from what precedes and follows.

Exegetes should learn to look for indications of the beginning and end of units of thought and expression in the Bible. They should choose texts that have a clear start and finish and that communicate a coherent sequence of thought or action. As one scholar puts it, a text for exegesis should be "at least relatively self-contained and intending a specific effect."[4] Sometimes the beginning and/or end of the unit will contain logical markers (such as "therefore") or chronological markers (such as "next"). Sometimes a unit can be identified by the way its subject matter is distinct from that of the surrounding text. One common indication of a self-contained unit is the presence of *inclusio,* in which a word, phrase, or theme found at the beginning of the unit is echoed at the end. Another indication of the presence of a self-contained unit is *chiasmus,*[5] in

---

[4]Werner Stenger, *Introduction to New Testament Exegesis* (ed. John W. Simpson Jr.; trans. Douglas W. Stott; Grand Rapids: Eerdmans, 1993), 24.
[5]From the Greek letter *chi,* X.

which thoughts are organized into an A-B-B'-A' pattern, with the initial thoughts mirrored back throughout the entire second half of the text. Sometimes there is a centerpiece or fulcrum in the middle of this structure (A-B-C-B'-A').[6]

One of the most obvious errors to avoid is selecting a passage that begins or ends in the middle of a thought or dramatic moment. Identifying units is often a matter of judgment. Consulting the divisions of the text in a Bible or a commentary may be a helpful starting point. Exegetes should not be bound, however, by the decisions of previous editors and commentators, nor even by the presence of verse and chapter numbers, which are not part of the text itself. Scholars introduced these tools for identifying and locating texts, but in doing so they made some mistakes. For example, they divided up 1 Corinthians in such a way that 11:1 begins a new chapter, when 11:1 is clearly the conclusion to chapter 10. If every Bible and every commentary you consult fails to see the integrity and unity that you perceive in a set of verses, your contribution to the conversation about that passage may consist in part in identifying its status as a unit—especially if that status can be plausibly argued and can be shown to be significant for understanding the text.

The Bible in Its Original Languages

If you can read the biblical text in its original language, you should obviously do as much of your exegetical work as possible with the Hebrew or Greek text. The main current Greek and Hebrew critical editions are listed in section 2 of chapter 11.

Preparing your own working translation of the original text, to the best of your ability, is also helpful. You will modify this working translation throughout the exegetical process. Various published translations can still help, of course, by indicating possible interpretations and by guiding you through any mazes of difficult grammar and vocabulary.

One popular middle ground between an English translation and a Hebrew Bible or Greek Testament is the "interlinear Bible," in which a very wooden translation of each word is placed above or below the line of Hebrew or Greek text. For readers who have some familiarity with the original language and use this tool as

---

[6] Further discussion of these sorts of text structures can be found in chapter 5.

a way to refresh their memories, it may have a useful function if employed cautiously. However, a little bit of knowledge of Hebrew or Greek can be dangerous, and combining such knowledge with the peculiar English renderings found in an interlinear Bible can be disastrous. People who do not read the original languages with some degree of competence should stay clear of interlinear Bibles and rely on good translations and solid research for their exegesis.

It is generally known that we do not possess the actual originals of the Bible. What we do possess are manuscripts that are copies of copies (and so on), and these manuscripts do not fully agree with one another. However, for the most part we have more and better copies of the biblical texts than we do of other documents from antiquity.

The art and science of studying these manuscripts, as well as early translations of the Bible, is called textual criticism. One of the goals of this field of study is to determine the most likely reading of every word of the Bible from among the several textual variants in each case. The judgments of textual critics about these variants appear in critical editions of the Bible in its original languages, and a very small percentage of them may sometimes be found in the footnotes of English translations.

Beginning exegetes should be aware of these issues, for they will be discussed in more technical commentaries and other works, and they do sometimes affect meaning in very significant ways. For example, some manuscripts of John 1:18 refer to Jesus Christ as the "only begotten son," while others read "the only begotten God," perhaps meaning "the only begotten one, who is God." Understanding how these differences may have arisen and how scholars argue about them is both fascinating and challenging. Some books about the topic are listed in section 2 of chapter 11. In general, beginning exegetes will need to rely on the judgment of textual critics and translators, and they should refrain from amateur textual criticism. However, more experienced exegetes should learn enough about textual criticism to understand and eventually to make their own text-critical decisions.

Bible Translations (Versions) and Editions (Study Bibles)

Not everyone has the luxury of mastering ancient languages before doing exegesis. For those who do not read (or remember!)

biblical Hebrew, Greek, and Aramaic, their first tool should be a good translation of the Bible. An additional aid is a scholarly, annotated edition of the Bible, or "study Bible." Many beginning exegetes do not understand why a professor recommends one translation or edition of the Bible and criticizes another, so this section attempts to explain the challenges of producing a good Bible translation and edition, and to comment on some of those available.

Translations

A Bible translation, or version, is a scholarly attempt to render the stories and thoughts of people from ancient cultures who spoke ancient languages into a modern language that is spoken by people who live in very different, contemporary cultures. Translation, like exegesis, is an art rather than a precise science. Every translation is itself an interpretation. Therefore, in a certain sense, every Bible translation is a kind of streamlined exegesis representing innumerable interpretive judgments and decisions. The artistic, interpretive character of translations is due to several factors, most of which we encounter when considering the various elements of exegesis. The analysis of words, grammatical constructions, contexts, and other factors in exegesis, and therefore also in translation, is seldom straightforward, always requiring intellectual agility and sensitivity.

The first factor is the words themselves, the lexical items, and how they are combined, the syntax. Some words have a very limited range of function or meaning in a language, but most words have a wide range of meaning. Furthermore, the function of many words changes when they are combined in phrases with other words or when used to serve particular rhetorical functions.

For example, the word *house* has quite different meanings in the following instances: "my friend's house"; "house of ill repute"; "house of David"; and "greenhouse." Similarly, the word *god* functions differently in each of the following phrases: "O my God, I am heartily sorry for having offended thee"; "Oh my God! What a beautiful dress!"; and "the god of this age." Even a simple phrase like "the love of God" is tricky: does it refer to human love for God or God's love for us? In the case of 1 John, one's rendering of this phrase is affected by, and will affect, one's interpretation of the document as a whole. As we will see in more detail in chapter 6, a word or phrase has a range of possible meanings; context narrows that range.

Further complicating the situation is the fact that the meaning of some words from ancient languages remains obscure, and the odd combination of words into idiomatic phrases (such as "pull the wool over my eyes") can turn individually clear lexical items into completely obscure phrases. The meaning of such words and phrases can sometimes only be guessed, using the context as a guide. In other words, meaning is not static; it is dynamic and dependent on context.

The second factor, therefore, is context—literary and rhetorical as well as historical, social, and cultural. The meaning of individual words, not to mention all the combinations of lexical items, depends on the greater literary context and rhetorical goals of the writing. Different writers use words differently, and the same writer may use the same word in different ways for different purposes. Moreover, the lexical items used by these writers point to historical, social, and cultural realities outside the text itself—extratextual items—that must be noticed and understood.

A third factor is the limitation inherent in all translation. The "target" language may not have a word or phrase to render accurately the meaning of a word or phrase in the "source" language. Even if appropriate lexical items exist in the target language, the resulting combination of words may be awkward, even to the point of being misleading. Good Hebrew syntax may yield horrible English syntax, and a good, literal English rendering may destroy the poetry or other artistic form and beauty of a Hebrew text. Furthermore, the target languages themselves evolve. For instance, the English spoken in the United States today differs markedly from that spoken in seventeenth-century England. Add to all of this the fact that frequently the translator and/or potential readers of the translation have no cultural phenomenon comparable to something mentioned or described in the text. For instance, how would one render the word *snow* for people who have never experienced it in person or via the media?

A "Good" Translation for Exegesis

Translators, it should be evident by now, have a daunting task. Good Bible translating demands a thorough knowledge of ancient languages and cultures as well as a sophisticated understanding of how best to bridge the linguistic and cultural gaps between then and now. It follows, therefore, that a translation produced by a team of reputable scholars drawing on years of study and research will be far superior to one produced by an individual or by a less qualified team.

What is unclear, however, is what the end-product created by such a scholarly team should look like. This lack of clarity is due to philosophical differences about the nature and purpose of translation. Should a translation aim primarily to convey *words* or to convey *ideas* into the target language? These two options have sometimes been called word-for-word or literal translations, on the one hand, and idea-for-idea, free, or dynamic-equivalence translations, on the other.[7] The two options really represent ends of a spectrum, and any existing translation can be placed somewhere along this spectrum. Some translators claim that a more literal translation has the benefit of allowing readers more room for their own interpretation of the words in the text, while others argue that an idea-for-idea translation is more likely to have the same effect on modern readers as it did on ancient ones.

Each of these positions, however, has its own particular problems. A wooden, word-for-word translation of an idiomatic statement would, in fact, be a mistranslation, for it would convey no meaning—or a very different meaning—to someone who does not use that idiom. For instance, if translators render the English phrase "take a walk" into another language by using the equivalent of the English word "take," their supposedly literal translation may wrongly convey the idea that the subject of the phrase is somehow acquiring something called a walk. This everyday linguistic phenomenon reveals that there is always a measure of interpretation involved in translation, even when it strives to be literal.

Similarly, it is highly problematic to suppose that a free translation that aims at conveying the general intent of a text would have the same effect on people who live in a very different set of social and cultural circumstances. For example, if translators decide to render references to the kings of Israel as "presidents" or "prime ministers" because most English-speaking readers have personal experience with these political figures, but not kings, their al-

---

[7]Ordinary Bible readers sometimes distinguish between a translation and a paraphrase, the latter being understood more or less as dynamic equivalence: a less exact retelling that aims at rendering the general intent of a text in very understandable English (or another target language). Some contemporary linguists would dispute this distinction, in part because all translation is interpretation. For our purposes, we will define as a translation any rendering of the Bible that is based on the original Hebrew, Greek, and Aramaic texts, no matter how "dynamic," even paraphrastic, it may be.

legedly dynamic-equivalence translation will not suggest to contemporary readers anything similar to what "king" meant to the people of Israel.

Despite their inherent problems, both kinds of translations exist—or at least the spectrum of translations that they define exists. Linguists now prefer the terms *formal equivalence* and *functional equivalence* to literal and dynamic equivalence. Formal-equivalence translations emphasize the similarity in the linguistic forms (such as vocabulary and grammatical structures) between the source language and the target language. Functional-equivalence translations, on the other hand, stress the similarity in linguistic function (meaning) between the two languages.[8]

Bible translators obviously approach the issue of formal versus functional translation theory differently, thereby yielding different kinds of translations. For instance, the principle of the translators of the New Revised Standard Version (NRSV) is "as literal as possible, as free as necessary." That represents a commitment to a largely formal-equivalence translation. On the other hand, the goal of the New Living Translation, which is the scholarly heir to the very popular Living Bible, was to produce a functional-equivalence, thought-for-thought translation that is accurate in both meaning and style.

No translation is perfect, and different kinds of translations fulfill different roles. For purposes of exegesis based on the English text of the Bible (as opposed to the original languages), a translation based on the theory of formal equivalence is best for two main reasons: (1) it allows more of the original ambiguities in the text to stand, and thus to be noticed, investigated, and interpreted by the exegete; and (2) it generally renders a recurring key word in the original biblical text with the same English word in the translation. Formal-equivalence translations are sometimes guilty, however, of creating odd, wooden renderings that do not sound much like English and that may even misinterpret the original text by giving precedence to form over function (meaning). But functional-equivalence translations, on the other hand, frequently (1) oversimplify complex or ambiguous texts and

---

[8]An example of the difference between these two kinds of translations may be seen in the case of the French phrase "au revoir." A formal-equivalence approach to translation might stress the "literal" meaning of the words ("until the [time of] seeing [each other] again") and render it "'til next time." A functional-equivalence approach would simply render the phrase "bye" or "see ya," depending on the context.

(2) substitute contemporary idiom for ancient biblical idiom, often resulting in inconsistent or misleading translations of key items. No matter how skillful the translators, the effect of these strategies on the exegete is prejudicial: one interpretation is given preference over another. This may be fine for the casual reader, but not for the serious exegete.

One possible strategy for addressing this problem is to use more than one translation. Reading several translations can indeed provide useful insights, but this approach is somewhat overrated and can lead to erroneous conclusions. Each translation still represents exegetical judgments, and the similarities and differences should not be given undue weight. Careful users of various translations should view the differences not as equally valid options but as possible renderings of the text, each of which has strengths and weaknesses that must be analyzed. In other words, translations suggest some (and not necessarily all) of a range of possible interpretations of particular texts. Only careful exegetical work will enable the reader to judge the various options. The notion that one translation is preferable to another because, on the surface, it is "easier to understand" or seems to "make more sense" is a mistaken one.

Choosing an English Translation for Use in Exegesis

The following discussion evaluates the strengths and weaknesses of popular translations for purposes of exegesis. In each of four categories, I have listed several versions in order of overall quality This evaluation is based on the criteria noted above: underlying translation theory; qualifications of the translator(s), including knowledge of biblical languages and contexts; and readability of the final result for readers of contemporary English. Only versions that contain both Testaments are discussed. Many contemporary commentaries are based on or keyed to one or more of these translations, even if the authors have worked with the original languages.

Versions Preferred for Exegesis

The **New Revised Standard Version** (NRSV), completed in 1989, is the successor to the RSV (see below) and follows a formal-equivalence principle that its translators identify in the words "as literal as possible, as free as necessary." The committee of superior scholar-translators, chaired by Bruce Metzger, made several major stylistic changes to the RSV. One was the elimination of archaic pronoun and verb forms (thou, thee, thine; art, hast, etc.). Another, more significant change was the introduction of gender-inclusive language for human beings whenever the pronouns or addressees implied either both men and women or any person, without reference to gender. This was accomplished, for example, by pluralizing singular male pronouns to "they"/"them"; replacing "brothers" with "brothers and sisters"; and substituting "mortal(s)" for "man"/"men." This was a minor concession to the principle of dynamic equivalence. Occasionally, however, the result is exegetically problematic, for example, when Paul's use of the word "brother(s)" is replaced, not by "brothers and sisters," but by "believer(s)" or "friend(s)."

The resulting translation, based on the best available critical editions of both Testaments (including the apocryphal/deuterocanonical books) and, for the most part, respecting the principle of formal equivalence, is excellent as a basis for English-language exegesis. It is not a perfect translation, of course, but it is by most accounts the best now available in English, especially for in-depth study.

The **New American Bible** (NAB) is, in the United States, the standard translation by and for Roman Catholics. It contains, therefore, the deuterocanonical books (what Protestants call the Apocrypha). Produced by a team of superior Roman Catholic biblical scholars, it first appeared in 1970. The New Testament was revised in 1986 and the Psalms in 1991, in consultation with non-Catholic scholars; a fully revised Old Testament is still underway. The NAB translators deliberately chose to reject a functional-equivalence approach and to follow a policy of formal equivalence, placing their work in the tradition of the RSV. Two of their stated reasons for this decision were to promote deeper study of the Bible and to avoid subjectivity (perhaps idiosyncrasy would be a better word) in the translation. Although the NAB is unknown to many non-Catholics, and its diction and vocabulary are often outside the mainstream of better-known biblical translations like the KJV and RSV/NRSV, it is generally a very good translation.

Today's New International Version (TNIV) is the successor to the popular NIV (see discussion below), again excluding the Apocrypha. It was released from 2002 (NT) to 2005 (full Bible). It was prepared by evangelical translators associated with the International Bible Society and published by Zondervan (as with the NIV). The new translation differs from the NIV in about 7 percent of the text, most notably in having more gender-inclusive (or "gender-accurate"—their term) language. More sensitive to a variety of translation issues, the TNIV is better for exegesis than the NIV, but it should probably be used in tandem with the NRSV.

The **New English Translation,** or the NET Bible (NET), is a version originally designed for electronic publication. Aiming to be readable, accurate, elegant, and "gender-accurate," this Bible contains more than 60,000 study, text-critical, and translators' notes. Free downloads are available at http://www.bible.org/net-bible. Published beginning in 1996 by the Biblical Studies Foundation under the leadership of Daniel Wallace, the NET's NT and OT are complete (for now—planned revisions will come about every five years) and also available in print (first edition, 2005), with a CD-ROM version included. Translation of the Apocrypha is in progress, and the results to date are available only online. The text itself is more functionally equivalent (but, generally speaking, rightly leaves ambiguous texts ambiguous), while the translators' notes provide the more formally equivalent renderings. The translators' notes also explain the reasons for the interpretive decisions that produced the translation. The overall result is quite useful for exegesis if both translation and notes are consulted.

Versions Useful for Exegesis, with Caution

The **Revised Standard Version** (RSV) was issued in stages from 1946 to 1977, with the first complete Bible, minus the Apocrypha, published in 1952. It continued the tradition of the King James Version (KJV) and its late-nineteenth-century revisions. The ongoing, first-rate translation committee, which was ecumenical in composition, assured wide acceptance of the final form of the RSV by many major Christian communions. The RSV translators worked with a formal-equivalence approach to translation in an age when functional equivalence was not a serious option. The result was an excellent formal-equivalence (self-styled "literal") translation informed by the best scholarship of the day and based on the best critical editions of the text available. In recent decades, of course, biblical scholarship, translation theory, and English-language usage have changed considerably, resulting in the need for an updating of the RSV. (For example, the RSV retained the KJV's use of "thees" and "thous" in address to God.) The RSV has been supplanted by the NRSV and other revisions, but it is still usable, with some caution, as the basis for exegesis of the English text.

The **New International Version** (NIV), now the world's best-selling Bible translation, was released by the International Bible Society in 1973 (NT) and 1978 (full Bible). It was intended in part, like the

NASB (see below), to be an evangelical Protestant alternative to the RSV for those dissatisfied with the KJV. Its team of translators was quite good, using the standard critical editions of the text rather than the less reliable texts that were the basis of the KJV. A team of reviewers for readability aided the process of translation. The NIV combines formal and functional equivalence in its approach. The preface to the NIV says that the translators' "first concern" was the "accuracy of the translation and its fidelity to the thought of the biblical writers" and that they have "striven for more than a word-for-word translation" in order to accomplish "faithful communication of the meaning of the writers of the Bible." They do this by means of "frequent modifications in sentence structure and constant regard for the contextual meaning of words."

Occasionally the theological perspective of the translators (or perhaps reviewers and editors) colors the translation a bit too boldly (a kind of functional-equivalence theory at work), but in general the NIV captures the substance and/or the spirit of the text well. With some notable exceptions, however, its renderings do not match the quality of the RSV-NRSV tradition. Moreover, its modifications of syntax and attention to context introduce a higher degree of interpretation into the translation than do the RSV and NRSV. The NIV appeared before gender inclusivity became a major issue in Bible translation. An attempt at a gender-inclusive edition (NIVI) in the late 1990s was squashed in the United States, though it appeared in Great Britain. The next version, Today's New International Version (TNIV; see above), took up the gender issue again.

The **New American Standard Bible** (NASB) was published by the conservative evangelical Lockman Foundation in 1971, with an update in 1995 (sometimes abbreviated as NAS95, NASBU, or NASU). The update improves the version's readability in many ways, most obviously in the elimination of out-of-date vocabulary, including "thees" and "thous." It is the Bible of choice in certain circles and completely unknown in others. The NASB/NASU is a formal-equivalence translation in the KJV-ASV (American Standard Version) tradition that is sometimes characterized as possessing a "wooden literalism." The publisher claims that this "word-for-word" translation is the "most literal" in English and that "at NO point did the translators attempt to interpret Scripture through translation."[9] Thus they claim to convey the word of God better than any other English translation.

---

[9] See the following page on the Lockman foundation website: http://www.lockman.org/nasb.

However, all translation is interpretation, and the NASB update continues the KJV tradition of supplying italicized English words for missing words in the Hebrew and Greek original. All translations must "fill in the blanks," so to speak (though italicizing the additions is no longer the norm), but to do so is clearly an act of interpretation. Thus the NASB/NASU is not as literal as it claims. Moreover, its translation team is not of the same scholarly caliber as those of the NIV, TNIV, or NRSV. All in all, however, the NASB update is generally an acceptable formal-equivalence translation.

The **Revised English Bible** (REB) is the 1989 revision of the disastrous New English Bible (NEB) from the 1960s and early 1970s. Its vivid style is distinctly British, and it frequently provides compelling reading by means of its turns of language while avoiding the excesses of its predecessor. Linguistically, it walks a kind of middle ground between formal and functional equivalence. Though it could be used as a last resort for exegesis, it is best used, not as the main basis for exegesis, but as a significant second translation and a source for well-worded interpretations of standard exegetical decisions.

The **English Standard Version** (ESV), published in 2001, was intended by its conservative evangelical translators and its publisher, Crossway Books, as another (formal-equivalence) revision of the RSV that would be different from both the NRSV and the attempts to make the NIV more gender-inclusive. Apart from eliminating the RSV's "thees" and "thous," making minor adjustments to enhance gender inclusivity and consistency in translation of words, and improving readability, the translators have not generally made major changes to the RSV. In fact, the RSV style is sometimes unwisely and unnecessarily preserved. The translators have, however, made some translation decisions that reflect certain theological convictions, making it useful for exegesis only with some caution.

The **Holman Christian Standard Bible** (HCSB) is the full Bible without Apocrypha and was published between 1999 and 2004 by conservative Southern Baptist translators, partially in reaction to evangelical translation efforts deemed to be linguistically and theologically inaccurate on gender matters. The translators attempted to combine formal and functional equivalence (which they call "optimal equivalence"). In addition to the goals of accuracy and readability in contemporary English within the framework of optimal equivalence, the translators sought "to affirm the authority of Scripture as God's Word and to champion its absolute truth against social or cultural agendas that would compromise its accuracy." In keeping with that affirmation, the translators attempted to preserve the Bible's alleged teachings on distinctive male and female roles. Among other things, the result is, naturally, less gender inclusive than the NRSV or TNIV. Despite the overall linguistic and scholarly competence of the translators, their reactionary agenda and the resulting theological influence on the translation makes this of value for exegesis only with a significant degree of caution.

Versions Unacceptable as the Basis for Exegesis, but Useful in Other Ways

The following versions, though unacceptable as the basis for exegesis, have specific merits that can assist in the interpretive process, and some of these merits are noted.

The **New Living Translation** (NLT) is a bold, vast improvement over the Living Bible (see below), issued in 1996 by the same evangelical publisher, Tyndale House. The NLT was produced by a team of excellent biblical scholars using the best available critical editions of the original languages and guided by an explicit principle of functional equivalence. This principle generated some criticism, with the result that a slightly more formal-equivalence approach was taken in the second edition, which came out in 2004. The translators' sensitivity to cultural context led them to render lexical items referring to measurement (weight, distance, time, monetary worth, etc.) and to everyday customs and realities of life in comparable English idioms. The NLT puts the contemporary equivalent in the text and the original words in a footnote, unlike formal-equivalence translations, which generally do just the opposite. Whether or not one agrees with the translators' functional equivalents, however, the result for exegesis is that too many exegetical judgments were made and too many cultural customs interpreted. The original NLT can and should be consulted as an interpretation, for it is usually a very insightful one, but it should not be used as the basis for careful exegesis. The second edition includes new notes and translational changes reflecting a hybrid of formal and functional concerns. Though an improvement, it too should be used with some caution and not as the primary basis for exegesis.

The **New Jerusalem Bible** (NJB), published in 1985, is the complete revision of the 1966 Jerusalem Bible (JB), an English translation of a French translation of the original languages. The French tended toward the functional end of the translation spectrum, and the English JB followed suit. As a translation of a translation, and a relatively nonformal one at that, the JB should never have served as the basis of exegetical work. The NJB translators worked directly from the original languages, but the product still tends toward the functional end of the spectrum. It is therefore a useful tool for exploring and expressing exegetical options, but it should not serve as the basis for exegesis.

The **Contemporary English Version** (CEV) appeared in 1995, published by the American Bible Society. Embracing the philosophy of functional equivalence, the CEV attempts especially to interpret sensitive biblical texts more appropriately and accurately, especially New Testament references to Jews. The translators argue that terms such as "the Jews" are better rendered, depending on the context, by phrases such as "the religious leaders" or "the people." The principle itself, as well as its application, causes problems for those doing exegesis, since it makes some very significant and debatable exegetical judgments. As in the case of the Good News Bible (see below), so also with the CEV: it may be consulted as one possible rendering of the text, both exegetically and stylistically, but it should not be used as the basis for exegesis. Of these two translations, the CEV is perhaps the better.

The **Good News Bible** (GNB) had also been produced by the American Bible Society, beginning with the New Testament (Today's English Version) in 1966 and the full Bible in 1971. The translators, who were quite sophisticated in their knowledge of the Bible and linguistics, employed a theory of functional equivalence and geared their translation to persons with a somewhat limited vocabulary. Its strengths for its intended audience, however, are its weaknesses for exegesis. If consulted at all, it should be viewed as one possible exegetical and stylistic rendering of the text. It should not be the sole basis for serious study.

The Message first appeared from NavPress as a New Testament in 1993, with the complete Bible (lacking Apocrypha) seeing the light of day in 2002. Now available in several editions, it is the translation project of the Reverend Eugene Peterson, a Presbyterian pastor with a significant degree of scholarly acumen (resulting, in part, from graduate studies at the Johns Hopkins University). Peterson's laudable goal is pastoral—to render the biblical text into contemporary idiom, operating with a clear theory of functional equivalence. The result is an exegesis, but it is not itself the basis for exegesis. Like the work of an earlier scholar-pastor, the British self-styled "paraphraser" J. B. Phillips, *The Message* is probably most useful to exegetes as an example of how one might express in contemporary idiom judgments made on the basis of work on the original texts or other English translations, and through research. Some of Peterson's idiomatic renderings, however, are rather odd.

Versions Unacceptable for Exegesis

The **King James Version** (kjv), or **Authorized Version** (av), was completed in 1611 by a team of translators convened by King James I of England. They generally followed an implicit theory of formal equivalence, but, unfortunately, they worked with generally late and less reliable biblical manuscripts. Since 1611, many older and better manuscripts of the Bible have been discovered, and modern research in the area of textual criticism (which includes comparing and contrasting manuscripts to produce a "critical edition" of the original text) has given us a different basis of original texts to translate than that used by the kjv translators. This means that an exegesis based on the kjv may sometimes be analyzing one or more words, phrases, or verses that did not actually appear in the original biblical text.

In addition, biblical scholarship and linguistics have both progressed significantly during the last four hundred years, providing countless pieces of data and perspectives for translating the text more accurately. During the same period, the English language has itself changed enormously, rendering much of the kjv's language obsolete. Taken together, these factors mean that the King James Version is completely unacceptable as the basis for serious scholarly study of the Bible. The **New King James Version** (nkjv), released in 1979 (nt) and 1982 (ot), updates obsolete language and attempts to be a more linguistically sophisticated translation than the kjv. However, because it is based on the same problematic manuscript tradition, it too is unacceptable for exegesis.

The **Living Bible** (lb), produced in the 1960s and published in 1971, is a paraphrase of the King James Version and is not based on the original languages. It reflects the theological perspective and lack of scholarly biblical training of its producer, Kenneth Taylor. While this paraphrase has made the Bible accessible to many, it possesses no scholarly value. Its successor, the **New Living Translation,** is discussed above.

To summarize the preceding discussion, we may list these versions in four categories: (1) those that are the best as the basis for exegesis (nrsv, nab, tniv, net); (2) those that can be useful for exegesis, if used with caution (RSV, NIV, NASU, REB, ESV, HCSB); (3) those that provide helpful exegetical or stylistic renderings but should not serve as the basis for exegesis (NLT, NJB, CEV, GNB, *The Message*); and (4) those that are unacceptable for exegesis (KJV/AV, NKJV, LB).

Preferred for Exegesis	Useful for Exegesis, with Caution	Unacceptable for Exegesis, but Helpful in Other Ways	Unacceptable for Exegesis
NRSV	RSV	NLT	KJV (AV)
NAB	NIV	NJB	NKJV
TNIV	NASB	CEV	LB
NET	REB	GNB	
	ESV	*The Message*	
	HCSB		

Of all these translations, the NRSV is probably the overall best to use for exegesis, but even this version can be usefully compared with other translations.

One helpful publication, ***The Complete Parallel Bible*** (New York: Oxford University Press, 1993), presents four major translations in parallel columns (NRSV, REB, NJB, NAB). This format will often alert the reader to major translational/exegetical options in the text. (For additional parallel Bibles, see under section 2, "Resources for Understanding the Text," in chapter 11.)

Editions (Study Bibles)

Most publishers that are licensed to publish the various translations of the Scriptures issue a variety of editions of the Bible. Some are "plain-vanilla" editions, containing only the notes that are provided by the translators. Others add section headings, cross-references to other biblical texts, pronunciation guides, abbreviated concordances (lists of key words and their biblical references), glossaries, and other helps for readers. There are still others, which we will call study Bibles, that provide some or all of the aforementioned helps as well as introductions to each book of the Bible. They also include footnotes explaining the gist of stories and arguments, illuminating historical and cultural references, presenting translational and exegetical options and difficulties, listing relevant cross-references, and offering brief interpretive commentary. Some even provide general articles on the Bible and biblical study and questions for study and reflection.

These study Bibles are, however, of uneven quality—even more so than the translations with which they are associated. Some are produced by well-meaning but academically unqualified people and publishing houses. Others are spiritually or devotionally oriented, products of a worthy enterprise that nevertheless should not be mistaken for encouraging scholarly exegesis.

The great value of a sound, scholarly study Bible is that it provides quick, reliable (though not infallible!), "context-sensitive" help. Every serious student of the Bible should use one on a regular basis. For purposes of exegesis, of course, a study Bible does not provide enough detail, but it can be suggestive for a variety of exegetical matters (especially context, structure, and synthesis). It also allows readers to peruse a particular portion of a biblical book, an entire book, or a series of books with some degree of comfort, in much the same way that they might use an annotated road map from one of the travel clubs. Finally, it normally provides readers with a very helpful array of cross-references at a glance, leading them to important parallel texts and possible sources in earlier writings.

There are several particularly helpful scholarly study Bibles from which to choose. Many of these appear in several forms (paperback, hardcover, student, electronic, etc.) for a variety of prices, but all have an excellent cost-to-value ratio. These study Bibles are grouped here according to the religious affiliations of those who have produced them: Jewish, ecumenical/interfaith, Catholic, and evangelical Protestant. One spiritually oriented study Bible also merits inclusion, and is therefore described at the end.

Jewish

The Jewish Study Bible (New York: Oxford University Press, 2004), edited by Adele Berlin, Marc Zvi Brettler, and Michael Fishbane, is a scholarly study edition of the Tanak (for Christians, the Old Testament) translation that was produced by the Jewish Publication Society. It represents a broad spectrum of Jewish scholarship: Orthodox, Conservative, and Reform. Each biblical book has a fairly substantive introduction, an outline, and both textual and interpretive notes. The interpretive notes vary in length from brief comments that take up about 5 percent of the page to much lengthier ones that cover half of the page. There are also twenty-one essays on various topics ranging from biblical backgrounds, to Jewish approaches to biblical interpretation and use, to modern critical methods of biblical study. The volume also includes tables and color maps.

This is a first-rate study Bible for students and others interested in the interpretation of the Old Testament/Hebrew Bible as the Jewish Scriptures rather than as part of the Christian canon. Its introductions, notes, and articles will be useful to serious students from any religious tradition.

Ecumenical/Interfaith

The New Oxford Annotated Bible (with or without the Apocrypha; augmented 3d ed.; New York: Oxford University Press, 2007) of the NRSV translation is the successor to the same title produced for the RSV, which combined *The Oxford Annotated Bible* and *The Oxford Annotated Apocrypha*. With the publication of the NRSV, the annotations and articles were reviewed and updated by an ecumenical team of superb scholars, with Michael D. Coogan as chief editor. The third edition (1991) had been a complete revision; the augmented third edition has slightly revised introductions to the biblical books. These introductions to each book are generally brief (a page or less) but insightful. The notes are also often brief (averaging 10 to 20 percent of the page), though in some documents, particularly in the New Testament, they consume an average of one-third of the page.

The greatest strengths of this study Bible are probably the other helps it offers, particularly the introductions to the various sections of the Bible (Pentateuch, Prophetic Books, apocalyptic literature, etc.), as well as the general articles on such topics as "Characteristics of Hebrew Poetry" and "Literary Forms in the Gospels." Tables, diagrams, and maps round out the volume, some of which were added for this edition, as was a glossary.

All in all, this is a good study Bible. Its quality is first rate, but its brevity makes it less desirable than some others.

The HarperCollins Study Bible (with the Apocrypha; fully revised and updated; New York: HarperCollins, 2006) of the NRSV was produced for the publisher by members of the Society of Biblical Literature, the world's largest and foremost association of professional biblical scholars, under the leadership of Wayne Meeks (first edition, 1993) and then Harold Attridge (second edition). The introductions (generally 2–3 pages) and notes (generally about 25 to 35 percent of the page, but sometimes 50 percent) reflect a range of contemporary scholarly opinion from a wide variety of Christian and Jewish faith traditions. The new edition has five brief but helpful general articles (there being none in the original edition), and it contains some helpful tables and more than twenty-five maps. Although the annotations are very responsible and reliable, they tend to focus only on historical and literary matters, to the neglect of theological concerns, though the revised edition is much more attentive to intertextuality (echoes of Scripture within Scripture itself). About 25 percent of the material in the 2006 edition is revised or brand new.

The New Interpreter's Study Bible (Nashville: Abingdon, 2003), published under the leadership of general editor Walter J. Harrelson, is an excellent study Bible, similar to *The HarperCollins Study Bible*. Based on the NRSV (including the Apocrypha), this study Bible includes introductions, outlines, and notes for each biblical book, plus excursuses and special notes on certain passages and topics. The introductory material for each book is about two to four pages in length, while the notes take up about 25–50 percent of each page. A few articles (on biblical inspiration, authority, and interpretation), a short glossary, and nineteen color maps appear at the end of the volume. The CD-ROM version includes the (quite dated) five-volume *Interpreter's Dictionary of the Bible,* maps, and the general articles from the recent and very valuable commentary *The New Interpreter's Bible.*

Catholic

The Catholic Study Bible (2d ed.; New York: Oxford University Press, 2006), edited by Donald Senior and John J. Collins, is a textbook, even a library, in one volume. Although produced exclusively by Roman Catholic scholars, it is not theologically biased and can be used with great profit by any student. The biblical text is the NAB. Each introduction to a biblical book (generally 1–2 pages) is supplemented at the front of the volume by a reading guide to the book. The reading guides, which have all been revised since the original 1990 edition, are all excellent, providing much longer introductions to each book's author, historical and sociopolitical context, structure, content, theology, and spiritual significance. Each reading guide concludes with a short bibliography. The brief introductions and reading guides are further supplemented by new or expanded general articles about various aspects of biblical study, each of the major divisions of the Bible, and biblical archaeology and geography. In addition to maps, the back of the volume has lectionary tables, indicating which texts are read throughout the Catholic Church's liturgical schedule.

The notes, also revised, take up anywhere from about 10 to 60 percent of the page, with an average of less than 20 percent for the Old Testament but 35 to 40 percent for the New Testament. These notes contain careful analysis of the structure and theology of the text and offer copious cross-references. The second edition also contains sidebars on special topics. All in all, this is the best study Bible on the market. Its notes are balanced and insightful, while its reading guides put the detailed comments into larger historical, literary, and theological perspectives.

The *Saint Mary's Press College Study Bible* (Winona, Minn.: Saint Mary's, 2007) is an attractive study Bible geared to the undergraduate or other beginning student. It contains the NAB text and its extensive notes; introductions to the biblical books, written for this volume; ninety short articles on topics such as social justice and spirituality; and lots of good graphics: color photos and maps, diagrams, etc.

Evangelical Protestant

The NIV Study Bible (fully revised ed.; Grand Rapids: Zondervan, 2002), edited by Kenneth L. Barker and associates, is a new version of a resource first released in 1985 and 1995. It was first produced at the initiative of some of the original NIV translators. (It is also available in a loose-leaf edition from Hendrickson Publishers.) The copious notes (averaging 30 percent, but frequently 50 percent of the page) sometimes reflect the "traditional evangelical theology" of the contributors. One major theme of the notes is the "interrelationship of the Scriptures," a legitimate concern that sometimes results in the drawing of parallels and theological conclusions that some may consider questionable, especially in notes on Old Testament texts that are seen as pointing ahead to the New.

In addition to the notes, *The NIV Study Bible* has introductions to each book (most of which reflect traditional views of authorship and date, such as Mosaic authorship of the Pentateuch); detailed outlines within the introductions; a cross-reference system for texts and themes; dozens of maps and tables related to various books; a few brief essays; indexes; and a very substantial concordance.

This study Bible's great strengths have been its helpful tables and notes, plus its inclusion of a concordance. The introductions and notes in the revised edition are improved, with strong emphasis on the theological and literary features of the text. Unfortunately, however, the introductions are still sometimes defensive (of traditional perspectives) in tone and the notes occasionally too biased in one theological direction. Used with awareness of the theological perspective and agenda of the contributors, this study Bible can be useful for providing a general survey, but its judgments need balance for serious academic study.

In 2006, Barker and Zondervan adapted *The NIV Study Bible* to the text of the TNIV, publishing the ***TNIV Study Bible.***

Similar in approach to *The NIV Study Bible* and the *TNIV Study Bible* is a unique resource called the NIV Archaeological Study Bible (Grand Rapids: Zondervan, 2006). Produced in collaboration with Gordon-Conwell Theological Seminary, a conservative evangelical institution, this study Bible with lavish graphics focuses on historical, cultural, and literary contexts, with supplemental articles, hundreds of photographs, a concordance, a glossary, and a companion CD-ROM. Its frequently apologetic tone, stressing the historical reliability of the Bible, also needs balance from other perspectives.

The ***NET Bible,*** which is technically a translation, is described earlier in this chapter. Though not a full study Bible, its various editions include one or more of the following: the 60,000 study, textual, and translators' notes; full-color satellite maps; a concordance.

Spiritually Oriented Study Bible

There are of course many "devotional" Bibles with introductions and annotations on the market, but few of these are produced by academic biblical scholars or theologians. ***The Renovaré Spiritual Formation Bible*** (San Francisco: HarperSanFrancisco, 2005), however, stands out as one attempt to bridge the gap between excellent scholarship and spirituality. Editors and contributors include well-known biblical scholars and theologians. The text is the NRSV, with Apocrypha, and the introductions and notes are supplemented by fifteen essays. Though not an appropriate choice for primarily academic use, this study Bible is worth considering for other purposes.

Summary

In the end, unfortunately, the best study Bible (*The Catholic Study Bible*) does not contain the best English translation for exegetical purposes (the NRSV). Students must therefore decide on the translation that best suits their purposes and then pick the best study Bible to match it—or vice versa.

Review & Study

Chapter Summary

- Students should select a passage for exegesis that interests them and that is a complete unit of manageable size with a clear beginning and end.

- Every translation is an interpretation, a kind of streamlined exegesis.

- The task of translation is rendered difficult by several complicating features of language.

- The two basic approaches to translation are formal equivalence and functional equivalence.

- Students who do not read the original languages should use an excellent version, preferably a formal-equivalence translation such as the NRSV or NAB, as the basis of their exegetical work.

- Study Bibles are a valuable tool, though none is without its limitations.

Practical Hints

1. Treat all translations, even the best, as carefully researched options, not as the final truth.

2. If you do not read the original languages, use a formal-equivalence translation such as the NRSV or NAB as the basis of your exegesis, and use other versions to supply possible translations or interpretations of various elements—any and all of which must be confirmed by careful exegesis.

3. Purchase a good study Bible for everyday use and for basic helps in the beginning stages of exegesis.

For Further Insight and Practice

1. Choose two favorite Bible texts and read them in at least three different translations. What differences do you notice among the translations? Are the differences signifi-

cant? Does the tone or thrust of either passage differ, in your estimation, from translation to translation?

2. Compare the treatment of these two passages in two different study Bibles, and record your observations about the differences in interpretation.

3. Review chapter 11, section 2, pp. 189–95, "Resources for Understanding the Text."

The
Elements

CHAPTER THREE
Survey

> Think of yourself as a detective looking for clues
> to a [text's] general theme or idea, alert
> for anything that will make it clearer.
> —*Mortimer J. Adler and Charles Van Doren,*
> How to Read a Book

On first reading, what seems to be going on in the text?

The careful reading and analysis of any text, whether textbook, essay, or poem, requires an initial survey of the contents of the document. Such a survey prepares the reader, alerting him or her to key aspects of the text for consideration in the process of closer reading. So too when reading the Bible. This very short (but very important) chapter introduces some simple strategies for surveying one's chosen passage in its context. Important tools for assisting in this part of the exegetical process are discussed in section 3 of chapter 11.

Survey and Question

When I was in elementary school, our teacher taught us a reading skill—actually a process—for "attacking" a chapter in a textbook. It was abbreviated SQ3R. The letters stood for *survey, question, read, recite,* and *review.* The starting point for SQ3R is obviously "survey": getting the lay of the land, so to speak. It is an initial overview of the contents of your chosen text in context.

In a similar way, today we have learned to navigate the electronic equivalent of a text, the website, by surveying its contents before plunging into the many layers of the site. A glance at the homepage, with its navigation bars and links, provides a bird's-eye view of the major components of the site.

Unlike textbooks or essays in newspapers and magazines, the Bible (apart from the Psalms) has no original chapter titles, headlines, or subheads to indicate the specific contents of a chapter or section—and certainly no navigation bars! The section titles found in many Bibles are the work—sometimes good, sometimes not so good—of the editors of each particular version or edition. Thus the first step in interpretation is to read the passage several times, ignoring the section titles—or at least recognizing that they are the work of other readers. You may even wish to give the passage your own preliminary title.

Many people find it beneficial to read the text in a few different translations (as well as in Greek or Hebrew, if you are able). It may also be helpful to read the text aloud, recalling that much biblical literature was actually heard before it was ever read. Furthermore, it is important to read the text within its context, to read (or at the very least, skim) the book or a major section of the book in which the text is found.

As you read, you should begin to record observations and questions that come to mind. These notes may be about the place of the text in the biblical book, the historical and social situation of the writer or audience, allusions to biblical texts or to extratextual items (place names, historical events and people, etc.) in the passage, the form and contents of the selection, and so on. This is the "question" step of the SQ3R process.

It is also helpful at this early point to read a brief introduction to the biblical book in which the passage is located, especially if you are reading it "cold"—that is, apart from the context of class discussion or reading assignments. Some study editions of the Bible provide good introductions of this sort. Other good sources would be a short article in an introductory textbook, a Bible dictionary, or a one-volume commentary. (These are discussed in section 3 of chapter 11.) Reading these items will likely raise additional questions that you will want to investigate as your exegesis progresses.

Do *not*, however, read much commentary on the text itself at this point in the exegetical process. Do your own work first! You may wish, nevertheless, to use the one-volume commentary or a similar resource to get a basic grasp of the themes and issues in the interpretation of your text before you proceed to more in-depth reading.

Exegetes who read the original languages should also make a provisional translation of the text at this stage. The translation process itself will raise all kinds of issues for the exegetical investigation.

First Impressions: Educated Guessing

As you execute and complete your first readings of the text and its contexts, you will begin to formulate some initial impressions of its meaning. Ask yourself, "What is the topic of this text? What perspective on the topic does it offer? What role might it play in the book as a whole?" At this point, answering such questions is often little more than educated guesswork—but it is an important first step in the process of exegesis. The great theorist of interpretation Paul Ricoeur said that there are no rules for guessing. However, the surveying and guessing process will lead you to continue with a more systematic investigation as you move on to the remaining steps of the process.

Furthermore, though there may be no hard-and-fast rules for guessing, Ricoeur also reminds us that this early encounter with the text in context provides a good opportunity for readers to acknowledge any prior understanding of—or bias about—the text. Do you know this text? Have you heard or read it before? Does its topic or perspective stir up any memories or feelings, whether positive or negative? This initial stage is also an opportunity to examine your own socio-theological location—your own social status, gender, culture, and religious beliefs—to see how they may affect your initial and ongoing encounter with the text.

The process of "educated guessing" should result in your formulation of a working thesis about the meaning of the text. This working thesis will be constantly revised and reformulated as your exegetical work continues. Scholars and good exegetes willingly seek out facts and details that might disconfirm their hypotheses. In fact, therefore, your final interpretation of a text may be quite contrary to your preliminary educated guess.

Writing an Introduction

In an exegesis paper, as in any paper, the first part should be a brief statement of the contents and thesis, or main point, of the paper. Your thesis statement, begun as an educated guess, will be honed and refined throughout the exegetical process. By the time you finalize your thesis statement for the introduction, it should be more than a guess. Although any biblical interpretation should be held with humility and an appropriate degree of tentativeness, a good paper presents a clear thesis and argues it vigorously.

This is sometimes a difficult point for beginning exegetes to grasp or to implement, for it is easy to think that writing about the Bible is like writing an encyclopedia article—just the facts, so to speak. But an exegesis paper is not a series of factoids or of good but unrelated observations about a text; rather, it is a series of inter-related observations that contribute to an overall interpretation of the text as a whole. This means that if several people (whether beginning students or established scholars) are working on the same text, their observations and interpretations will be at least slightly, and sometimes radically, different from one another. It also means that if the *same* person works on a text, over time, in different personal, ecclesial, or political contexts, his or her interpretations will also, in all likelihood, differ from one another. (The variety of possible interpretations for one biblical passage is illustrated in chapter 7 on synthesis.)

An exegesis paper begins, therefore, with a thesis—a claim to be unpacked and demonstrated. Practically speaking, the opening of the paper may contain highlights from one or more of the main sections of the paper, but it will draw especially from the sections on context and synthesis. In fact, the thesis is really an advance statement of the synthesis. For this reason, of course, the introduction will be written after the process of interpretation is completed. An exegesis paper without a thesis indicates that the writer has not come to any conclusions but has simply accumulated a lot of data or ideas. This is really not exegesis, nor is it acceptable paper-writing at either the undergraduate or graduate level.

One final point. Some exegetes today also feel the need to identify their own socio-theological location in the introduction to a paper or longer work. Although this is unobjectionable in principle if handled carefully, the introduction to an exegesis paper is not the place for an extended self-description or confession.

Review & Study

Chapter Summary

- The process of initially surveying and questioning the text in context gives the reader the "lay of the land" and encourages preliminary observations and questions to investigate.

- The initial survey includes taking an educated guess at the text's meaning.

- Eventually in exegesis, an original educated guess must be honed and sharpened (or occasionally even discarded!) through careful work, and replaced by a well-thought-out, clearly articulated, and (in a paper) convincingly presented thesis.

- The introduction to an exegesis paper, finalized at the conclusion of the exegetical process, presents the thesis of the paper in light of the results of the exegetical process.

Practical Hints

1. Begin recording thoughts and questions from your very first encounter with the text.

2. Remember that guessing is not a bad reading strategy—as long as you remember to allow your first impressions to be refined, expanded, and corrected.

3. Once you formulate a guess or working thesis, begin to note potential supporting evidence for, as well as challenges to, your hypothesis. Be prepared to be corrected.

For Further Insight and Practice

1. Using a Bible with section or chapter titles, read the following well-known passages, noting the title supplied by the editors and writing one of your own.

Passage	Editor's Title	Your Title
Genesis 1:1–2:3		
Exodus 12:29–42		
Luke 15:11–32		
John 3:1–21		

2. Review chapter 11, section 3, pp. 195–202, "Resources for Surveying the Text."

3. Choose a one-volume commentary and learn as much as you can about the book of Isaiah and the basic contents of Isaiah 40–55 in fifteen minutes. Then look at Isaiah 40:1–11 and make an initial guess at the gist of its message.

4. Read carefully the introductions to the sample exegesis papers at the end of this book in Appendix C.

CHAPTER FOUR

Contextual Analysis
The Historical, Literary, and Canonical Contexts of the Text

> A text without a context is a pretext.
> —*Anonymous*

> The devil can cite Scripture for his purpose.
> —*William Shakespeare,* The Merchant of Venice

> Oh that I knew how all thy lights combine,
> And the configurations of their glorie!
> Seeing not onely how each verse doth shine,
> But all the constellations of the storie!
> —*George Herbert, "The Holy Scriptures (II)"*

In what historical, sociopolitical, and cultural situation was the passage written?

How does the passage relate to what precedes and follows it, and to the document as a whole?

The Bible did not just "drop out of heaven," nor was it written in a special language with unique literary forms by some strange class of humans unaffected by their social and historical situation. No, the Bible was written by and for real people, living in specific historical contexts, to address particular individual and community needs. (This does *not* necessarily imply, however, that the Bible is *merely* a human book. Jews and Christians have always believed that the Bible was the result of some combination of human and divine effort.) Close analysis of a biblical text requires, to the greatest degree possible, careful attention to its historical and literary contexts.

Indeed, context is so crucial to interpretation that it is no exaggeration whatsoever to say that if you alter the *context* of a word or sentence or paragraph, you also alter the *content* of that text. Sometimes the effect is relatively minimal, but often it can be very significant. For example, the meaning conveyed by a person shouting "Fire!" will be very different depending upon the circumstances in which he or she shouts that word: while running out of a house engulfed in flames, while sitting inside a movie theater that is not burning, or while standing beside a line of men armed with rifles facing a lone man who is blindfolded. The meaning of that one simple word is clearly very context-dependent.

In this chapter we consider the historical (including sociopolitical and cultural) and the literary (including rhetorical) contexts of a text. We also note briefly the subject of the canonical context of a text—its place in the Bible as a whole.

Historical, Sociopolitical, and Cultural Contexts

People and communities are constituted in large measure by three things:

- the significant events they experience (either personally or vicariously through stories) and retell
- the private and public relationships in which they are engaged
- the values that they embrace, consciously or not

These three facets of human life—our historical, sociopolitical, and cultural contexts—were also, of course, facets of life in "Bible times." Of all elements of exegesis, understanding the historical, social, and cultural contexts—which we will refer to collectively as "historical context" for short—is the most difficult for the non-scholar (and even for the scholar!).[1] Reconstructing the historical contexts of the biblical writings is a never-ending task in which professional biblical scholars, historians, and others are engaged. Because historical reconstruction is an arduous task, because it

---

[1]There is no one ideal term to refer to the complex reality that is embodied in the long phrase "historical, sociopolitical, and cultural contexts." To those who emphasize the sociopolitical or sociocultural dimension, "historical" is sometimes taken to refer only to events, with insufficient attention to political realities, cultural values, and networks of social relationships. Because I find the term "social context" inadequate and the terms "sociopolitical context," "sociocultural context," and "socio-rhetorical context" a bit cumbersome, I have chosen to use the term "historical context," but I mean it in the broadest sense possible.

is in part art as well as science, and because it is always changing as new discoveries are made and new theories are advanced, some readers of the Bible conclude that the real-life context of the biblical writings can be ignored. Some would even argue that we imperil ourselves and our readings if we make interpretation dependent on historical, social, and cultural contexts.

This book affirms that the task of understanding the worlds of the Bible and of particular texts is necessary, albeit difficult. Texts are often the product of specific occasions, composed to address certain needs, and neglecting these contexts is more perilous than the risk of making mistakes in our historical reading. People communicate within a social network located within a particular culture and political situation at a specific point in time. Our goal, in part, is to discover the social network within which the writers and hearers/readers of biblical texts communicated. We also want to discover the common cultural beliefs and values—the "presupposition pool" as some have called it—that authors and hearers/readers of the original text would have brought to their production of or encounter with the text. Making this challenging process all the more complex is the fact that the authors and readers/hearers of the text may well have all had different social networks and presupposition pools! The same applies for the authors of the sources underlying the text.

It should be noted that frequently we cannot reconstruct the exact or even an approximate "occasion" for a biblical text.[2] That is, we cannot always discern precisely which event in precisely which year, or even what kind of event and what kind of circumstance, triggered the writing of a passage. This does not, however, remove the need to attend to a text's historical context, more broadly understood. In the biblical texts we find references to the historical, political, religious, and symbolic worlds that their writers and readers/hearers inhabited. In order to understand these worlds, an exegete may need to understand something about, for example, ancient Near Eastern covenant treaties, ancient attitudes toward death and dying, honor-shame relations, or Roman imperial ideology. These contexts may be conceptually and even chronologically rather broad, but they add much to our understanding of the text even when there is no way to identify the text's exact date and occasion.

---

[2] The specific situation of the author and readers/hearers of a biblical passage or document has often been called the "occasion" of the text. More recently, it has been referred to as the "rhetorical situation."

The average reader cannot possibly know in detail the complex stories of ancient nations, communities of faith, and individuals that are the concern of biblical scholars and historians. Most people must rely on the technical works or more popular publications of these scholars. These can be found in books, Bible dictionaries, commentaries, scholarly journals, and certain magazines written by scholars for nonscholars. (Some of these works are listed in section 4 of chapter 11.) Modern scholars adopt not only more traditional approaches to history but also relatively new approaches that are indebted to such social sciences as sociology and cultural anthropology. Some are interested primarily in *social description,* or *what,* while others are interested in *social analysis,* or *why,* often utilizing standard models and procedures from the social sciences. The goal of all of these approaches is to understand the contexts of the biblical texts as thoroughly as possible—the social and political environment in which texts were written, the cultural values expressed in or challenged by the texts, and so on.

As you read a biblical text, questions about these sorts of topics will naturally arise. They should be noted carefully for investigation. Using one or more of the kinds of resources noted above, you should attempt to answer these questions as well as find out as much as you can about the historical, social, and cultural situation in which the author and readers lived. Ask yourself these kinds of questions:

- What are the chief characteristics of the people (often referred to as the "community") addressed by the passage? What can be known of their history? social location? beliefs and practices?

- What ancient events, political realities, places, customs, values, and beliefs are mentioned or alluded to in the text (sometimes called "historical background" or "extratextual realities") that must be understood in order to comprehend the text?[3]

- What circumstances, or what kind of situation, might have prompted the author to write this text?

The last of these questions may be the most challenging, for discerning the occasion or rhetorical situation of a text is often tricky

---

[3]When writing an exegesis paper, one is always faced with decisions about where to discuss such matters—in the contextual analysis or in the detailed analysis. In general, the contextual analysis should only consider the aspects of historical, social, and cultural context that affect the whole passage, and should normally do so relatively briefly. Discussion of extratextual realities not associated with the whole text should usually take place in the detailed analysis, which may also require more in-depth discussion of certain aspects of the context first mentioned in the contextual analysis.

business. In fact, sometimes even the broader historical context in which the text was written cannot be known with any certainty. For example, the same Old Testament psalm may be dated to the tenth century B.C.E. by some scholars and to the fifth century B.C.E. by others. Certain New Testament letters are believed by some to have originated in the mid-first century and by others to have derived from imitators working in the mid-second century. Indeed, the authorship and audience are quite disputed among scholars for many biblical books, including the books of the Pentateuch, the Historical Books, the Gospels, and several of the Letters. In some cases, what used to be called "the assured results of criticism" are no longer assured.[4]

Nevertheless, the exegete needs to explore the scholarly options for situating the text historically and, at the very least, identify those references in the text to extratextual realities that can be determined. Many of these references—for example, to kingship or covenants in the ancient Near East, or to wedding banquets or adoption in the Roman Empire—should actually be discussed in the detailed analysis. But noting them at this stage will often help the exegete discern the rhetorical situation that seems to give rise to the writing of the text at hand.

In your attempts to discern the historical context, be careful not to stray beyond the evidence. Many times, for instance, exegetes assume that a word or phrase in a narrative text about Israel or Jesus alludes to a particular belief, situation, or problem in the later community for which the text was written. While the existence of such connections is plausible, even likely, the burden of proof is on the exegete to demonstrate specific connections. An important example of this is the occurrence of three references in the Gospel of John to believers in Jesus being put out of the synagogues (John 9:22; 12:42; 16:2). Many scholars have argued or assumed that these references reflect the situation of disciples in the time the Gospel was written rather than that of disciples in the time of Jesus. These arguments and assumptions are now being questioned.

A related problem is sometimes called "mirror reading," the attempt to reconstruct the beliefs and practices of a community on the basis of what is said not only *about* it but also *to* it, especially in

---

[4]In the second half of the twentieth century, for instance, scholars made bold assertions about the nature of the individual communities to which the four Gospels were addressed. These scholarly "certainties" are now increasingly disputed and even dismissed.

a New Testament letter. For example, the presence of an injunction to brotherly/sisterly love does not necessarily mean that the community being addressed is full of friction or hatred. The careful exegete wants to make sure that such reconstructions do not result in one's exegesis being built upon a house of cards.

You need also to be careful not to let the introductory questions of biblical studies—the who, what, when, and where of the biblical writings—divert you from the main task of exegesis. Your assignment in exegesis is to engage the text, not to review the academic debates about the book in which your text is located. Do not turn the first part (or any part) of your exegesis paper merely into a list of possible scholarly positions.

Nevertheless, despite these words of caution, understanding as much as possible of the historical, social, and cultural contexts is absolutely essential to exegesis. For example, you cannot grasp either the irony or the message of the story of the Good Samaritan (Luke 10:25–37) unless you understand something of first-century Jewish–Samaritan relations. Nor can you understand Ezekiel's vision of dry bones coming to life (Ezekiel 37) without some knowledge of his people's spiritual and political destruction, exile to Babylon, and consequent despair.

Since in preparing a basic exegesis of a text you cannot, and should not, read (or write!) a lengthy history book or review of research about the historical context of your text, ask yourself, "What are the *key* facts and issues related to this passage (and the book in which it is found) that will help me interpret it?" It is these key things that you must focus on in your research and, when you write an exegesis paper, point out to your reader, either in broad strokes in the discussion of historical context or in more detail in the detailed analysis. A hermeneutical circle will be at work: the more you learn about the context, the sharper your questions will become and the more able you will be to zero in on that which really matters.

Literary and Rhetorical Contexts

It has been said that a text without a context is a pretext—an excuse for finding one's presuppositions confirmed by the text. In other words, many misinterpretations of the Bible are due to neglect of the literary context. To understand a passage, you must try to see how it fits into the larger literary unit(s) in which it occurs: for instance, the chapter, the section of the biblical book, and the book as a whole. Literary context, therefore, is really contexts—plural. The text is often like the center of a set of concentric circles, each circle representing a larger section of the biblical book. These contexts are usually referred to as the *nearer,* or *immediate,* context and the *larger* context(s).

The nearer, or immediate, context is that which directly precedes and follows the passage. The larger context of a passage is the major division of the biblical book in which it appears and then the biblical book as a whole. For example, the immediate context of the story of Nicodemus's encounter with Jesus (John 3) includes the events narrated and interpreted in chapter 1 and especially chapter 2, as well as the subsequent encounter of the Samaritan woman with Jesus in chapter 4. The larger context includes the first half of the Gospel, often called "the book of signs" (John 1:19–12:50, following the prologue) and beyond that the Gospel of John as a whole.

One helpful, almost necessary, tool in the task of contextual analysis, especially for the larger context, is an outline (even a brief one) of the book of the Bible in which the passage occurs. Outlines can be found in many editions of the Bible and in Bible dictionaries, introductory texts, and commentaries. Ideally, however, students should construct their own outlines of biblical books that they study.

In addition to the literary context, a text also has a *rhetorical* context. Rhetoric is the art of effective (and therefore often persuasive) speaking and writing. According to Cicero, the purpose of rhetoric is to teach, delight, and move hearers or readers. Rhetorical context, therefore, refers to the place of a passage in the document's overall strategy of rational, artistic, and/or emotional influence and persuasion. Rhetorical context is a function of literary context, but it is more. Analyzing the literary context means asking *where* a text is located; analyzing the rhetorical context means asking *why* a text is located where it is. The fundamental question is what *effect* the text has, or might have, on readers by virtue of its situation within a larger discourse. For example, the relationship of John 3 to each of the other small and large text segments mentioned above will affect the way we understand the narrative of the encounter of Nicodemus with Jesus.

The average exegete, and even the biblical scholar, cannot be expected to grasp all the intricacies of rhetorical criticism. Some of the basic structures of rhetoric indicated in the next chapter are helpful to know, but perhaps the single most important tool for rhetorical analysis is the disciplined imagination. Constantly ask yourself, as you look at the text, "Why *this* and why *here*? If I am the hearer/reader, what do I sense this text trying to do to me?"

As you consider literary and rhetorical contexts, then, you will be asking yourself the following kinds of questions:

For the Immediate Context

- What is the subject of the paragraph or two immediately preceding this passage? How does this material lead into the passage at hand?

- Does the material following the passage connect directly to it or help explain it?

- Does this passage work in connection with its immediate context to achieve a particular rhetorical goal?

For the Larger Contexts

- Where does this passage occur in the structure of the book? Of what major section is it a part? What significance does this position have?

- What has "happened" (whether in narrative, argument, etc.) in the book so far, and what will happen later?

- What appears to be the text's function in the section and in the book as a whole? How does this passage appear to serve the agenda of the entire work?

Brief observations about the literary-rhetorical context of two biblical texts may be helpful here, as examples of how the immediate and larger contexts can inform an understanding of a specific passage.[5] Sometimes it is more helpful to begin with the larger context of the entire book and work inward, so to speak, and sometimes it is more beneficial to begin with the nearer context and work outward. An illustration of each follows.

A study of Genesis 15:1–6, the famous text in which God promises Abram (later Abraham) descendants like the stars and then reck-

---

[5]Of all the biblical books, only in the book of Psalms (a collection of hymns) is there really anything resembling a series of independent, isolated texts without an overarching context. It should be noted, however, that scholars have recently paid more attention to the structure and organization of the book of Psalms and thus to the literary context even of these individual psalms.

ons Abram's response of faith as righteousness, only makes sense in light of its larger and more immediate contexts. Genesis is a book of origins, dividing neatly into two major parts: the origin of the world and its peoples and problems (chs. 1–11) and the origin of Israel through God's covenantal promises made and fulfilled (chs. 12–50). The first section of the second part focuses on Abram/Abraham and is sometimes called the "Abraham Cycle" (Genesis 12:1–25:11). Thus Gen 15:1–6 appears near the beginning of a major cycle and of a major part of the book. Yet this short narrative must also be read in connection with more proximate parts of the grand story: God's call of Abram and God's original promise (Genesis 12:1–9); the unfolding story of Abraham through the end of chapter 14; the ratification of the covenant in ritual, including circumcision (15:7–21; ch. 17); and the lack of faith that led to Isaac's birth (ch.16)—all before the promise made in 15:1–6 is fulfilled in the birth of Isaac (ch. 21).

An examination of 1 Corinthians 13, the "love" chapter read at weddings, would require consideration of the structure and contents of the letter to discern its function within the document. Chapter 13 stands right in the middle of a discussion about the use and abuse of spiritual gifts in the body of Christ (ch. 12), especially the divisive gift of speaking in tongues (ch. 14). Much of the second half of the letter (chs. 8–14) deals specifically with several issues related to worship, and chapter 13 provides a way of operating as faithful members of the one body of Christ in the middle of the original "worship wars." In 1 Corinthians more broadly, Paul deals with various forms of confusion in the practice of the gospel at Corinth, and self-giving love seems clearly to be part of the solution to a set of multiple problems (e.g., divisiveness in chs. 1–4 and litigious behavior in 6:1–11). In fact, one might argue that for Paul love is the principal solution to the entire array of issues in Corinth.

It should be clear that the process of analyzing the literary context of a text entails hard work. It means carefully reading more than the short passage you are trying to understand or analyze. But it is necessary hard work if you really want to grasp something of the original significance of a biblical text and if you want to interpret the text responsibly. (Thus, those who use a lectionary for preaching must be especially faithful in reading the passages for the week in a Bible, not just in the lectionary.) In the cases where little or nothing can be said with certainty about the historical context, the literary and rhetorical contexts—which are always very important—become even more so.

More often than not your subsequent detailed analysis of the text will cause you to modify your initial conclusions about the literary and rhetorical contexts—as you would probably have expected by now.

Canonical Context

For those who read the Bible theologically, one of the contexts within which a text may be considered is the Bible, or canon, as a whole—the canonical context. This does not mean that theological interpreters may ignore the historical and literary contexts discussed above but, rather, that they may also supplement or expand these contexts by viewing the text as part of the one book called the Bible.[6]

If you decide to consider the canonical context, you will be asking yourself the following kinds of questions:

- What role (if any) does this text, and/or its primary theme(s) and character(s), play in the rest of Scripture?
- What, specifically, is the relationship (if any) between this text and texts in the other Testament (Old or New)?
- With which other biblical texts or themes does your text stand in harmonious relation?
- With which other biblical texts or themes does your text stand in tension? Can or should this tension be resolved?

That is to say, considering the canonical context allows the exegete to put biblical texts in conversation with one another.

For example, in considering the canonical context of Genesis 15:1–6, discussed above, you might wish to note the role of God's promise to Abraham and Abraham's response of faith as a significant motif in one or more other parts of Scripture: later in the book of Genesis, in Exodus and Deuteronomy, in 1–2 Chronicles, in Acts, and in Paul's letters. On the other hand, if you are doing an exegesis of Paul's use of Abraham in, say, Romans 4, you not only will have to consider the narratives in Genesis (since Paul does), but you also may wish to address (and maybe even try to resolve!) the apparent tension between the "faith alone" perspective of Paul and the "faith + works" perspective of James.

---

[6]For further discussion of theological interpretation and the role of canonical considerations within it, see chapter 8.

These canonical concerns should not preoccupy you as an exegete, but neither should they be dismissed as irrelevant to the larger goals of exegesis when it is done for theological ends. In an exegesis paper, the discussion of canonical context can take place in the section on contextual analysis and/or elsewhere, as appropriate; often it fits well into the final section of the paper on theological reflection. In a sermon or homily based on solid exegesis, attention to the canonical context is especially relevant, as people in the pews often wish to know how one text or theme fits into the big picture, the greater economy of God.

Conclusion

A text without a context—a text isolated from its various contexts (plural)—is a potentially dangerous weapon. Responsible exegesis acknowledges the difficulty of discovering those contexts, whether historical, social, cultural, literary, rhetorical, or canonical in nature, but refuses to abandon the task. The alternatives to engaging in the hard work required by this element of exegesis are too costly.

Review & Study

Chapter Summary

- The exegetical process includes the difficult but necessary task of discerning the historical, social, and cultural contexts of the text.

- Analyzing the literary context of a text means asking where the text is situated in its nearer as well as larger contexts.

- Considering the rhetorical context means asking why a text is where it is and what effect it has on readers/hearers by virtue of its location.

- Considering the canonical context means thinking about the role of the text in the Bible as a whole and about its relationship to certain other portions of the Bible.

- A text without a context is a pretext.

Practical Hints

1. When considering the historical, sociopolitical, and cultural contexts, which can encompass a vast quantity of information, always ask yourself, "Of everything I could learn and say about these contexts, what are the key facts and issues related to this passage that will affect my interpretation of it?" In writing a paper, eliminate, or at least greatly abridge, all other data.

2. When considering the literary and rhetorical contexts, again ask yourself, "What do I need to know (and to say, in a paper) about the literary and rhetorical situation of the text that will enhance my understanding of the text itself?" As you work through the text, keep asking yourself, "Why *this* and why *here*?"

3. When considering the canonical context, keep in mind that the Bible contains diverse, even if ultimately complementary, voices and that the biblical authors did not always know the works of their fellow "contributors"—even their contemporaries and near-contemporaries.

For Further Insight and Practice

1. Isaiah 9:1–7, which contains the words "For unto us a child is born," is celebrated in Handel's oratorio *Messiah* and is read especially during the Christmas season as a prophecy of the birth of Jesus. Skim the first nine chapters of Isaiah and consult a one-volume Bible commentary to find some information about the original historical context of this eighth-century B.C.E. text. (This assignment, by the way, raises the very significant question of how much the meaning of a biblical text is tied to, or dependent on, its original context.)

2. Read Mark 3:1–6, a story early in the narrative of Mark's Gospel that ends shockingly with the Pharisees plotting to kill Jesus. Then read carefully Mark 1–2 (and other parts of Mark, if time allows) and a Bible dictionary or encyclopedia article on the Pharisees. Based on your reading, explain in a few paragraphs the importance of the literary and social contexts for understanding the intense conflict between the Pharisees and Jesus that is portrayed in this story.

3. Review chapter 11, section 4, pp. 202–7, "Resources for Contextual Analysis."

4. Read the sections on historical and literary contexts in the sample exegesis papers in the back of this book, Appendix C.

CHAPTER FIVE

Formal Analysis
The Form, Structure, and Movement of the Text

> Let chaos storm!
> Let cloud shapes swarm!
> I wait for form.
> —*Robert Frost*

> It is impossible to play any game without a
> thorough knowledge of the laws that govern
> it, and you are at fault in making the attempt.
> —*Emily Post,* Etiquette, *chapter 31, "Games and Sports"*

What is the literary form of this text?

What is the literary genre of the document within which the text is situated?

How is the passage structured?

How does the text "move" from beginning to end?

Many people, especially when reading casually, simply "jump into" a text, whether it is a newspaper article, a book, a fund-raising appeal, or a love letter. If, however, a reader merely reads each of the words, sentences, or paragraphs individually, without paying attention to how the whole piece is put together, it is quite possible to "miss the forest for the trees." Moreover, as we know from daily experience, different kinds of printed and electronic media must be read with different principles of interpretation in mind, like the rules of a game.

In this chapter, we consider the form and shape of texts. We will look at how biblical texts are put together. This involves considering the type of writing that the text itself is as well as the type of writing within which it is found. It also involves studying the text's structure and its "movement" from start to finish. As one literary critic puts it, elements of design—structure, patterns, and so on—manifest both the artistic beauty of a text and its function or intended impact.[1] The general term we will use for the careful consideration of the literary form, structure, and movement of a text is *formal analysis.*

Literary Form

Formal analysis begins with the question of the literary form of the passage—what kind, or type, of writing it is. Biblical specialists and other scholars use various terms to refer to the type of literature that a particular text is: *literary form, form, genre,* and even *subgenre.* Whichever terms are used, in each case what is meant is a set of texts with common distinguishing features and with commonly recognized principles, or conventions, for their interpretation. Some people, including myself, prefer to use the term *genre* for larger literary units (e.g., prophetic book, letter, gospel), *subgenre* for more specific categories of a genre (e.g., friendship letter), and *form* for smaller literary units (e.g., prophetic oracle, parable, miracle story, thanksgiving). Others, however, use the term *genre* to refer to smaller as well as larger units. In each case, however, the principle is the same: with respect to format, or formal features, much writing shares common traits with other pieces of writing.

For our purposes, we must consider both the specific literary form of the text being analyzed and the broader literary genre of the writing in which the text appears. While recognizing different uses of the terminology, in this book we will use the term *form* narrowly to mean the literary form (type) of a smaller, specific kind of text (normally the actual passage under consideration) and *genre* broadly to mean the literary form (type) of the entire document within which the passage is situated.[2]

From common experience, we realize that it is important to know the literary form of a text because its form affects the way we read and interpret the text. For instance, when we read a newspaper,

---

[1] Ryken, *Words of Delight,* 91.
[2] This means also that we will not use the word *form* to mean the specific, unique structure or outline of a text. We will reserve the word *structure* for that aspect of the text.

we recognize (consciously or subconsciously) that the front-page news, the comics, the advice columns (such as "Miss Manners"), the advertisements, and the editorials are different types of literature and must be interpreted as such. We understand, even if subconsciously, that each type of "literature" in a newspaper has its own characteristics as well as its own rules of interpretation. We expect an editorial to editorialize, and we look for it; we do not expect it, however, in a front-page news story. We allow for hyperbole in advertising; we do not tolerate it in the crime reports.

Similarly, when we go online we expect to find different kinds of websites and blogsites, and we develop appropriate reading strategies for the various types. For example, there are several main types of blogs. The title of the blog, its appearance and format (structure), and of course its contents reveal its character and purpose—which in turn suggest ways to navigate, or interpret, the narrative "facts" and interpretive perspectives we encounter. There are "pure" blogs, personal online diaries in which we expect and allow for a mixture of narrative and soul-baring. Slightly different are "family news" blogs, in which we expect and allow for a bit of hyperbole and appropriate family pride. Then there are news blogs for particular places (e.g., a school or town or company), which we take seriously but for the most part hardly expect to be CNN, and we probably expect to find a little bit of propaganda. With personal-interest blogs (e.g., Meg on Ice Skating), we look for some combination of expertise, passion, and advocacy, but we probably do not get too emotionally invested if we disagree with the post. Then there are ideological blogs, which function to express a particular social or political perspective; we may approach these with a bit more caution and even suspicion, not to mention passion when we disagree. And, of course, there are commercial and quasi-commercial blogs, where we know to expect hyperbole, and we practice a healthy suspicion as we encounter exaggerated claims.

The way we handle these everyday encounters with differences in literary type in print and electronic resources is helpfully analogous to reading the Bible. The Bible is not, from one perspective, truly a single book; it is a library. The books of the Bible exist in many different genres (e.g., historical narratives; collections of hymns, proverbs, visions, and oracles; and letters[3]), and within the

---

[3]There are even several types of letters and letter fragments in the Bible ("subgenres")—letters of friendship, letters of recommendation, parenetic (advice) letters, and so on.

books there is also a wide variety of forms (e.g., short stories, poems, parables, proverbs, sermons, laws). Responsible readers of the Bible must attempt to identify the literary genres and forms of the texts they study and to understand the principles of interpretation that govern each type. To do anything less is to confuse the comics with the op-ed page, or a personal blog with a commercial one.

Exegesis, because it focuses on a relatively short text, is more concerned about the form of that particular text than about the genre of the document in which it is found. Nevertheless, the question of genre cannot be ignored. We need to ask:

- What kind of writing is the document (biblical book) in which our text is found?
- Are there general principles for the interpretation of this kind of writing that need to be employed?

For example, people wreak all kinds of havoc in the interpretation of the books of Daniel and Revelation when they do not realize that these are *apocalyptic* writings that freely use lavish symbolism and need to be read more like poetry, or even a series of political cartoons, than historical narrative or video footage of the future.

Once you have determined the literary genre of the document—and some research may be needed to make the determination and discern how that affects interpretation—you are ready to look at the form of your specific passage. The first question to ask about literary form is, Is the passage *prose* or *poetry?* Prose is ordinary, everyday speech or writing, whether formal or informal. Poetry is speech or (usually) writing that is metrical, full of images, and often structured in segments called verses or strophes. It does not have to rhyme, though it may. Biblical poetry is often called "thought rhyme," meaning texts consisting of parallel phrases that are similar, or opposite, to each other in meaning.[4]

If the passage under consideration is prose, is it a historical narrative? a symbolic narrative? a short story or tale? a parable? a miracle story? a speech? part of a letter? If it is a speech or part of a letter, is the passage an argument? a definition? an explanation? moral instruction? an apology (self-defense)? a prayer?

If the text appears to be poetry, does it just contain some rhythmic or poetic language, or is the entire text a poem or hymn? If it is a hymn or psalm, what type of hymn is it? Possibilities include praise, instruction, confession, and lament.

---

[4]For instance, Matthew 7:7: "Ask, and it will be given to you; / search, and you will find; / knock, and the door will be opened for you" (NRSV).

Your answer to these questions will affect the way you read and interpret the text. Just as you do not read and interpret the various parts of a newspaper or the various kinds of blogsites in the same way, you should not read all parts of the Bible the same way. It would be a mistake, for instance, to read an evocative biblical poem in the same way you read a prose historical narrative! Therefore, once you determine the literary type of a biblical text, you must approach the details of the text in an appropriate way, especially taking care, for instance, not to interpret poetic or symbolic language (e.g., "the face of God" or "the lamb that was slain") literally.

Individual books of the Bible sometimes incorporate an astonishing variety of forms. In some cases, the different forms are not merely aesthetically impressive, but they may also signal different theological emphases within the book. For instance, in 2 Corinthians, Paul's opening chapters (1–7) contain largely apologetic (self-defense) arguments mixed with conciliatory messages. Chapters 8 and 9 consist of two brief, theologically grounded fund-raising appeals. Chapters 10–13 contain highly charged rhetorical speeches, including a famous "fool's speech" (11:1–12:13), which is dripping with irony but is also full of theologically profound insights about weakness and suffering. These shifts in form and theological emphasis within one letter raise the possibility that different forms might at times correspond to different historical periods within the life of the biblical writer(s) and/or audience(s). Do the various forms and theological emphases within 2 Corinthians mean that this letter is really a pastiche of several letter fragments from different times in Paul's relationship with the Corinthians (the older, more diachronic scholarly view)? Or are they the single work of a very talented and rhetorically powerful writer who employs literary variety within a single letter with several different but related purposes (the newer, more synchronic scholarly perspective)?

The wide variety of literary forms exemplified in 2 Corinthians can be found in other biblical books as well. For instance, the book of Psalms contains several different types of psalms (e.g., praise, lament, confession). The Gospels contain genealogies, hymns of praise (such as the "Magnificat," Luke 1:46–55), birth narratives, parables, discourses, healing stories, accounts of nature miracles, passion narratives (elaborate accounts of Jesus' suffering and death), stories of resurrection appearances, and other literary forms, each of which has a fairly standard format. In the controversial and eclectic book of Revelation we find visions, prophetic messages, and hymns of praise just in the first five chapters.

Prophetic books (including Revelation, but also many OT writings) contain call narratives, oracles, vision reports, historical narratives, and more.

The first few chapters of the prophetic book of Jeremiah provide us with another example of a dazzling array of intriguing literary forms, both prose and poetry, including:

- a prose superscription introducing the prophet's historical context (1:1–3)

- a call narrative, part poetry and part prose, reporting Jeremiah's commissioning by God (1:4–19)

- a poetic oracle (message from God) in the form of a lawsuit (Hebrew *riv*), indicting the people of Israel and Judah, and full of provocative imagery (2:1–37)

- and a collection of prose and poetic oracles, again filled with vivid images, on the theme of repentance, or returning (Hebrew *shuv*) to the Lord (3:1–4:4)

This combination of prose and poetry at the beginning of Jeremiah (and elsewhere in the book) includes material written at various points during (and perhaps after) Jeremiah's prophetic ministry. In appreciating the various literary genres, we become attuned to the various historical circumstances in which Jeremiah worked and the book was composed, the interrelated theological messages of the prophet, and the literary and rhetorical artistry of the book's compilers. In other words, attention to form can be helpful to all aspects of the exegetical task: historical, literary, and theological.

Structure

After many years of reading and writing various kinds of literature (including student essays and research papers), I have become absolutely convinced that the key to good writing is organization, and the key to good reading is discovering that organization. On many occasions, after contemplating and applying the material in this chapter on form, structure, and movement, students have said: "It's all so clear now. The rest is easy. Once you see the structure, the movement, you understand the whole thing." This is often true, and more than one professor of biblical studies thinks that discerning the structure of a text is the key to exegesis. On the other hand, sometimes structure, like beauty, is in the eye of the beholder. The rest of this chapter should therefore be studied very carefully.

Some writing specimens may appear to be composed rather haphazardly, and sometimes that is in fact the case. Most writers, however, whether consciously or subconsciously, write with some kind of organizing principle or pattern that appears in their writing. The pattern or principle may be inherited from the writing conventions of the culture (as it often is), or it may be unique to the writer, or it may be (and very often is) a combination of tradition and creativity. Very few kinds of writing, and very few writers with even a minimal amount of training, are basically unorganized and incoherent. There is meaning and purpose to a writer's activity and thus to the final product—the text itself. Discerning the structure that expresses this purposeful activity is, of course, challenging and—as one might expect—often more art than science.

Formal analysis includes consideration not only of the general form of a text but also of its specific structure and movement. We are interested here, not in the structure of the biblical book as a whole (that has to do with context), but with the structure of the passage itself that is the focus of the exegesis. The *structure* of a passage refers to its parts, its main divisions and subdivisions, while the *movement* of a passage refers to the progression of the text, through those parts, from beginning to end. This section of your study is like the old Triptiks from AAA (the American Automobile Association) that would guide you step by step, showing where to turn and pointing out local attractions, as some Internet software and GPS systems now also do. The divisions of the text correspond to the main intersections and points of interest along your route, while the description of the text's movement corresponds to the routemaker's directions as well as commentary on the scenery and road conditions between the points of interest.

The notion of a road map may sound a bit pedestrian (no pun intended!). A text, however, can be a beautiful thing, a work of art. To discern its structure is, in part, to pay attention to its literary beauty, to the aesthetics of the text. Discerning structure and movement is one function of rhetorical analysis or criticism, because rhetoric is sometimes defined as "literary artistry." A careful reader will be sensitive not only to the location of a text (context) but also to the formulation of the text itself (structure and movement). Both aspects of the text contribute to the meaning, beauty, and effectiveness of the text—that is, to its rhetorical power.

Outlines

Many students have found it very helpful to construct a phrase outline of a biblical text with one or two levels (e.g., I, II, III and A, B, C), so as to discern and express the text's structure and movement. Further subdivisions are not always necessary but can be helpful. The purpose of these phrase outlines is not merely to repeat the words of the text but to *summarize* their content and, if possible, their purpose or function in the passage. When constructing an outline, you should indicate which verses of the text correspond to each part of the outline.

The first part of an outline from a hypothetical text in one of the prophets might look like this:

> I. Condemnation of injustice (vv. 3–7)
>   A. Hatred for the poor (vv. 3–4a)
>   B. Mistreatment of orphans and widows (vv. 4b–6)
>   C. Use of unfair scales (v. 7)
> II. Announcement of God's wrath (vv. 8–10)
>   A. Reminder of God's holy intolerance of evil (v. 8)
>   B. Proclamation of God's coming punishment (vv. 9–10)
> III. Plea for repentance to avoid punishment (vv. 11–12)

The designations "4a" and "4b" refer, respectively, to the first and second parts of v. 4.

An outline of the Disciples' (Lord's) Prayer from Matthew 6 might be done this way:

> I. Disciples' address to God as personal yet holy (v. 9)
>   *"Our Father who art in heaven"*
> II. Disciples' praise (v. 9) *"hallowed..."*
> III. Disciples' prayer for the world (v. 10)
>   *"Thy kingdom come, thy will be done on earth..."*
> IV. Disciples' prayer for themselves (vv. 11–13)
>   *"Give us this day ... forgive us ... lead us...."*

In preparing an outline, you should be sure to follow normal outlining conventions (e.g., no "I" without a "II," no "A" without a "B," etc.). In addition, at each level of the outline, the relevant verses should be presented in sequence, with no omission of verses and no repetition of verses at the same level of the outline. (In the first example above, "A," "B," and "C" under "I" cover all of vv. 3–7 in order. It would be incorrect either to omit, say, v. 6, or else to include v. 6 both in "B" and in "C.")

Common Structural Patterns

Discovering a structure or outline or organizational pattern in a text is something of an art. There is seldom only one "right answer," one correct way to outline a text; two people may discern two different, but equally legitimate, patterns in the text. It is helpful to know, however, that there are several common structural patterns that occur in many biblical texts; indeed, they occur in many texts outside the Bible, too.

Perhaps the most basic structural pattern of human communication is *repetition*. Repetition of a key word, phrase, or grammatical feature can be a clue not only to the structure of a text but also to the central concern of that text, as we will note again in chapter 7 on synthesis. The repetition of a previous element is sometimes an exact repetition and sometimes an allusion or briefer mention of some concept. We may refer to the fundamental pattern of repetition as A-X-A-Y-A-Z, in which X, Y, and Z are those sections not comprised of repeated material. If repetition occurs at structured intervals in a text, especially a longer text, it can be called a refrain (as in a poem or hymn).

Another simple but common structural pattern of expression is *contrast* or *antithesis*. The contrast may be between ideas, actions, characters, times (e.g., past and present), or other elements of human experience and expression. We may refer to this pattern as A [-A] for "A and the opposite of A." For example:

> So then, remember that *at one time* you Gentiles by birth . . . were *at that time* without Christ, being aliens from the commonwealth of Israel. . . . *But now* in Christ Jesus you who *once* were *far off* have been brought *near* by the blood of Christ. (Ephesians 2:11–13 NRSV)

A specialized form of both repetition and contrast that is very common in the Bible is *parallelism*—the expression of similar, related, or contrasting things in parallel ways. As noted earlier, it is often said that biblical poetry is "thought rhyme," or parallelism. Psalms, for instance, are often structured in sequences of paired statements, with every second line reiterating or elaborating the previous line or else expressing an antithesis:

> Wash me thoroughly from my iniquity,
> And cleanse me from my sin.
>
> For I know my transgressions,
> and my sin is ever before me.
> (Psalm 51:2–3 NRSV; synonymous parallelism)

> The LORD watches over the way of the righteous,
> but the way of the wicked will perish.
> (Psalm 1:6 NRSV; antithetical parallelism)

It is not only a sentence or verse that may be structured in parallel (synonymous or antithetical) form but also an entire text or a segment of the text. We may refer to this as the A//A' pattern.

Another form of parallelism commonly marks the opening and closing of a text, thus indicating that what is in the middle is all interconnected. In many texts, a particular word, phrase, image, or idea both introduces and concludes a paragraph or a stanza, a story or an argument. This phenomenon of beginning and ending on the same note is known as *inclusio* ("inclusion"). It can be illustrated by Psalm 8, which starts and finishes on the exact same note of praise: "O LORD, our Sovereign, how majestic is your name in all the earth" (vv. 1, 9 NRSV). It can also be seen in Romans 5:1–11, where the inclusio is clear even though the key words that begin ("justified . . . peace with God") and conclude ("reconciliation") the passage are not an exact repetition:

> Therefore, since we are *justified* by faith, we have *peace with God through our Lord Jesus Christ, through whom* we have obtained access to this grace in which we stand; and we *boast* in our hope of sharing the glory of God.
>
> . . .
>
> But more than that, we even *boast* in God *through our Lord Jesus Christ, through whom* we have now received *reconciliation.* (5:1–2, 11 NRSV)

We may refer to this as an A-B-A' pattern. The beginning and the ending elements function like bookends around the rest of the text.

Sometimes a text characterized by inclusio is further structured in parallel fashion from both ends, so that the second element of the text is somehow parallel to the next-to-last element. We may refer to this as an A-B-B'-A' pattern. This structural pattern is known as *chiasmus*, from the Greek letter *chi*, which looks like an English *X*. Consider the form of Psalm 51:1 (NRSV):

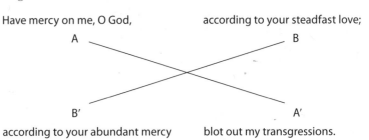

The *X* or *chi* shape becomes evident if the A elements are joined by a line and the B elements are similarly joined, as above.

Also like an *X*, a longer text that is chiastically structured has two or more parallel elements at its "top" and "bottom." This pattern may continue, moving in (so to speak) from both ends, for the entirety of the text, so that the text appears to have a complex and complete parallel structure of, for example, A-B-C-D-E-E'-D'-C'-B'-A'. This is sometimes referred to as a *concentric* arrangement of the text or *ring composition*. The chiastic or concentric pattern often has one element in the center that has no parallel element; this pattern may be represented as A-B-C-B'-A', in which the C element is the focal point, center of gravity, and fulcrum of the text as a whole.

Occasionally, what at first appears to be an inclusio at closer inspection turns out to be a larger concentric pattern. For example, the text from Romans 5 cited above may actually be structured chiastically:

A   Justification by faith, peace with God through Christ (vv. 1–2a)

   B   Hope for glory (vv. 2b–5)

      C   Christ's death as the manifestation of God's love (vv. 6–8)

   B'   Certain hope of future salvation (vv. 9–10)

A'   Reconciliation with God through Christ (v. 11)

Some students of human language and thought believe that all human expression is naturally concentric or chiastic, having a beginning, a middle, and an end with several parallel elements on either side of the middle. In fact, some biblical commentaries propose that all the units of a biblical book, from the smallest to the largest—including the complete book—are structured chiastically.[5] The motto of other scholars is "a little bit of chiasmus goes a long way." Sometimes two chiastic outlines of the same text, even a relatively small text, will identify two very different center points and thus yield two very different readings of the text.

Many texts probably do possess a loose chiastic structure, being marked by inclusio and a clear center point, without having a one-for-one correspondence of all the elements on either side of the

---

[5]For example, Norman Gottwald outlines the entirety of Isaiah 56–66, or Third Isaiah, chiastically (*The Hebrew Bible: A Socio-literary Introduction* [Philadelphia: Fortress, 1985], 508). Peter F. Ellis does the same with the Gospel of John and all of its subparts (*The Genius of John: A Composition-Critical Commentary on the Fourth Gospel* [Collegeville, Minn.: Liturgical, 1984]).

middle. The best guideline is probably to be alert to the likelihood of some kind of parallelism in every text and then to proceed carefully to look for signs of synonymous and antithetical parallelism, inclusio, and concentrism or chiasmus, but without forcing a text into following any of those patterns or into following them exactly and consistently.

There are of course other general ways that texts, whether ancient or modern, can be structured. For example, an introductory thought, image, or character can be developed or revealed in some systematic or unsystematic way. My own experience with texts suggests that careful study of most texts will reveal some structural pattern, even if the pattern is only that of a series of loosely related aspects of one central item.

Patterns Common to Certain Literary Forms

In addition to generic structural patterns that may occur in any text, many literary genres follow somewhat regular patterns. Space permits only a few examples.

Exposition

Expository or argumentative writing, whether ancient or modern, usually sets out a thesis, for which support of various kinds is offered. The support may include arguments for the thesis itself as well as arguments against the opposite of the thesis (its antithesis).

Ancient writers and speakers often followed a regular rhetorical pattern as they attempted to persuade and move their audiences:

- **introduction**—defining the speaker and topic *(exordium)*
- **narration** of relevant events *(narratio)*
- **thesis** or proposition *(propositio)*
- **arguments** for the thesis *(probatio)*
- **refutation** of counterarguments *(refutatio)*
- **recapitulation and appeal** *(peroratio)*

Within this standard pattern speakers or writers might insert other major elements (such as the *digressio,* or digression) and sprinkle various tools of the trade, such as appeals to reason (logos), emotion (pathos), tradition, authority (including sacred texts), and analogy.

Narrative

Although stories may convey a thesis or argument, that is not normally their primary intent, and they do not follow the structure of a piece of rhetoric. But stories, or narratives, do generally follow a predictable format: they always have a beginning, a middle, and an end. Within this basic structure they normally follow a pattern of "rising and falling action" that may be pictured as follows:

```
                        climax

    rising action;                 falling action
    development/
       conflict

 introduction;                        dénouement;
 setting/occasion                     closure/resolution
```

An example of this sequence may be found in Mark 3:1–6 (NRSV):

```
                    He looked around at them with
                    anger; he was grieved at their hard-
                    ness of heart and said to the man,
                    "Stretch out your hand." He stretched
                    it out, and his hand was restored.

    They [the Pharisees] watched him to see        The Pharisees went out . . .
  whether he would cure him on the sabbath,
  so that they might accuse him. And he said to
  the man who had the withered hand, "Come
  forward." Then he said to them, "Is it lawful
  to do good or to do harm on the sabbath, to
  save life or to kill?" But they were silent.

     Again he [Jesus] entered the              . . . and immediately conspired
     synagogue, and a man was there              with the Herodians against
     who had a withered hand.                    him, how to destroy him.
```

Part of the brilliance of this story, of course, is that the ending does not fully resolve the conflict but invites the reader to "stay tuned" for more. Thus this story is undoubtedly one episode of rising action and conflict within the greater narrative of the Gospel of Mark as a whole, the climax of which has not yet been reached.

Narratives are comprised of three basic kinds of text segments: narration of action, speech, and commentary. The way these segments are arranged helps to define the structure of a narrative text.[6]

Specific kinds of narratives may display particular structures. For instance, healing stories such as those recorded in the gospels often follow this pattern:

1. description of the illness

2. request for healing/expression of faith

3. narrative of the healing

4. reaction from the person healed, crowd, and/or opponents

A text selected for exegesis may encompass all or part of one of these patterns. For example, your text may be the *propositio* in a rhetorical piece of writing, or it may be the presentation of the conflict in an extended narrative. On the other hand, a text may tell a complete miracle story that simultaneously is both a full narrative, from introduction to dénouement, and a *narratio* within a larger rhetorical work.[7] For emphasis, drama, or some other effect, the writer may not only *adopt* a typical structural pattern but also *adapt* it, that is, alter it, usually with significant rhetorical impact. Furthermore, a text may follow both a structural pattern common to its literary form and one of the patterns of repetition, contrast, or parallelism discussed above.

Movement

The way a writer uses or alters the structural patterns is often very significant, and the resulting structure indicates also the *move-*

---

[6] For typical story patterns, or archetypal plot motifs, see Ryken, *Words of Delight*, 49.

[7] This does not contradict the point of chapter two that passages selected for exegesis should be relatively self-contained units with clear starting and ending points, communicating a coherent sequence of thought or action. Because almost every text (e.g., a paragraph) is part of a larger text (e.g., a chapter), which in turn is part of a still larger text (e.g., a book), a text has various functions within the larger texts in which it is situated.

ment of the text from beginning to end. Identifying the structure of a text is like labeling the parts; discussing the movement of the text is describing the relationship among the parts and especially how that relationship unfolds step by step in linear, or diachronic, fashion. For example, identifying and labeling the parts of Romans 5:1–11 outlined above reveals a chiastic structure that can be described as moving from the *present* experience of God's grace to the hope of *future* salvation, both rooted in the love of God seen in Christ's death in the *past*—the fulcrum of the text. The text then returns to the subject of hope for *future* salvation and ends where it began, on the subject of the *present* experience of God's grace.

Structure and movement are of course closely connected. For example, when one identifies the various parts of a narrative (as seen in the graphic presented above), from introduction through climax to dénouement, one can hardly avoid speaking of movement. Yet there is still a difference. Simply to identify a part of the narrative as the climax is not necessarily to describe its relationship to any other part of the narrative's structure. Thinking about movement forces the exegete to consider the dynamics of a text—its inner energy, so to speak.

There are, of course, many ways in which a passage can move from beginning to end. The following are some common general patterns, other than narrative, with an example of each:[8]

- **description**—general identification to specific details; Leviticus 25:1–7, the Sabbatical Year

- **explanation**—announcement of topic followed by a sequence of ideas or emotions; Isaiah 1:2–20, the divine lawsuit

- **repetition**—Deuteronomy 27:11–26, the Mosaic covenantal curses

- **logic**—if *or* since . . . then; Romans 6, the consequences of baptism

- **catalogue**—list; Galatians 5:19–23, works of the flesh and fruit of the Spirit

- **comparison/contrast**—Hebrews 9:1–14, the two sacrifices

To discover the structure and movement of a text, it is especially helpful to look for key words that express the main ideas and the relationships between the main ideas. For the main ideas, look principally at the main subjects and verbs; for relationships, look especially at words that indicate relationships between actions or

---

[8]Adapted from Ryken, *Words of Delight*, 209.

ideas. These include such words as "next," "then," "while," "but," "therefore," "for," "because," "although," "in order that," and so on. (This process of looking at the relationships between parts of a text is described more fully in the next chapter on detailed analysis.) Look also for any evidence of repetition and/or contrast, or theme and variation, or point and counterpoint. As always, the discoveries made in looking at the details affect the understanding of the structure of the whole, and vice versa—such is the nature of exegesis as a hermeneutical circle.

In the typical four-part healing story outlined above, the movement is from illness to faith to wholeness to, perhaps, praise by some and hatred by others. Other kinds of stories may also move from bad to good by the time of the dénouement (a basic narrative pattern known as "comedy"), like the story of Joseph or the narratives of Jesus' death and resurrection. Stories can also move from good to ill ("tragedy"), like the narratives of Adam and Eve, the fall of King Saul, and Jesus' suffering and death (apart from the resurrection).

Hymns (like the psalms) move from contemplation to praise or to complaint, from self-examination to confession, from fear to hope, and so on. Other texts may present a thesis, followed by pieces of evidence, culminating in a warning or instruction. Still others may present a command followed by a promise for those who obey, or describe a problem and offer a solution.

In an exegesis paper, it is helpful to writer and reader alike if the paper includes a brief phrase outline that indicates the basic content of each of the parts that a student discerns in the text.[9] (See the examples above of the fictional prophetic text and the Lord's Prayer.) The outline should be followed by a short statement of the movement of the text. This outline of the biblical passage becomes the outline for the detailed analysis of the text, which is the next part of the paper. Although consideration of form, structure, and movement takes much time in study and preparation, it should take up relatively little space in the paper. Otherwise (and this is a common problem) the paper becomes repetitious. However, if you have done a good job analyzing the structure and movement of the text, *your work is nearly half over*— in part because you have already been forced to begin the work of detailed analysis!

---

[9]For more guidelines for writing a research exegesis paper, see Appendix B.

Review & Study

Chapter Summary

- The formal analysis of a text refers to the consideration of its literary form, its structure (divisions and subdivisions), and its movement from beginning to end.

- There are particular principles of interpretation appropriate to every literary form and genre.

- Common general structural patterns include repetition, contrast or antithesis, parallelism, inclusio, and chiasmus.

- Some literary forms and genres have common structural patterns specific to the genre, including such comprehensive genres as rhetorical speech and narrative, as well as specific forms such as miracle stories.

- Some general ways in which a text can move from beginning to end include description, explanation, repetition, logic, catalogue, and comparison/contrast.

Practical Hints

1. Some basic literary genres, and the principles of interpretation that accompany them, are common from culture to culture, reflecting universal human ways of communication. Therefore, draw on your experience with literature and life generally as you read a text carefully with respect to its literary and rhetorical shape.

2. Become familiar with the basic literary forms in the Bible. Some suggested books on this topic are listed in chapter 11, section 5, pp. 207–9, "Resources for Formal Analysis."

3. The best way to discern the structure and movement of a text with any degree of precision is to "play with" the text on paper. This can be done by circling and underlining portions and marking connections you perceive, by rewriting the text phrase-by-phrase in outline form, or by creating some other kind of visual representation of the text as a whole.

For Further Insight and Practice

1. Carefully read Psalm 19. What kind of literature is this? Compose a brief outline of the three or four major sections of the psalm, indicating their basic content. Describe in two or three sentences the movement of the psalm.

2. Read the brief but powerful narrative in Acts 9:1–9 about Saul, known later as Paul the apostle. (To understand the immediate context, skim Acts 6–7 and read carefully 8:1–4.) What kind of literature is this? Create an outline of the story following suggestions in this chapter, and then briefly describe the structure and movement of the story.

3. Compose an outline of the parts or "scenes" in the story of the golden calf in Exodus 32. Try to correlate the scenes you identify with the five stages of a typical narrative sequence described in this chapter. Describe the movement of the story and how this movement gives shape to the various characters in the story.

4. Describe the literary form, structure, and movement of Isaiah 1:21–31.

5. Review chapter 11, section 5, pp. 207–9, "Resources for Formal Analysis."

6. Carefully read the sections on form, structure, and movement (or literary structure) in the sample exegesis papers in Appendix C.

CHAPTER SIX

Detailed Analysis of the Text

It is not in the interest of extravagant ambition
that we trouble ourselves with this detailed
exposition, but we hope through such painstaking
interpretation to train you in the importance
of not passing over even one slight word or
syllable in the Sacred Scriptures. For they are not
ordinary utterances, but the very expression of
the Holy Spirit, and for this reason it is possible
to find great treasure even in a single syllable.
—*John Chrysostom*

*What are the main points of each of the parts of the text, and
how does the text/writer make these points?*

*What do the details mean in the big picture, and how does the
big picture affect the meaning of the details?*

In some respects, detailed analysis is the very heart of exegesis.
It is the *sine qua non,* or most essential feature, of close reading:
careful scrutiny of every word, phrase, allusion, grammar point,
and syntactical feature in the text. Should you randomly open to
a page in the middle of almost any biblical commentary, you will
likely discover discussion of details. In this chapter we will explore
various aspects of performing an in-depth analysis of the text.

The Pieces of a Puzzle

Attention to detail is indeed the stuff of commentaries and the
heart of exegesis. Nevertheless, a shift in commentary writing, and
in scholarly understanding of exegesis, occurred in the last twenty-
five years or so of the twentieth century. Many earlier commentaries

took a very narrow, word-by-word, phrase-by-phrase approach that did not give much attention to the larger units of thought or the contexts in which the words and phrases appear. The danger of these commentaries was of missing the big picture. Most recent commentaries place a great deal of emphasis on the form, structure, and context of texts as a way of interpreting the meaning of the details.[1]

The beginning exegete may face the same temptation to which older commentators succumbed. Overwhelmed by the quantity of words in the text, the numbers of questions these words raise, and (eventually) the extraordinary amount of scholarly ink spilled over every jot and tittle of the text, you can easily get so bogged down in the details that you miss the big picture. This is not to say that the details can be dealt with casually or ignored—quite the opposite! But the careful interpreter is always asking the question, "What do these details mean in the big picture, and how does the big picture affect the meaning of the details?" At the same time, he or she will ask, "How do the details give shape to the big picture?" This is the hermeneutical circle at work.

In some ways, exegesis is like doing a puzzle. To put together a puzzle, you must find and arrange the small pieces (details) in order to create a picture (the whole). The process involves identifying the parts and discovering how they fit together. Without the little pieces, there would be no puzzle picture. But the little pieces alone are only a very small part of the picture; their ultimate value lies in their contribution to the larger picture.

The Art of Selectivity

As mentioned in the last chapter, the detailed explanation of a passage normally corresponds to the outline of the text devised during the formal analysis. The detailed analysis is therefore logically divided into two or more (usually three to five) sections corresponding to the major parts of the outline. In these sections, you carefully examine (and discuss, if you are writing a paper) the key ideas of each segment of the text.[2]

---

[1] In addition, there is now something of a trend in commentary writing away from verse-by-verse analysis and toward the analysis of larger text segments (e.g., paragraphs). This trend, however, suggests that we can dispense not with the careful consideration of details but only with the notion that individual sentences (or words) alone bear the most significant semantic weight.

[2] It is wiser for the beginning student to move systematically through the text in smaller chunks than to follow the emerging trend in com-

This section of a written exegesis can become very long if every phrase of the text is analyzed. That is precisely what you will find in most scholarly commentaries, some of which contain a thousand pages or more on one biblical book. In your investigation of the text, first on your own and then in researching the work of others, you must observe and analyze as much as you possibly can. Like a detective, attempt to leave no stone unturned, no question unexplored.

In writing an exegesis paper, however, you must be *selective,* commenting in detail only on the most significant features of each verse in the passage, making more concise observations about other features, and ignoring still others. Deciding what is and is not important is partly a matter of intuition, partly a matter of overall careful study of the text and its contexts, and partly a matter of experience. Once again, the hermeneutical circle will be at work. As you carefully engage the details of a text, an understanding of the whole passage will begin to emerge. As it does, you will begin to have a feel for what elements of the text deserve the most attention and emphasis in an exegesis paper (or, for that matter, in a homily or sermon). Indeed, careful attention to details— sometimes the details others have overlooked—is very often what creates and supports an exegetical thesis. Thus exegesis of a text, even when using appropriate historical and literary methods, is more like an art than a science.

Some Basic Questions

Every genre, indeed every passage, of the Bible is unique. Still, there are some basic questions about every passage that you need to ask yourself. Examples of these fundamental questions are:

- What does the text communicate, and how?
- What are the key terms and images? What do they mean?
- Are there any key terms or ideas whose meaning may be explained by looking elsewhere in the book?
- Are there any literary or rhetorical devices (simile, metaphor, hyperbole, personification, repetition, irony, etc.), and if so, what is their effect?
- What kinds of sentences are used? What are the major components of each sentence? What verbal actions or states appear in these sentences, and what subjects are associated with them?

mentary writing (toward analysis of larger units) mentioned in the previous note.

- Does the text include appeals to tradition or Scripture, such as stories, beliefs, laws, and well-known historical figures? If so, how do these appeals function?

- Does the text appear to use sources, whether written or oral? If so, how are the sources used?

- If the text is a narrative, what elements of setting, plot (conflict, suspense, resolution), and character development does each part of the text, and the text as a whole, convey?

- Which elements of the text work, individually or together, to instruct, delight, or move the reader?

- What is the tone, or mood, of the passage, and what elements convey that tone?

- How do the various parts of the passage reflect and/or address the situation of the readers?

- How does each part of the passage relate to the other parts?

- How does each part contribute to the whole?

- How does my emerging understanding of the whole affect the meaning of the parts?

This is a broad range of questions, and more could be added to the list. Some of these questions are directed primarily at each part (word, sentence, etc.) of the entire text. Others are directed at the text as a whole. Readers who ask and answer these kinds of questions will have much to say about a text.

These questions may, in fact, be sufficient for this element of the exegetical process. The rest of the chapter, however, provides more detailed guidance on the task of detailed analysis. Specifically, we will look at what the various parts of a text are and at how the parts relate to one another. Then we will consider some important aspects of the text as a whole, especially in light of the sources it may contain or use.

The Whole and the Parts

A text obviously exists as a whole, as a "relatively self-contained unit of meaning," but it also consists of numerous parts. The units of meaning that an exegete will normally analyze, from the smallest to the largest, are the following:

- **words**—lexical items
- **sentence segments**—phrases

- **sentences**—or utterances
- **text segments**—paragraphs, stanzas, and smaller clusters of sentences
- **the text itself**—as a whole

What these various units of meaning have in common, apart from words, is that each has a sort of completeness: each is a unit of meaning with a beginning and end. They differ with respect to size and degree of completeness and thus with respect to the kind and quantity of meaning they convey. Students of language generally view the sentence, or utterance, as the basic unit of meaningful, complete communication, what we sometimes refer to as a "complete thought." Sentences usually consist of phrases, which are made up of words. Sentences work together, so to speak, to form larger segments of a text, and the text segments combine to form the text (sometimes called the "discourse") itself.

The process of exegesis works, as we have seen, as a hermeneutical circle, a back-and-forth movement between one dimension of the text and another—in this case, between the whole and the parts. One can begin the process of detailed analysis in several ways—with key words or phrases, for instance, or with sentences. Eventually, every part of the text needs to be examined. In the presentation of one's exegesis in a paper, however, the normal procedure is to work systematically text segment by text segment,[3] within each segment to work sentence by sentence (which often means verse by verse), within each sentence to examine each phrase, and within each phrase to analyze each key word.

Since many people are fascinated with the smallest unit of meaning in the Bible, the word, we will begin our discussion of the parts with it. The length of your paper will determine the amount of detailed analysis of the text and its words to include. The shorter the exegetical project, the more crucial it is to be selective.

Key Words and Images

One of my best teachers of exegetical method used to urge us to treat every key word or image (word-picture) in the text like

---

[3]Given the normal length of exegetical studies, a text segment will usually be a cluster of a few sentences/verses but may be as short as one sentence or as long as a paragraph.

an unknown variable—the x or y—of an algebra equation. For example, in examining the following verse we should clearly treat the italicized words, and perhaps others, as such unknown variables:

> And the *Word* became *flesh* and *lived* among us, and we have seen his *glory*, the glory as of a *father*'s *only son*, full of *grace* and *truth*. (John 1:14 NRSV)

The suggestion to treat key words as unknown variables is good advice, but some caution is needed in analyzing these words as "lexical items" or "dictionary entries." What scholars sometimes call "lexical analysis" and others "word studies" is an area of exegesis full of potential land mines. The following discussion suggests why this is true and how to avoid the dangers of "word studies" while still taking words seriously.

Meaning in Context

Many people assume that words are the most important conveyors of meaning. Both modern linguistics and ordinary experience, however, teach us that meaning is context-dependent. The exclamation "Oh, my God!" has one meaning in the context of praying and quite another in the context of admiring someone's new car. Popularly, people recognize that a word's denotation ("literal" meaning) and its connotation (implied or suggested meaning) can differ, and that a word can mean different things to different people and in different social locations or contexts. The study of meaning is called semantics.

Even apart from the issue of connotation (discussed briefly below), the meaning of a word is more complex than one might at first imagine. Linguists suggest that although a word, or lexical item, may have some core semantic features, it has a spectrum of possible meanings, called its semantic range.[4] The meaning or function of the item depends on a variety of factors, but especially on

---

[4] The English word "girl" might be said to have core semantic features that include "human," "female," and (one would think) "young." Yet the word has a range of possible meanings that can be found in any comprehensive English dictionary: any female child, daughter, girlfriend, one of a group of adult female friends, etc. In at least two of these meanings, this word is no longer marked for the feature "young." In a specific instance of the word, only one of these dictionary meanings will be the correct one, and that meaning becomes evident only in relation to its context.

the various contexts in which it occurs. These contexts include especially the speaker's or writer's social location, his or her personal word bank and style (i.e., what this person normally means when using this term), and the literary and rhetorical setting in which the term appears. What is the speaker or writer trying to accomplish, and how does this term serve those purposes? A word has a range of "dictionary" or commonly recognized meanings (lexical senses), only one of which is its meaning *in context* (contextual sense). Furthermore, if a person or group uses a word for particular purposes and invests its own meaning into the word, it may take on a new and distinctive meaning for that person or group (specialized sense). This is sometimes called a technical term.

For example, the lexical sense of the word *fellowship* may be "association of people with common interests" or "specialized academic appointment with stipend." Its contextual sense in the sentence "The church is a fellowship" is clearly the former, not the latter. However, the general dictionary sense is further refined in its religious context and may, in some churches, take on a peculiar, specialized sense, as in "a time of fellowship after church." Here the specialized sense is "informal conversation with light refreshments"—and the conversation may not even be of a religious nature. Other churches would not use, or perhaps even understand, the term in that way; it has become a technical term for certain churches.

A "biblical" word, therefore, should not be treated as an unchanging, homogeneous unit of meaning. The distinctive ways in which a word or phrase is used within a text impart distinctive contextual senses to that lexical item within that text. For instance, the Psalms use the title *son of God* primarily to refer to the king in his special role as God's representative; the Gospel of Mark uses this title to refer to Jesus in a way that invokes associations with kingship and the power of the Holy Spirit, yet also with suffering and death; and the Gospel of John associates the title with Jesus in his eternal closeness to God the Father and, indeed, his divinity. Similarly, the word *salvation* has different meanings among the various biblical writers: political deliverance, forgiveness of sins, and wholeness, to name a few possibilities. It probably does not mean exactly the same thing for Isaiah that it does for Matthew, even when Matthew is quoting Isaiah. And *salvation* may not mean the same thing for Matthew that it does for another New Testament writer such as Luke or Paul. It is even possible—and here is why context is so important—that one writer can use the same word differently in different contexts.

Further Principles for the Analysis of Words

A biblical word, then, does not mean the same thing in every place it occurs. Neither does a word ever mean everything it could possibly mean at one time. The erroneous notion that a word in a particular context means the sum total of all (or even some) of its possible meanings is called *illegitimate totality transfer,* a term coined by the British biblical scholar James Barr.[5] Illegitimate totality transfer occurs when, for example, a significant biblical term such as *faith* or *salvation* is interpreted in a specific passage as the conglomeration of all meanings of the word in the Bible, not according to the usage of the author or according to the context. That kind of universal synthesis is bad exegesis.[6]

Nor, finally, does a word mean what its origin and history (etymology), or its component parts, might suggest. Words take on a life of their own (like texts!) and naturally break away from their roots. For example, the contemporary usage of the word *enthusiasm* has nothing to do with "being in God," despite its roots in the Greek words for "in" *(en)* and "God" *(theos).* This common misinterpretation of words is called the *etymological fallacy.*

The meaning of a word, then, depends upon a combination of the dictionary meaning and the context. The importance of these various contextual principles may be illustrated by consideration of the word(s) *green* + *house.* Let us imagine for a moment that English, like ancient Greek, were written without breaks between the words, such that the two words *green house* and the single word *greenhouse* would both be written as *greenhouse.* If we came upon this lexical item while reading a newspaper column about trends in exterior home decoration, we could probably assume that *green house* (two words) is meant. However, if we saw it while reading a column about trends in plant care, we could probably assume that *greenhouse* (one word) is intended. In neither case, however, would we be correct to transfer the meaning from one context to the other (i.e., there is no new trend to grow plants in houses with green exteriors) or to add up the two meanings and conclude, for example, that people are starting to live in hothouses painted green. To draw either conclusion would be to engage in illegitimate totality transfer.

---

[5] James Barr, *The Semantics of Biblical Language* (Oxford: Oxford University Press, 1961; repr., Eugene, Ore.: Wipf & Stock, 2004), 218.

[6] One "translation" of the Bible, the *Amplified Bible,* is based on this thoroughly flawed understanding of language.

Similarly, it would be erroneous to suggest that the words *green house,* or even *greenhouse,* must have something to do with growth simply because the word *green* is related to the Old English verb "to grow." This error is an example of an etymological fallacy. If a green house or a greenhouse has anything to do with growth, it is due to factors other than the history of the word *green.*[7]

When analyzing the key variables in the literary equation—the words—it is important to gather as much basic information about these main words as possible in order then to determine their meaning in context. This information would include the normal semantic range (possible meanings) of the word, as well as the usage of the word elsewhere in the particular book or writer. There are three main types of tools to assist in the interpretation of words: dictionaries, or lexicons; wordbooks that contain essays on important biblical words; and concordances, or alphabetically arranged indexes of biblical words. Of particular importance is the concordance, which can identify all the places where a word and its linguistic relatives ("cognates") occur. Concordances and other lexical tools are discussed in section 6 of chapter 11.

Connotation and Figurative Language

Two additional aspects of word usage that are important for exegesis may also be mentioned briefly here: connotation and figurative language, or imagery.

We all know that sometimes a word functions outside its normal semantic range. A word's "connotation"—the additional meanings the word suggests within a general cultural context or a particular rhetorical situation, as well as associated emotions and value judgments—is particularly difficult to grasp. Knowledge of the historical and social setting of a text is the only thing that can

---

[7]An example of this problem in biblical interpretation is the meaning often assigned to the Greek word translated "church" or "assembly," *ekklēsia.* Etymologically, the Greek word is derived from the verb "call" *(kaleō)* and the preposition "out" *(ek),* but its primary significance is probably to be found not in its etymological roots but in its cultural contexts. The word *ekklēsia* was used of the body of citizens, or members of a guild or other group, assembled to make decisions for the body; a good translation might be simply "assembly" or "council." The word was also used in the Greek Bible to translate the Hebrew word *qahal,* meaning the assembly of the people of Israel. In each case the idea of being called or called out might be present, but the primary significance is that of being assembled.

help. For example, many Americans think that they may summon a French waiter by calling "Garçon," but in contemporary France that term connotes disrespect for the server (even though a French–English dictionary might include "waiter" as one translation of "garçon"). The appropriate address nowadays is "Monsieur," even though most French–English dictionaries do not provide "waiter" as a translation of "Monsieur."

Figurative language is also a universal phenomenon. Some images are very culturally conditioned, while others are more universal because they are based on universal human experiences (such as light and darkness). The Bible is full of evocative images. These words (and even phrases, sentences, and longer units) must be interpreted by means of a disciplined imagination in light of the context in which they appear. Readers should be particularly attentive to the presence and function of metaphors (e.g., "God is a rock") and similes (e.g., "God is like a rock") in the text. It is not unusual to find that the key term in a text is in figurative language. Such a term is sometimes referred to as the *governing image* or the *ruling metaphor*. For example, the first half of Psalm 23 is governed by the image of the Lord as "my shepherd."

Interpreting a Word in Context

We have stressed that the meaning of a key word or image in a text depends on its context(s) and that any kind of "word study" that ignores this principle will likely misrepresent the word's significance, at least in part. It is both possible and important, however, to interpret specific terms in context—to do word studies in this more nuanced sense—as part of the exegetical process.[8] The following steps may be followed to do so:

- Consult a good dictionary of biblical words, preferably a lexicon of the original language, to determine the range of possible meanings (semantic range) of the word. Note also any interpretation offered by the dictionary for the specific occurrence(s) of the word in your text and/or for the general use of that word by that writer or in that book.

- Select a concordance based on the translation that is the primary basis for your exegetical work (preferably one that links translated words to the Greek, Hebrew, or Aramaic terms) or, if you read the original languages, a Greek or Hebrew/Aramaic concordance.

- Locate the word in question in the concordance, and identify all the occurrences of that word and closely related words from the same fam-

---

[8]I am grateful to Fr. Michael Byrnes for the suggestion to include this section.

ily (if possible, only those occurrences representing the same Greek, Hebrew, or Aramaic word or family of words) in the biblical book or author from which your particular text has been selected.[9]

- Carefully examine each occurrence of the word/word family in its context in an attempt to identify its meaning in each context. (There may be consistency, but there may also be difference.)

- Using the insights gathered from the dictionary/lexicon and from the study of other occurrences of the word and its relatives, return to the word in your selected passage. Carefully examine the usage of the word in this context and in relation to the other occurrences you have studied, to determine, as best you can, its meaning in the context of your passage.

In preparing an exegesis of a text, this process will often need to be repeated for several key terms in the passage. In the research phase of your exegesis (see chapter 9), allow your conclusions about the word's significance in context to be affirmed, corrected, or expanded by the work of scholars.

The Arrangement of Words into Larger Units (Phrases, Sentences, and Text Segments)

Words do not normally stand alone; they are arranged into larger groupings, which we may call phrases or sentence segments. The arrangement of words into phrases and of phrases into sentences is referred to as syntax. The primary linguistic unit for expressing meaning is not the word or even the phrase but the sentence. Sentences, in turn, are arranged into larger units of thought and expression that can be called text segments, which may be as few as two sentences and as many as a dozen. Such larger text segments are called paragraphs (prose) or stanzas (poetry). Exegesis requires careful analysis of all of these units.[10]

---

[9]For instance, in choosing words to examine, one should normally look at "righteous" as well as "righteousness" in a particular book (say, Malachi), and "rejoice" as well as "joy" in a particular book (say, Philippians). In choosing which specific occurrences to examine, the exegete should remember that a word like "Zion" might have different meanings in Isaiah 1–39 and Isaiah 40–66 if the second half of the book was not written by Isaiah of Jerusalem in the eighth century B.C.E., as most scholars think. On the other hand, when studying a passage in Acts, it might be legitimate to look at occurrences of, say, "peace" in Luke as well, since most scholars believe that Luke is the author of both books.

[10]Some would argue that the paragraph, not the sentence, is the basic unit of meaning. In fact, all discourse units, from smallest to largest,

Phrases are ordered combinations of words that follow patterns of usage within themselves and in relationship to one another (rules of grammar and syntax). It is of course impossible to grasp all the nuances of Greek or Hebrew grammar and syntax in translation, so precise exegesis depends on in-depth knowledge of the original languages. Nevertheless, exegetes who do not read the original languages can still pay close attention to questions of syntax and sentence structure. One can begin the analysis of each verse or sentence by dividing it into its several segments: the noun phrase, the verb phrase, and any qualifying or expanding phrases such as prepositional or adverbial phrases, which perform a kind of "fine tuning" on the language of the text and are often crucial to the meaning and function of the text.

As you begin to think systematically about the several verses of your passage, you will start asking yourself such questions as:

- What are the main phrases in this text?
- How are these phrases related to one another?
- Is their order significant?

Once the phrases that contain the subject(s) and verb(s) are identified, it is also important to determine the type of verb(s) (action or state of being) as well as the tense (time) and mood (e.g., indicative [declarative] or imperative) of each. What is the significance of these aspects of the verbs? Are the verb tenses all the same, or are past, present, and future tenses mixed? If they are mixed, why?

Are there verb phrases that relate closely to each other? Are they coordinate phrases (equal partners), or is one subordinate to another? What word or other device indicates this relationship? How is the coordination or subordination important to the meaning of the text?

As for the sentences themselves, what kind are they? Each sentence will be either a declaration, an imperative (either command or counsel), a question, or an exclamation.[11] What is the type of each sentence, and what is the meaning of that sentence as a unit?

---

bear semantic significance. My point here is simply that, contrary to some people's thinking, meaning is primarily borne not by words in isolation, or even by a few key words, but by words in relation to one another in larger units.

[11] Declarations, questions, and exclamations generally use verbs in the indicative mood, whereas imperatives generally employ verbs in the imperative mood (e.g., "He goes," "Does he go?" and "He is going!" versus "Go").

As these questions are addressed to the text, and tentative answers come to mind, it is helpful to create a two-column phrase table. In such a table, you set out the text phrase by phrase in the left column, skipping several lines between phrases. In the right column, opposite each phrase, you note your perception of the meaning and function of each phrase in the text. The following is an example, for just one verse:

Text Phrase	Meaning and Function
In the beginning	—adverbial phrase indicating time of action and (perhaps) the action to follow as the beginning of time
God created	—identifies subject and verb; limits creation to God alone; narrates character of God (creative)
the heavens and the earth	—two objects/products of creation; encompasses all of known reality

If you create this table using your computer, you can more easily adjust the columns and rows to accommodate the additions and revisions that you will make as you start to think more systematically about the relationships that exist among the various parts. If you would like to do "sentence diagramming," you may wish to try it on part or all of the passage.[12]

The Interrelationships among the Parts

We have already considered the fact that exegesis is a "circular" endeavor, a process of moving back and forth between the parts and the whole (a "hermeneutical circle"). To understand a text, one must consider not only the meaning of each of the parts, but also the meaning of the parts to one another:

- What are the explicit and implicit relationships of the key words to one another? of the phrases in each sentence to the other phrases in that sentence?

- How do the sentences relate to one another?

---

[12]Some exegetical handbooks stress sentence diagramming, while others criticize it as a linguistically flawed approach to sentence analysis. My view is that it can be helpful but that a phrase chart like the one illustrated in this book is more accessible to most students and can serve equally well, if not better.

- How do the sentences work together to become a larger unit of meaning? Are there any contradictions or discrepancies among the sentences?

Indeed, we must again stress not only that meaning is dependent on context but also that meaning is dependent on *relationships*. Words, phrases, sentences, and so on do not have meaning in isolation but in relationship and in context. Some of these relationships are largely explicit, while others are largely implicit in nature.

Explicit Relationships

There are several typical ways in which the various segments of a text relate, more or less explicitly, to other segments. These relationships may exist, for instance, among the phrases of a sentence or among the sentences within a larger text segment.

One obvious set of interrelationships is the one that exists among the subjects, verbs, and other "participants" in the action of a sentence. For example, in the opening sentence of the Bible quoted above, one word indicates the actor ("God"), another word indicates the action ("created"), and a phrase indicates the resulting product of the action ("the heavens and the earth"). (These interrelationships are sometimes indicated in biblical languages by grammatical forms, though the translation of those forms often requires phrases in English and other languages.)

In addition to these interrelationships, there are also phrases and sentences that expand or qualify other phrases or sentences. These segments of the text identify, define, describe, or limit other segments. In the example above, "In the beginning" qualifies the action with respect to time.

We may also distinguish between *chronological,* or *narrative,* relationships, on the one hand, and *logical* relationships on the other. The relationships are sometimes—though not always—indicated by verbal markers, including such narrative markers as "before," "while," and "after," and such logical markers as "because," "so that," "therefore," and "by" or "through." The forms of chronological or narrative relationships among parts of a text, and some of the markers,[13] include:

---

[13]The markers noted in the lists are English words. Obviously, the markers will be different words, or sometimes grammatical forms, in the original languages.

- **simultaneous action**—"while," "when"
- **prior action**—"before"
- **subsequent action**—"then," "next," "after this," "when"
- **reaction**—"then"
- **consequential action**—"therefore"
- **location of action/setting**—e.g., "on Zion"
- **time of action**—e.g., "on the third day"

The forms of logical relationships among parts, and some common markers, include the following:

- **condition**—"if"
- **reason**—"because"
- **purpose**—"so that," "in order to"
- **result or consequence**—"therefore," "so that," "then"
- **means or instrumentality**—"by," "through"
- **concession**—"though," "although"

There are also some relationships that can be either chronological or logical in character. These include comparison (similarity) and contrast (difference). It should also be noted that certain texts, such as the poetry of the psalms and certain of Paul's arguments, have both a logical and a narrative character to them.

Implicit Relationships

Not all relationships among the parts of a text are explicit. For example, the reasons for a character's action or a writer's exhortation may not be stated. Careful analysis may be able to discern important connections that are not explicitly made in the text; in a paper, the existence of such connections must not only be asserted but also demonstrated.

According to some theories of language, relationships exist in every text between that which is said and the opposite of that which is said. Every assertion, in other words, implies the negation of something else. The Pauline acclamation "Jesus is Lord," for example, means that Paul is not Lord, Caesar is not Lord, and so on.

One form of the method known as structural exegesis assumes that every text contains an inherent pattern, or structure, of opposing convictions. Daniel Patte, the foremost practitioner of this method, seeks to identify both the various interrelated beliefs, or "faith convictions," expressed in a text and the explicit or implicit "oppositions" to those convictions. Patte and others look not only for what the author says but also for what the author means *not* to say. Thus these exegetes find contrasting subjects, actions, locations, and so on in every text, all representing a text's faith convictions and its explicit or implicit oppositions.

Looking for implicit contrasting relationships in a text can generate very significant insights. Exegetes must be careful, however, in drawing inferences about opposites, because sometimes two apparently opposite affirmations can both be true. The Pauline acclamation cited above, for instance, does *not* mean for Paul that "YHWH is not Lord"; in fact, quite the opposite is true. With this caution in mind, however, a good reader will always look for implicit relationships in a text, whether relationships of contrast or the kinds of chronological or logical relationships discussed above.

Summary

The astute exegete will look carefully at the text to discern and describe its many interrelationships. Recording observations and questions allows the kind of "playing with the text" or "thinking on paper" that is necessary for careful close reading of the text.

Dimensions of the Text as a Whole

It is unlikely that most of the books of the Bible were written without the use of prior sources, whether oral, written, or both. Quotations, allusions, and evidence of reliance on other materials abound in the Bible. The question for exegesis is, What do we do with these phenomena?

Sources and Redaction

The historical-critical method developed and flourished in large measure because scholars recognized discrepancies and disjunctures within texts. This led them to conclude that most biblical texts were like an onion, with many layers of literary and pre-literary material buried within them, or like jigsaw puzzles constructed from many discrete pieces, some of which do not quite seem to fit. The purpose of the historical-critical method was and is, in large measure, to determine the origin, development, compilation, and editing of these various sources.[14]

The tasks of the historical-critical method have specific names attached to them. *Source criticism* is the task of uncovering the various sources, especially written sources, that have been used within a text. *Form criticism* is the task of identifying small units of tradition (especially oral tradition, but also written) within a text and classifying them with respect to type or form (such as hymns, laments, etc.). Form critics also attempt to identify the kind of situation within Israel or early Christianity in which such a form would originate and prove useful. *Tradition criticism* is the discipline that seeks to identify the ways in which specific forms or oral traditions may have evolved as they were passed on from place to place and time to time. Though all of these criticisms focus on the preliterary and/or prefinal form of the text, they are not particularly interested in the composition of the text itself. That is the subject of *redaction criticism,* which is the discipline devoted to how the final "redactors," or editors, of the biblical texts adopted and adapted their available sources for their own purposes. Redaction criticism also traces the writer's interests throughout the biblical book, as evidenced by trends in the use of the sources and themes. Appendix A lists some specific examples of the kinds of questions these various criticisms address.

Reactions to the historical-critical method, as defined by these criticisms, range from staunch defenders and practitioners, to uncompromising critics who dispute its methodological presuppositions and/or theological value, to those who see its value but also its limitations and problems. This volume takes the last of these three positions.

No matter how one feels about the methods in principle, in practice they are difficult to execute, especially for the beginning exegete, but even for the advanced student or seminary-educated clergy person. Unless an exegete has detailed knowledge of the original languages, of ancient cultures and patterns of communication, and of early Israelite and Christian history, he or she simply cannot carry out these criticisms responsibly.

---

[14]For further discussion of the historical-critical method, see the table in Appendix A, certain resources discussed in section 1 of chapter 11, and John R. Donahue, "Modern and Postmodern Methods of Critical Biblical Study," in *Scripture* (ed. Gorman), 147–62.

The one possible exception to this problem may be redaction criticism. If an exegete has good reason to suspect that a writer has used a source,[15] and the source can be identified, then by comparing the text with its source in the original languages, or even in a good translation, the average exegete can engage in redaction criticism with some degree of success. For instance, if the majority of scholars are correct in thinking that Matthew used both Mark and some other written source, called "Q," then we may be able to learn from Matthew's editing of Mark something of what Matthew wished to highlight or play down in his Gospel.

Redaction criticism asks the following kinds of questions of a text:

- What evidence of sources is there in this text? Are there differences in vocabulary, style, and/or literary form? Are there "seams" or other problematic points in the flow of the narrative or logic? Is there an introductory formula indicating a quotation (e.g., "Moses says . . . ")?

- For what purpose has the writer used the source?

- How has the source been altered? Has it been abbreviated or expanded? Has it been rearranged? Have words or phrases been replaced by other words or phrases?

- Do these alterations seem to have an intended effect? Are they unusual for the writer or document, or are they consistent with other aspects of the writing in question?

The problems, of course, with redaction criticism are that (1) we cannot always know for sure that there was a source, (2) we can seldom know for sure why the source was used and changed, and (3) we cannot assume, if a writer uses a source, that any differences from the source are either intentional or significant. Moreover, even if the differences are deemed significant, we cannot conclude that the differences represent the most important dimensions of the writer's literary or theological perspective. Furthermore, sometimes what redaction critics identify as seams or other evidence of sources and redaction, literary critics identify as literary or rhetorical devices.

Critics of redaction criticism stress the gravity of these problems and advocate exegesis of the final form of the text alone, as a literary whole. While exegesis of the final form of the text is the general approach taken in this book, it is important to acknowledge both that there are recognizable sources in the biblical writings and that, with care, the identification of these sources and the

---

[15] For example, if it is the scholarly consensus or if the biblical writer quotes a known document.

analysis of their use contribute to the exegesis of a text. In other words, proceed with caution! It would be a mistake to build a complete exegetical house of cards on a source theory, but it would be equally grievous to ignore quotations of and allusions to various sources in the Bible.

Intertextuality: Literary and Cultural

Recent study of the Bible and other literature has emphasized the reality that much of what people write is a kind of weaving together of the new and the old. Human literary creativity almost always includes quotations and allusions to texts, ideas, and images from the culture in which it is nurtured. That is, texts contain echoes of other texts, as well as reverberations of additional nonlinguistic items from the cultural environment.

This phenomenon is called *intertextuality,* and it permeates the Bible. As one scholar says, "the Bible itself is an intertextual fabric within which later texts elaborate on earlier texts."[16] For example, Isaiah 61 ("The spirit of the Lord GOD is upon me. . . . He has sent me to bring good news to the oppressed"), probably written after the Babylonian exile, appears to echo Isaiah 42, probably written during the exile, and is clearly echoed by Luke in his account of Jesus' "inaugural sermon" at Nazareth (Luke 4:16–21). Interest in intertextuality among biblical scholars is extraordinarily high at the moment, and will be for the foreseeable future.

If we limit the term intertextuality, as some scholars do, to mean the use of known written texts, then clearly the most important dimension of intertextuality for the New Testament is its hundreds of quotations of and allusions to the Scriptures (i.e., the Old Testament). Fortunately, many editions of the Bible indicate these in cross-references and notes. Even the books of the Old Testament, or Hebrew Bible, however, seem constantly to take up and refer to earlier texts or traditions (such as the exodus) that now are part of the Bible. While this may not always be intertextuality in the narrow sense of the word, the final product is clearly a woven fabric. Those attentive to scriptural intertextuality will ask themselves questions such as:

- Which biblical texts, themes, and/or images does this passage quote, echo, or allude to? If it cites a text, does it do so verbatim or does it appear to make changes?

---

[16]Wim (Wilhelmus) Weren, *Windows on Jesus: Methods in Gospel Exegesis* (trans. John Bowden; Harrisburg, Pa.: Trinity, 1999), 200.

- What aspects of the context of the cited text(s) may have informed the usage of the text in this passage?

- To what ends does the passage incorporate, modify (if it does so), and utilize a particular biblical text, theme, or image?

In addition to the Bible itself, biblical writers sometimes draw on texts besides Scripture (both religious and secular) and often on extratextual sociocultural realities. They may quote an ancient proverb or hint at a famous historical character or event. Or they may allude, for instance, to royal or imperial images and practices, or to paternal and maternal images and customs, to portray God.

This latter kind of "intertextuality" (drawing on nontextual sources) is sometimes referred to as *cultural intertextuality*. The investigation of such echoes extends the concern for historical context, or "background" (chapter 4), into the detailed analysis of a text.[17] Questions similar to those noted on page 72 of chapter 4 should be raised again during the process of detailed analysis, but now with more specificity and focus. That is,

- What are the cultural and political realities, places, customs, values, and beliefs to which the passage makes explicit or implicit reference?

- What can be known of the significance of these items at the time in which the passage was written?

- How does the passage incorporate, modify, challenge, or otherwise utilize these cultural realities?[18]

To ignore the Bible's quotations of and allusions to such texts, ideas, realities, and images is to neglect one of the most significant aspects of almost any particular text. The meaning of many texts depends in part—and sometimes in large measure—on

---

[17] It has been a commonplace of biblical studies to speak of the "background" of a biblical text, meaning the general or specific contextual factors about which one needs knowledge to understand the text. The term "background," however, is problematic. It erroneously suggests that there is a distance between the world narrated in the biblical text and the actual ancient Near Eastern or Mediterranean world, with its beliefs, practices, institutions, etc. Thus I prefer to speak of cultural intertextuality rather than background.

[18] In an exegesis paper, the contextual analysis will briefly consider the aspects of historical, social, and cultural context that affect the whole passage, while the detailed analysis will treat extratextual realities that may be associated with only one part of the text (e.g., one verse), and it may treat in more depth something mentioned only briefly in the contextual analysis.

their "interaction" with other texts and with extratextual cultural realities. For this reason, it is not merely the historical critic but also the literary critic and the average reader or exegete who must attend to the "sources"—defined in the broadest sense possible— that are woven into biblical texts.

One problem to avoid, however, is the error of what the Jewish biblical scholar Samuel Sandmel termed "parallelomania": the excessive hunt for parallels as sources for, or as points of contrast to, the biblical text.[19] Although there may be many allusions to or apparent quotations from other sources, this happens in part because a text, idea, or image is "in the air," part of the cultural pool of presuppositions. The wise exegete does not fall into the trap of thinking that similarity automatically means either interdependence or deliberate citation. On the other hand, a direct scriptural quote by a New Testament writer should be understood for what it is and analyzed for how it has been used by the writer.

Narrative Detail

A good writer weaves influences and sources together rather seamlessly, even instinctively. This is especially true of good writers of narrative. Since so much of the Bible is narrative literature, the analysis of narrative detail requires some special attention.

In some older discussions of exegesis, the term "literary criticism" meant the analysis of (literary) sources in a text—picking it apart, so to speak. Today literary criticism can mean many things (from the general study of the literary aspects of a text to the use of specialized literary theories), but it does not mean looking for the original forms embedded in the text, its stages of development, or the purely editorial work of the supposed redactor. Rather, contemporary literary criticism is interested in the final form of a narrative text and, more precisely, in how it communicates *as a narrative*. The best term for this kind of analysis is *narrative criticism*. Narrative criticism is not inherently interested (though neither is it necessarily disinterested) in the actual community that stands behind the text and within which the author wrote. Narrative analysis deals with the story as story and with the author/narrator and reader/hearer that the text implies—which may not be synonymous with the actual writer and audience. (These

---

[19]Samuel Sandmel, "Parallelomania," *Journal of Biblical Literature* 81 (1962): 1–13.

are often referred to as the "implied author" and the "implied reader.") It deals with the final form of the text.

As noted in the chapter on form, structure, and movement, narrative literature follows a pattern of (1) introduction (setting, occasion), (2) rising action (development, conflict), (3) climax, (4) falling action, and (5) resolution (dénouement, closure). Together this sequence of elements forms the narrative's plot. The detailed analysis of a narrative text includes careful attention to which of these elements are present in the text. (These may be some or all.) It must also include consideration of other narrative elements of the text, such as character development:

- Who are the characters?

- How are they developed (through description? their actions?)?

- What are their roles in the story? Is a character a protagonist (leading character), an antagonist (opponent), or a supporting character?

Attention to invisible characters and forces (such as supernatural powers, including God) is crucial in the exegesis of many biblical narratives.

Astute exegetes will do everything in their power to enter the "narrative world" of the story. In light of the context of the narrative within the biblical book as a whole, try to imagine the setting, the characters, the interrelationships among the characters (including conflict), the mood and emotions that the story contains:

- How does the story begin?

- What is the climactic moment of the story?

- How does it end?

After doing this imaginative work, you will be better prepared to engage the story more critically and creatively. You may wish to consider one or more of the following in more depth:

- What aspects of setting are presented in the story and why?

- What elements of the story explicitly or implicitly depict characters and their interrelationships?

- What is the conflict in the story, and what is the literary and theological significance of that conflict?

- What words, phrases, and sentences convey the mood of the story and its central motif or apparent purpose?

- How do the characters and actions within this narrative relate to other parts of the larger narrative of which this story or section is a part?

These and similar questions are the questions most of us learned to ask of literature in school. Some of us have not always been encouraged to ask them of biblical texts, but they can, indeed must, be asked. Two final points must be made, however. First, narrative criticism and intertextual analysis or even redaction criticism are not mutually incompatible. One may inquire both about how a text adopts and adapts other sources *and* about how the text works together as a whole unit and as part of a larger literary entity. Second, narrative analysis of a text need not be restricted to texts that are obviously stories. Many texts that are poetic or expository in form contain a story within or behind them, complete with characters, conflict, and resolution. Other texts allude to stories or contain parts of large, master narratives, such as the story of God's salvation through the exodus or the cross and resurrection.

In some important sense, as many recent scholarly studies of the Bible have suggested, much of the Bible is narrative literature, and the Bible as a whole tells a set of interrelated stories. The careful exegete will always be attentive to the elements of narrative in every biblical text, as well as the larger narratives to which the biblical texts persistently refer.

Conclusion

The quantity and character of questions to be considered and addressed in doing the detailed analysis of a text can be overwhelming. One should not, however, give up. For one thing, like doing anything else, exegesis requires practice. As the French say to convey the idea that "practice makes perfect," "C'est en forgeant que l'on devient forgeron": "It is by smithing that one becomes a blacksmith." Or, "It is only by doing exegesis that one becomes an exegete."

For another, the more you look, the more you will see. The story is told of a fifth-grade science teacher who once had her class stare at a frog in an aquarium. The students were supposed to record everything they observed. When they all thought they had finished, she made them keep staring and recording. When she told them to put their pencils down, they all replied, "But we're not done!"

Review & Study

Chapter Summary

- Exegesis involves balancing attention to the big picture and attention to the details.

- It is important to select carefully which details to analyze.

- There are some basic questions of detail to ask of every text concerning key words, images, literary devices, sentence components, appeals to tradition, sources, narrative and rhetorical elements, tone and mood, and the relation of the parts to the whole.

- The exegetical process is a hermeneutical circle, moving back and forth from the parts to the whole.

- Key words and images in a text are like unknown variables in an equation; their meaning is dependent on context and relationship to other elements.

- Careful analysis of the phrases in a text, and the function of each phrase, is an essential part of the exegetical process.

- The parts of the text have both explicit and implicit relationships to one another.

- Exegesis includes the attempt to identify any sources used by the text and *how* they are used.

- Exegesis must also address intertextuality, both literary and cultural, or the phenomenon of texts echoing both other texts and extratextual realities.

- Detailed analysis of narrative texts includes attention to plot, character development, and the "narrative world" of the text.

Practical Hints

1. Recording observations and questions allows the kind of "playing with the text" or "thinking on paper" that is required to read the text carefully. A two-column phrase table, with the phrases of the text on the left and space for your observations on the right, may be especially helpful.

2. Constantly ask yourself, "What do these details mean in the big picture, and how does the big picture affect the meaning of the details?"

For Further Insight and Practice

1. For an idea of the kinds of things you might want to discuss in an exegesis paper, take a look at what several commentaries say on the same passage. (Among other things, this exercise will likely reveal how even scholars disagree with one another on the meaning of a text!)

2. Read Psalm 1. Compose a brief outline of this psalm and then analyze the text according to your outline. In your analysis consider especially the main point of each section, the images and their respective functions, and the overall meaning of the psalm in light of these parts.

3. Read carefully Luke 2:1–21 and then divide the story into scenes. Identify and note briefly the significance of each of the following aspects of the pericope: date; location (city, "manger"); characters (human and nonhuman); reactions of the characters to the birth; the content of the angels' message. Answer the following questions: What is the action in each scene? What is the theme of this story? What is the tone? Is there any irony in the story? How do the scenes you identified work together to produce a complete narrative? Does the story hint at any themes or conflicts that you might expect to find in the remainder of the book of Luke?

4. Reread Psalm 19. Make a list of about ten to fifteen key words, phrases, or images whose significance you would need to explore and explain if you chose to write a paper on this psalm.

5. Read Revelation 21:1–8. Make a list of possible examples of literary (especially biblical) and cultural intertextuality in this passage, and note what kinds of questions you might need to answer about these examples in order to understand the passage.

6. Review chapter 11, section 6, pp. 209–25, "Resources for Detailed Analysis."

7. Read carefully the sections of detailed analysis in the sample exegesis papers in Appendix C.

CHAPTER SEVEN
Synthesis

We shall not cease from exploration,
And the end of all our exploring
Will be to arrive where we started
And know the place for the first time.
—*T. S. Eliot,* Four Quartets

What is the punch line?
—*J. Christiaan Beker, who asked this of every text and in
every class at Princeton Theological Seminary*

What is the main point, or what are the main points, of the text?

In analyzing the details of the text with the greatest amount of
care and precision possible, you have been dealing with the proverbial trees rather than the forest. After doing so, however, you
must now turn to the forest and attempt to see what the trees look
like as a whole. To return to another metaphor we have used, it is
time to look at the big picture, at the puzzle as a whole.

Formulating a Synthesis of the Text

To synthesize is to pull various elements together into some kind
of unified whole. Synthesizing, then, is a disciplined but creative
act of integration. In formulating a synthesis of the passage, you
are bringing together all that you have thought or said so far. You
are not, however, simply making a summary; you are drawing a
conclusion about the text's essential meaning, about its purpose
or function, as you have come to understand it. In literary terms,
you are looking to say something about the topic and the theme
of the text—both its subject matter and its slant or perspective on
that subject. Harking back to your original guesswork, you are

now turning your guesswork and careful analysis into a coherent reading of the text as a whole.

As you attempt to synthesize your findings, ask yourself questions like these:

- What is the main point of each part of the text, and how do the parts make a whole? Can the main point be located accurately in one word, phrase, image, or verse, or does it come only from the content and/or structure of the text as a whole?

- Why do you think the passage was included in this biblical book? What might have been the purpose(s) or function(s) of the text for its original authors and hearers/readers?

- What claims did the text make upon its original hearers/readers? What response might the author have desired from these hearers/readers? What effects—intentional or not—might the text have had on them?

As you ask yourself these questions, never forget that you are reading religious literature; the authors and their texts are making religious (theological and spiritual[1]) claims that are intended not merely to inform but also to transform their readers.

The search for a "main point" does not begin at the end of the exegesis or at the end of the paper. It is part of the process, part of the hermeneutical circle, as you look at the parts and the whole, the whole and the parts. Nevertheless, as you approach the conclusion of your work on the text, you may wish to look back again at the contexts, structure, and details of the text with the specific purpose of formulating your understanding of the main point of the text. Some specific questions to ask—which may already have been asked of the text—include:

- Is there any repetition of words, ideas, or images that might indicate not only the structure but also the theme of the text? Is there a governing idea or metaphor? a central motif?

- Does the structure of the text indicate its focus? Is there a center point? inclusio? contrast?

- Does the beginning or the end of the text reveal its main concern?

- Are there significant relationships among the various components of the text that might indicate the overall rhetorical purpose of the text?

After considering the questions suggested above, state your conclusions clearly and creatively. In the writing of an exegesis paper, there is of course a close relationship between the synthesis and

---

[1]That is, claims about God and about people's relationship with God.

the introduction, for each presents your thesis, and the introduction is usually written (or at least finalized) after the exegetical process is complete. A good, rhetorically effective synthesis, however, does not only restate the main points you have made in the detailed analysis or repeat the introduction verbatim. Instead, it should set out in new (and hopefully memorable) language what the passage is all about.

The art of synthesis should not be undervalued. Although detailed analysis is very important, one's synthesis of the passage is an important indication of the fruits of the exegetical process. As we have said before, exegesis is not merely the accumulation of unrelated facts and observations; it is, rather, the production of a reading, an interpretation, of the text. No reader of the biblical text should be unable to "see the forest for the trees." For those who read the Bible as sacred Scripture, this step of synthesis is extraordinarily crucial, since the task of theological reflection will be heavily influenced by the reader's overall understanding of the passage.

Synthesis and the Plurality of Interpretations

Different interpreters are going to arrive at differing interpretations, or syntheses, of the same text. And the same interpreter, whether exegete or preacher, will likely have various interpretations of a text depending on the contexts within which the interpretations take place. Indeed, most of us hope that a preacher does *not* say the same thing about a text year in and year out.

In formulating and writing a synthesis—which in effect is the interpreter's thesis about the text at a particular point in time—good exegetes present their interpretations with vigor, but also with humility. They argue against inferior interpretations when necessary, but they also recognize the value of other interpretations (and interpreters) and the limitations of their own knowledge and perspectives. (Admittedly, this last point is not always embraced by biblical scholars or preachers.)

To illustrate both the importance of arriving at a synthesis and the variety of possible syntheses, we may look at several possible interpretations of a famous text in Paul's Letter to the Philippians. Philippians 2:6–11 has been the subject of great scholarly inquiry and theological reflection for a very long time. It has often been called a hymn or poem, and it has frequently been said to predate Paul. The passage famously begins, "Though he [Christ] was in the form of God, he did not count equality with God as something to be exploited [or grasped], but emptied himself. . . ." After marking the voluntary descent of Christ from equality with God to humanity to a slave's death—"even death on a cross"—the text says that "therefore, God highly exalted him" and that all creation will confess that "Jesus Christ is Lord."

Every aspect of this text has been in dispute: the basic meaning of key words, such as the one translated "exploited" or "grasped"; the theological significance of startling claims, such as "form of God" and "emptied himself"; the "background," or scriptural and cultural echoes present in the text; the reason Paul quotes or composes the text for a particular historical and literary context; and the theological implications of the text's apparent claims about God and Christ, about their relationship to each other, and about our relationship to them as readers.

As a result, the interpretations of this passage are numerous. A synthesis, or thesis statement, for the text could legitimately take any of the following forms (and more):

- Philippians 2:6–11 is a Christian reinterpretation of the fourth Servant hymn of Isaiah (52:13–53:12), presenting Christ as the debased and then exalted Servant of God.

- Philippians 2:6–11 narrates the story of Christ as the preexistent Son of God whose incarnation and death led to his exaltation by God.

- Philippians 2:6–11 depicts Christ, not as the preexistent Son of God, but as the true human being in contrast to Adam.

- Philippians 2:6–11 is a Christian reinterpretation of a Gnostic redeemer myth.

- Philippians 2:6–11 presents Christ in his self-emptying as the ultimate revelation of true divinity.

- Philippians 2:6–11 presents Christ's incarnation and death as an example of love and humility for Christians to imitate (see 1:27–2:5).

- Philippians 2:6–11 does not present Christ as someone to imitate but as the sovereign Lord of all who is worthy of Christian devotion.

- Philippians 2:6–11 presents Christ's death and exaltation as a promise of resurrection to eternal life for those who suffer as Christians now (see 3:10–11, 21).

As an exegete, your primary task is to arrive at, argue for, and present *one* persuasive interpretation of a text, not to catalog all possible interpretations, even though you may acknowledge the existence of other views—sometimes in order to show their deficiencies. Although some (though clearly not all) of the interpretations offered above may be mutually complementary rather than mutually exclusive, they are still distinctive interpretations. Elements of more than one interpretation may be combined in an exegesis, but no synthesis can or should include the full range of possible interpretations, not least because some ways of reading a text are in fact exclusive of other ways.

To be sure, not every biblical text is as rich and open to various perspectives as is this passage, but many are, and the meaning of a text is never simply an objective, one-dimensional reality that everyone who reads it will discover and agree upon. This is true both with respect to historical, literary, and theological analysis and with respect to the application of the text to contemporary life, as we will see in the next chapter.

At this point, you may be wondering if there is any hope of arriving at a definitive interpretation of any biblical text. If you are a preacher or future preacher, you may be asking yourself, "Does all this mean that I cannot preach with clarity or conviction? If scholars cannot agree on the meaning of the text, is there any hope for me? Will I ever be able to hear or preach a word from the Lord?" I believe that there is actually great comfort and both theological and spiritual vitality in the plurality of biblical interpretations. But to defend that claim, we need to consider the phenomenon of plurality in interpretation both linguistically and theologically.

Ambiguity and Polyvalence

Despite all that we have said about variety in interpretation, well-meaning students of the Bible sometimes—understandably—hope that careful exegesis, attention to all the details, will produce a definitive interpretation of the text: *the* meaning of this or that favorite, troubling, or otherwise significant passage. Perusing several commentaries or articles on a particular Bible passage ought to defuse this understandable but erroneous hope. In addition to natural differences in approach or emphasis among interpreters, there is another factor. Despite—or even because of—careful investigation of every detail of the text, a good exegete may conclude that this or that aspect of the text, or even the text as a whole, is ambiguous, or uncertain, as to its meaning. In some cases, the ambiguity will be due to insufficient knowledge of the historical and cultural situation in which the text was produced. In other cases, it will be due to insufficient knowledge of the vocabulary or grammar used in the text or to unclear arrangements of words, phrases, or sentences.

Ambiguity, however, is not always in the eye of the beholder. It is not always the "fault" of the reader. Sometimes the text itself is inherently ambiguous, and sometimes the author intended it to be that way. Deliberate ambiguity is evocative, allowing or even forcing readers to ponder the text more carefully, asking "What in the world does this mean?" Ambiguity can be an invitation to engagement. Readers of John's Gospel will recall that Jesus' ambiguous statement "You must be born anew" or "from above" (John 3:3, 7) prompted one of that gospel's most significant exchanges.

Ambiguity, whether intentional or not, also allows for various interpretations of a text, all of which—if arrived at responsibly—have some claim to validity. In fact, since there is ambiguity and tentativeness in every historical reconstruction and every literary analysis, and since exegesis is more like an art than a science, we should expect a text to mean different things to different people, even if those people employ the same basic methods of reading the text. A text, in other words, inherently has a sort of open-ended character that permits a variety of readings. The process of exegesis brings together a text, a set of contexts in which the text was created and is now situated, and a reader located in yet another context. The results of this process are bound to vary. In fact, as suggested above, my own careful reading of a text this year and next may be quite different. This is because nearly every biblical text is so richly multidimensional, and its readers and their contexts so richly varied, that we should speak of the meanings—plural—of a text rather than the meaning—singular.[2]

Specialists in hermeneutics (interpretation) often refer to this phenomenon as the "surplus of meaning" in texts. Christian (especially Catholic) theologians speak, particularly with respect to Old Testament texts that have been understood by Christians to point to Christ, of a text's *sensus plenior*. This Latin phrase means "fuller sense," or the meaning intended by God but not necessarily by the human author. For example, since the first century, Chris-

---

[2]Some interpreters prefer to speak of a text's singular meaning and its multiple applications. Even if this understanding of meaning were theoretically correct, it would not functionally alter the way in which we seek and discover the rich multiplicity of dimensions of meaning that any text bears.

tians have understood Isaiah 52:13–53:12, about the suffering of one servant of God for the sins of many, as a prophecy about, or at least a text fulfilled in, the death and exaltation of Christ. This claim does not necessarily mean that the original author intended a reference to any future figure at all, much less Jesus of Nazareth. Rather, it means that whatever the original referent of the Suffering Servant (e.g., a prophet or the people as a whole), for Christians the fuller meaning intended by God and legitimately heard by Christians centers on Christ.[3]

For those who hear in and through the Bible the voice of God, this conviction about the meanings (plural) of a text does not mean that God is fickle but that God's voice is not only constant and faithful but also fresh, new, and creative. The "word of God is living and active" (Hebrews 4:12 NRSV). Nevertheless, a theological account of the surplus of meaning must include the conviction that there is a significant degree of congruence between original textual meanings (as far as we can determine them) and later readings. A suffering servant cannot be morphed into the inspiration for a military campaign.

All this is not to say, then, that a text imposes no limits on our interpretation of it, or that a text can mean anything we want it to mean. It does mean, however, that a text has multiple possible readings, both in terms of its original meaning in context and in terms of its abiding significance, and that several of these possible interpretations may be legitimate. In the list of interpretations of Philippians 2:6–11 provided above, there are some that are different from one another because they look at the text from different angles, but these interpretations are still compatible with one another. There are also a few interpretations that are mutually exclusive, such as the two that give radically different perspectives on the question of Jesus' preexistence. The task of the exegete is, in part, to discern legitimate from illegitimate readings of the text by demonstrating through good historical, linguistic, literary, and theological analysis that certain interpretations do not do justice to the historical, linguistic, literary, and theological phenomena associated with the text. In other words, an interpretation is a claim, a thesis, and it must be demonstrated. The notion that a text is, or can be, polyvalent does not excuse sloppy reading or obviate the need for careful exegetical work.

---

[3] It is of course also true simply to say, without making any theological claim about divine intention, that Christians have seen in Jesus the fulfillment of, or ultimate referent in, the Suffering Servant text.

With respect to Philippians 2 and the question of preexistence, the exegete is faced with numerous phenomena requiring careful analysis in order to demonstrate the legitimacy of one interpretation or the other. The task of exegesis will include identifying, interpreting, and weighing the significance of phrases such as "[being] in the form of God," "equality with God," and "emptied himself" (verses 6–7). These phrases need to be understood in light of first-century Greek usage, in connection with similar phrases elsewhere in Paul, and in relationship to the rest of the poem (Philippians 2:6–11). In my view, these factors all point strongly in the direction of the text's affirming Christ's preexistence, and I would therefore argue that a denial of Christ's preexistence in the poem is an illegitimate reading of the poem. This position, as well as the position it rejects, must be argued carefully and convincingly (though not here!), not merely claimed. But if the case for an interpretation is made well, certain other interpretations will thereby be ruled out even as a variety of compatible interpretations is allowed.

Another textual example may serve to illustrate these two points about the legitimacy of multiple interpretations and the illegitimacy of unconstrained interpretation. In this case, we look less at historical and linguistic data and more explicitly at literary and theological issues. The image of a "city on a hill" from Matthew 5:14 has a long history of interpretation, much of it within American religious and especially political contexts. A careful reading of the text in context is quite provocative. There are echoes of Isaiah 2, which declares that the nations shall ascend to Jerusalem (Zion) and live in peace at some future date. This intertextuality suggests Israel's—or a renewed Israel's—eschatological witness to the Gentiles. The image of city lights on a hill (Matthew 5:15) would be vivid to residents of both Judea and Galilee. The nature of this light as "good works" (Matthew 5:16) gives focus, though not specificity, to the manner of the witness. The images in the text point to the exemplary mission of a community, specifically Israel or the early disciples and church as the continuation of Israel.

The Christian church legitimately inherits that image and applies it to itself in various times and ways. Thus "community" and "light" (= "good works"), the text's two dominant images, have been subject to a variety of legitimate readings. However, the application of these images to a nonreligious entity (e.g., the United States) for its nonreligious deeds (e.g., political freedom, democracy) stretches the limit of interpretation to the breaking point.

Some readings, it has been said, do violence to the text. There must be some limits to what the text can mean.

To use an old analogy, a text is like a diamond with many facets, and no single observer will see every facet from his or her particular vantage point. We may refer to this phenomenon as the *polyvalence* of a text. Polyvalence is the condition of possessing multiple senses. More precisely, since a text does impose some restrictions on our interpretation, we should speak of its *limited* polyvalence.[4] One cannot look at a diamond and legitimately claim to see an orange, or analyze twelve sentences of prophetic lament and claim that the prophet is describing the joy of the Lord. But different people can identify and emphasize different phenomena associated with a text and therefore offer different, but all legitimate, interpretations.

Some people will object to the notion of even limited polyvalence and argue that what the writer intended to say is what a text meant and means. The job of the exegete is therefore to discover "authorial intention." I do believe that in some cases we can approximate authorial intention and should therefore state as the synthesis of a text what Paul, for example, seems to have wanted to say. More often, however, we can only describe what the text might have communicated to a first-century c.e. audience in Roman Corinth or to an eighth-century community in Israel, and also what it communicates to us with our informed, but still limited, understanding of the ancient contexts.

Discerning authorial intent, as everyday experience teaches us, is always difficult and sometimes impossible to do. Furthermore, as everyday life again instructs us, meaning is not equivalent to authorial intent because communication involves at least two parties,

---

[4] I am less comfortable with the evocative term "restricted infinity"— though I understand its appeal. See Tate, *Biblical Interpretation*, 211. Stephen E. Fowl has proposed the term "underdetermined" reading to describe a variety (though not an unlimited variety) of possible textual functions, in contrast to "determinate" reading (i.e., determined and restricted, normally by authorial intent, to one meaning) and "indeterminate" or "anti-determinate" reading (i.e., determined fully by the reader, without constraint). He also argues for a "multifaceted literal sense" of scriptural texts. On the first point, see his *Engaging Scripture: A Model for Theological Interpretation* (Challenges in Contemporary Theology; Oxford: Blackwell, 1998). On the second, see his essay "The Importance of a Multivoiced Literal Sense of Scripture: The Example of Thomas Aquinas," in *Reading Scripture with the Church: Toward a Hermeneutic for Theological Interpretation* (ed. A. K. M. Adam et al.; Grand Rapids: Baker Academic, 2006), 35–50.

the sender (author) and the recipient. Although the notion that meaning is created exclusively by the *recipient* of a communication is a misguided overreaction to the claim that meaning is limited to authorial intent, this kind of reaction does rightly acknowledge the fact that various people receive various messages from a single communication. Human communication is polyvalent.

It is also important to note that many forms of communication are evocative, rather than merely propositional, and evocative speech or writing inherently generates several meanings. This is especially true of poetry, and much of the Bible is poetic litera-ture of one sort or another, from the first chapter of Genesis, to the prophets, to the psalms; and from the gospels, to poems such as Philippians 2:6–11, to the book of Revelation. In these cases, ironically, although authorial intent may not be precisely discern-ible, it is very likely that the author intended to evoke a variety of responses simply by using evocative language.

Finally, it is important for those who think about exegesis theo-logically to remember that the ultimate author of Scripture is God, and to recall once again that the word of God is living and active. Divine authorial intent may be much greater, and yet at times less precisely defined, than the intent of the human au-thors. While that conviction does not give readers or preachers license to engage in eisegesis, it should liberate them to be ready to hear the voice of God speaking once again through the words of Scripture when they are read with care and in dependence on the Spirit who inspired those words and continues to breathe life into them.

So where does this leave us in the task of synthesis? As each of us attempts to integrate the various details in the text that we have observed and analyzed, the different minor conclusions to which various readers have come begin to add up, and the "grand total"—the understanding of the text as a whole—begins to emerge. And it may very well be much more than the sum of the various parts. We can attribute that to human powers of insight, to the power of the text itself, to the inspiration of the Spirit, or to all of the above.

To conclude: A synthesis creatively expresses one interpreter's well conceived, well developed, and well defended conclusion about the meaning and function of a text. This synthesis will be unique to the interpreter who offers it. In an exegesis paper, it is the sum-mation of the argument and the bridge to theological reflection.

Review & Study

Chapter Summary

- Synthesizing is not merely summarizing but rather a creative act of drawing a conclusion about the meaning and function of a text.
- Several features of a text may provide hints as to its essential topic and theme.
- For various reasons, including the inherent character of the text itself, the meaning of a text may be ambiguous.
- Because exegesis is an art (a craft with an inherently subjective dimension) as well as a science (a technique), and because every biblical text is multifaceted, a text has a variety of legitimate readings; it possesses limited, though not infinite, polyvalence.

Practical Hints

1. Keep a record of the possible key point(s) as you work through the exegetical process, but save your formulation of the synthesis until you have time to step back and look at all your details holistically.

2. When you have a sense for the text as a whole, write it down in one good (even if complex) sentence, trying to use the key terms or images of the text itself as much as possible while also analyzing the way the key parts interrelate and constitute the whole.

For Further Insight and Practice

1. Reread Psalm 19. In one well-written sentence, state your understanding of the meaning of this psalm, making sure to include the results of your outline work from your earlier study of it.

2. Read the story about the prophet Elijah, King Ahab, and the prophets of Baal in 1 Kings 18:1–40. What are the chief religious claims being made in and through this

story? What political and social functions would this text have had when it was first told or written? Why might the compiler of 1 Kings have preserved this story for future readers?

3. Read the collection of short stories in Luke 8:22–56. How are these stories related to one another? What seems to be the main point of each and the point of the collection as a whole?

4. Read carefully Romans 8:28–39 and make a brief outline of the text. Then state, in one or two sentences, the main point of the text as you understand it.

5. Review chapter 11, section 7, pp. 225–26, "Resources for Synthesis."

6. Carefully read the sections on synthesis in the sample exegesis papers in the back of this book, Appendix C.

CHAPTER EIGHT

Reflection: Theological Interpretation
The Text Today

> Search the Scriptures, not as though thou
> wouldst make a concordance but an application.
> —*John Donne*

> Apply yourself wholly to the text;
> apply the text wholly to yourself.
> —*Johann Albrecht Bengel*

> Theological exegesis is not a "method." . . . It
> is a complex *practice,* a way of approaching
> Scripture with eyes of faith and seeking to
> understand it within the community of faith.
> —*Richard B. Hays,*
> "Reading the Bible with Eyes of Faith"

What does this text mean for readers other than the original ones?

What does it mean to you? What does it mean to your faith community?

Reflection on a biblical text hardly begins at the end. The exegetical process is, of course, a process of reflection from start to finish. After careful analysis and synthesis have occurred, however, you are in a better position to think carefully and systematically about the significance of the text. At this point, the primary question shifts from "What?" to "So what?"

This stage, or dimension, of exegesis, though avoided by some readers, is really a natural final element in the process. Great works of art (including religious literature) inescapably invite engagement. They have an inherent capacity to inspire the imagination and to create new possibilities for thinking and living. The ultimate goal of exegesis, of "leading out" from the text, is to consider carefully the text's invitation to the imagination, to the spirit, and especially to the community that calls the Bible "Scripture"—sacred text and divine address. In this chapter we look at some possible goals in and methods for such reflection on the text, and we enlarge our understanding of exegesis to include what is now called theological exegesis or theological interpretation of the Bible.

This chapter contains more theory and theology than most of the other chapters in the book. This is needed to provide an appropriate foundation and framework for the practical work—about which there are also numerous suggestions in the latter part of this chapter.

Five Possible Interpretive Postures

In chapter one we briefly suggested that there are two basic types of existential approaches to exegesis, or approaches that wish to do more with the biblical text than analyze its historical and literary features. We said that one approach was characterized fundamentally by suspicion and the other by trust or consent.

We may now expand that discussion by recognizing that not everyone reads the Bible in one of those two ways. These two ways, as different as they are from each other, each reflect interpretive experience within a religious tradition and/or community. But there are three other types of approaches that do not presume experience in biblical interpretation within a religious framework. I would suggest that people reflect on and respond to biblical texts coming from one of five different basic perspectives, or "interpretive postures,"[1] ranging from antipathy to trust/consent. The technical term for such a basic interpretive perspective or posture is "hermeneutic," a word derived from the name of the Greek god Hermes (the Roman god Mercury), the messenger or interpreter of the other gods. Each group of readers looks for, and finds, something different in the biblical texts. Each hermeneutic has a legitimate role in the ongoing interpretation of the

---

[1]Tate, *Biblical Interpretation,* 167, uses the term "interpretive framework."

Bible as a literary classic of the human spirit and has something to contribute to the other hermeneutical readings. They differ significantly, however, in their ability to foster growth in a believing community.

1. A Hermeneutic of Antipathy

A hermeneutic of antipathy (opposition) is the perspective held by those who find the Bible itself, or its effects, to be dangerous to human freedom, the quest for truth, or another principled, cherished ideal. Those who approach the Bible from this point of view are apt to be critical not only of the "premodern" worldview of the texts but also of what they perceive as the (un)ethical consequences of living according to the values expressed in at least some of its texts: violence and war, intolerance and hatred, and so on. (History, unfortunately, provides many examples of evil and injustice committed by people who claimed the Bible as their guide, and these examples make a hermeneutic of antipathy understandable even to those who do not share it.) A typical question from this hermeneutical perspective might be, "What erroneous view of the world and what deleterious consequences for human life together does this text perpetuate?"

2. A Hermeneutic of Appreciation or Noncommitment

A hermeneutic of appreciation or noncommitment is the perspective held by those whose primary interest in the biblical text is not religious but literary or historical. They have no prior antipathy to the text nor any prior commitment to the text as an inspired or authoritative document—though they may find various parts of it either disturbing or inspiring. They read the Bible with at least as much seriousness as they read, say, Aristotle or Shakespeare. Sometimes, in fact, such interpreters read the Bible more carefully and creatively than those who are steeped in a tradition or community that formally takes the Bible to be its authoritative guide but is unable to read the text in new and different ways. A typical question that a person operating with a hermeneutic of appreciation or noncommitment might ask is, "What does this interesting text tell me about an ancient people's view of (some aspect of) reality?" Going a bit further, this person might also ask, "What does this text ultimately tell me about the universal human quest for meaning in life, and to what degree do I, or do I not, resonate with its point of view?"

3. A Hermeneutic of Discernment or Inquiry

A hermeneutic of discernment or inquiry is the point of view held by those who have neither rejected nor avoided a formal commitment to hearing the Bible as sacred text, nor made such a commitment. They are "looking for answers," and the Bible is one place (perhaps one of many places) in which they are seeking perspective for life. A typical question from this point of view might be, "What mode of life does this text suggest, and how satisfying is its suggestion—intellectually, spiritually, ethically—compared to others with which I am wrestling?"

4. A Hermeneutic of Suspicion

A hermeneutic of suspicion is typically employed by those who have been part of a religious community or tradition and who have reacted against what they perceive to be the misuse of the Bible as a source of religious authority by traditions and communities (their own and/or others). The suspicion may be directed against readings that are believed to neglect the historical contexts and cultural conditioning of the Bible or, more often today, against readings that have been used to marginalize or oppress minorities. The oppressed may include the poor, women, African-Americans, Jews, gays and lesbians, the colonized or enslaved, or other groups not within the mainstream of society or of the interpretive tradition. A hermeneutic of suspicion characterizes methods of biblical study that go by the names ideological, postcolonial, and advocacy criticism (especially liberationist exegesis).

Those who embrace a hermeneutic of suspicion believe that the interpretive tradition and (usually) the text itself are subject to criticism and even potentially dangerous. Typical questions that a person operating with a hermeneutic of suspicion might ask are, "How does this text and/or its interpretation in history condone or promote oppression? Is there some way to retrieve or salvage this text so that it can liberate the very people that it was written to oppress or the people who have been oppressed by later interpretations?"

5. A Hermeneutic of Consent or Trust

A hermeneutic of consent or trust is the interpretive framework within which most practicing Jews and Christians generally read the Bible. They give the Bible the benefit of the doubt and conclude that because the people of God known as Jews and Christians have heard "the word of the Lord" in the Bible for thousands of years, they also may still hear from God through this book.[2] A typical question that a person operating with a hermeneutic of consent or trust might ask is, "What is the word of God for us in this text?" or "How might the situation of God's people addressed in the text be analogous to our situation today, and what is our appropriate response of faith and life to this word?"

Those who read Scripture in this manner continue the ancient Jewish tradition of seeing the study of Torah as a form of prayer and worship, as well as the biblically rooted practice of invoking the Holy Spirit to guide and illumine the interpreter. Christians read the Bible as Scripture because they seek to find in it the mind of Christ, and thus they do so prayerfully, no matter how academic the task is at the moment. A hermeneutic of trust guides exegetical practice that acknowledges God as the ultimate *source* of good interpretation and acknowledges faithful living before God as the ultimate *goal* of good interpretation. Such exegetical practice is one form of embodying the biblical injunction to love God with one's mind as well as one's heart.

Reading with Trust, Listening to the Other

The view explored in the rest of this chapter is a form of the last interpretive posture, a hermeneutic of consent or trust. As a general posture, the approach of consent is not so fixed, so static, that one who reads with a fundamental hermeneutic of consent will never read texts with some hesitation and even suspicion. Faithful women, for example, have legitimate difficulty with certain texts, as do readers who have experienced, say, slavery, colonization, or other forms of oppression. It is important for all readers of the biblical text—whatever their interpretive stance—to listen to readers with differing hermeneutical approaches, for in so doing they will hear questions and gain insights that would not otherwise occur to them. This may, at times, take a certain degree of courage, but taking the risk of hearing the other almost always

---

[2]A very important essay on the hermeneutic of trust is Richard B. Hays, "Salvation by Trust? Reading the Bible Faithfully," *Christian Century* 114 (February 26, 1997): 218–23, reprinted in *The Conversion of the Imagination: Paul as Interpreter of Israel's Scripture* (Grand Rapids: Eerdmans, 2005), 190–201.

pays off with the fruit of greater appreciation both for the text and for the other.

These various fundamental interpretive postures naturally vary in their appropriateness for believing individuals and communities. Indeed, it is difficult to imagine believers being able to sustain themselves as a community for long without a basic hermeneutic of consent or trust toward their sacred texts. Nonetheless, it would be wrong to think that operating with this kind of hermeneutic means a closed-minded approach to other perspectives. Those who have examined other hermeneutical stances and found them either unwarranted or inappropriate as their fundamental interpretive posture must still take others' views very seriously. Their decision to give the Bible the benefit of the doubt as a source of religious authority is not made easily and should not be interpreted as simplistic, antiquated, or anti-intellectual. Such readers may, in fact, share some of the concerns of those who read with suspicion and even with antipathy.

As noted in chapter one, we may refer to the interpretation of the Bible with a basic hermeneutic of consent or trust as the *theological* interpretation of Scripture, which we now explore in some detail.

Theological Interpretation of Scripture

Arguably the most significant development in academic biblical interpretation in the first years of the twenty-first century has been the meteoric rise in interest in theological interpretation of the Bible—biblical interpretation that takes the Bible not just as a historical and/or a literary document but as source of divine revelation, witness to God's creative and salvific activity, and/or (minimally) significant partner in the task of theological reflection—thinking about God and about the world and humanity in light of God. Theological interpretation is hardly a new phenomenon—it was by most accounts the only way of reading the Bible before the Enlightenment, and it has survived the Enlightenment in many communities of faith—but it has recently received more attention in biblical studies after a long time of marginalization, at least in some academic circles.

This renaissance can be accounted for by noting a number of factors that converged at about the same time. Among these were widespread dissatisfaction with purely historical-critical (diachronic) and even purely socio-rhetorical and literary (synchronic) approaches to biblical study; the sense of a new freedom, granted by postmodernism, for biblical interpreters to make their theological interests (as well as other "ideological" interests—feminist, liberationist, etc.) explicit; and the desire among many biblical scholars and systematic theologians to reconnect their respective disciplines.

The rebirth of theological interpretation has been marked by a number of significant scholarly ventures that are helping to reshape the field of biblical studies. These include:

- a growing number of groups within the professional societies of biblical scholars (especially the Society of Biblical Literature) that are devoted to theological interpretation of Scripture

- the launching of several new commentary series with specifically theological purposes (and titles), including at least one series being written, not primarily by biblical specialists, but largely by theologians[3]

- an increasing interest in the recovery and reappropriation of earlier (patristic, medieval, reformation, etc.) theological readings of the Bible[4]

- the publication of numerous books in various formats—monographs, multi-volume series, and multi-author volumes—dedicated to defining and doing theological interpretation of the Bible

- the publication of a major reference book entitled *Dictionary for Theological Interpretation of the Bible*[5]

- the 2007 launching of a significant new journal called *Journal of Theological Interpretation,* edited by one of the leading voices in theological interpretation, Joel B. Green

Despite the rapid and widespread rise in interest in theological interpretation, its theoreticians and practitioners (among whom the present author should be counted) sometimes quip that no one knows exactly what it is. That is not quite true, but there is in fact great diversity of opinion about what constitutes theological interpretation or exegesis. One thing that seems to be generally agreed upon, however, is that theological interpretation is

---

[3]See the discussion of commentaries in chapter 11, section 6, "Resources for Detailed Analysis."

[4]This revived interest is manifesting itself in several ways, including the publication of "commentaries" that are really anthologies of earlier sources. See once again chapter 11, section 6, "Resources for Detailed Analysis."

[5]Kevin J. Vanhoozer, gen. ed.; Craig G. Bartholomew, Daniel J. Treier, and N. T. Wright, assoc. eds., *Dictionary for Theological Interpretation of the Bible* (Grand Rapids: Baker, 2005).

not primarily about exegetical *methods* but about exegetical *goals*. What is the goal, or *telos*, of biblical exegesis? If the exegete is seeking only to understand a biblical text as an ancient text, as a purely human text—whether using diachronic or synchronic methods—that exegete is not doing theological interpretation. On the other hand, if the exegete seeks to understand a biblical text in order to appropriate its message as a guide for contemporary belief and behavior within a community of faith (either Christian or Jewish)—whether that goal is achieved with historical-critical, social-scientific, narrative, or other methods—that exegete is doing theological interpretation.

One of the major goals of all theological interpretation is to bridge the gaps that have developed between academic biblical studies and the church, on the one hand, and between academic biblical studies and systematic theology on the other. One way to achieve this two-part goal, according to many theological interpreters, is to balance (or even replace) the modern preoccupation with *methods* with a focus on theological dispositions and practices. That is, theological reading requires a hermeneutic of trust that is grounded in such dispositions as humility and receptivity, as well as such corollary practices as prayer and Christian virtue.

Defining Theological Interpretation and Its Goals

The chief editor of the *Dictionary for Theological Interpretation of the Bible*, systematic theologian Kevin Vanhoozer, says that theological interpretation is "reading to know God," the God revealed in Israel and Jesus.[6] Its goal is to overcome the modern gap between exegesis and theology and to express the "joint responsibility of all theological disciplines" to interpret Scripture "with a governing interest in God" and a "broad ecclesial concern." Vanhoozer insists, however, that theological interpretation is not the imposition of a confessional system (e.g., Catholicism or Calvinism) onto the biblical text, and he opposes what he perceives to be the postmodern tendency to turn exegesis into ideology.[7]

Joel Green contends that the most important difference between reading the Bible and reading the Bible as *Scripture* (theological interpretation) is that in the latter case we read the Bible as a word addressed to *us;* it assumes that we are part of the same

---

[6]Vanhoozer, *Dictionary for Theological Interpretation*, 24. His entire introduction to the dictionary is valuable reading (19–24).

[7]Vanhoozer, *Dictionary for Theological Interpretation*, 19–21.

community—God's people throughout space and time—to which the biblical text was originally addressed. In other words, when we read a biblical text we are not reading someone else's mail but our mail. And that "mail" is not merely part of a book or collection of books—"Bible"—but part of the sacred authoritative text for God's people—"Scripture."[8]

Theological exegesis, therefore, is biblical interpretation that takes place in an ecclesial context[9] and is grounded in certain fundamental theological principles, especially (1) the principle of divine self-revelation and address and (2) the principle of the unity and catholicity, or universality, of the church. (We will have more to say about these, and other principles, momentarily.) Together, these two basic principles encourage the theological interpreter of Scripture to develop (or learn) and use appropriate methods of diachronic and synchronic analysis of texts, while also mandating a spiritual sensitivity to the texts.

The great saint Augustine (354–430) famously stated the purpose of scriptural interpretation in the following poignant words:

> Whoever, therefore, thinks that he understands the divine Scriptures or any part of them so that it does not build the double love of God and of our neighbor does not understand it at all. (*On Christian Doctrine* 1.35.40)

Stephen Fowl, another leading voice in theological interpretation of Scripture, echoes Augustine in saying that the goal of theological interpretation is ever-increasing communion with God and with one another.[10]

Another way of describing theological exegesis is to reflect on the kinds of questions the reader seeks to answer. In summary form, we may describe those questions as the following:[11]

---

[8]See Joel B. Green, *Seized by Truth: Reading the Bible as Scripture* (Nashville: Abingdon, 2007), and further discussion below.

[9]That is, "church community," broadly understood to include academic and other contexts associated with the church.

[10]See Fowl, *Engaging Scripture*, vii, 3, 7, and throughout.

[11]These questions, as noted in chapter 1, are rooted in the medieval church's fourfold exegetical method that considered first of all the literal meaning of a text, and then also its doctrinal, eschatological, and moral dimensions. See discussion in Burnett, "Interpretation," 138–41. For an approach to the biblical text that places these three questions at the center of the interpretive enterprise, see Michael J. Gorman, *Apostle of the Crucified Lord: A Theological Introduction to Paul and His Letters* (Grand

- What does the text urge us to believe? *(faith)*

- What does the text urge us to hope for? *(hope)*

- What does the text urge us to do? *(love)*

In asking these sorts of questions, however, we are acknowledging that the goal of theological interpretation is not merely, or even primarily, to read and question the text, but to allow the text to read, question, and form us. Christian theological interpretation is interpretation in, with, and for the church so that the church may in fact be the kind of church in the world that is appropriate to the Christian gospel.

Eight Principles for the Theological Interpretation of Scripture

Theological interpretation of Scripture, then, is biblical interpretation grounded in certain fundamental theological and hermeneutical (interpretive) principles. For many lay and ordained readers of the Bible as Scripture, most of these principles may not seem particularly revolutionary and may already be operative, either explicitly or tacitly, in their own interpretation. Nevertheless, they represent a growing consensus among some biblical scholars and theologians about how Scripture has *not* been read but *should* be read even by scholars. The coming together of non-academics and scholars in the reading of Scripture *theologically* may be one of the fruits of the renewed interest in theological interpretation in the academy.

Beginning with the two noted briefly above (divine self-revelation and address; the unity and universality of the church), we may identify eight principles for the theological interpretation of Scripture, all of which are closely connected to one another.[12]

Rapids: Eerdmans, 2004). At the end of each chapter on Paul's various letters, the final question for reflection is "In sum, what does this letter urge us to believe, hope for, and do?"

[12]These principles are my own formulation. I have added, in footnotes, some of the parallel theses from the important work of the Scripture Project, found in Ellen F. Davis and Richard B. Hays, eds., *The Art of Reading Scripture* (Grand Rapids: Eerdmans, 2003), 1–5. I write here as a Christian practitioner of biblical exegesis, but very similar principles could be adopted within a Jewish framework. For a discussion of recent shifts in Protestant interpretation of the Bible that have paved the way for theological interpretation, see my "The Interpretation of the Bible in Protestant Churches," in *Scripture* (ed. Gorman), 177–94.

1. The Chalcedonian (or Incarnational) Principle

This first principle, as an aspect of the conviction that God engages in self-revelation (otherwise humans could not know God), has to do with the nature of Scripture as simultaneously fully divine and fully human. It is divine address in human dress. This view of the nature of Scripture is analogous to the theological doctrine of the incarnation, the Christian belief that the eternal second person of the Trinity became human in Jesus of Nazareth, and that he was therefore both fully divine and fully human. Since this theological doctrine was articulated at the Council of Chalcedon in 451 and is called the Chalcedonian formula, its hermeneutical corollary can be called the Chalcedonian principle.[13]

This principle affirms that Scripture is first of all part of God's self-revelation. The Christian tradition has consistently affirmed, in the words of the late Yale biblical scholar Brevard Childs, that the Bible is "God's means of telling God's story."[14] As such, Scripture is a divine word, or address, to us and an invitation (indeed a summons) to join the divine story, the divine drama.

This principle does not, however, ignore the human dimension of Scripture. Rather, it both permits and requires us to read Scripture as a collection of human writings, with all their historical and literary dimensions, and thus to develop and use appropriate methods of diachronic and synchronic exegesis. At the same time, the theological interpreter, sensitive to the Scriptures as a vehicle of divine address, seeks to hear the voice of God through the human voices; the theological interpreter also remains open to a surplus of meaning that does not limit the significance of texts to the results of diachronic and synchronic study.[15] This principle,

---

[13] Readers should note that there are diverse ways of understanding the nature, inspiration, and function of Scripture. Some would prefer to use terms like "witness" or "testimony." This is not, however, the place for a full-blown theological account of Scripture. The view briefly and partially developed here and throughout this chapter is to me both persuasive and helpful in the task of theological exegesis. As will be clear, this view does not underestimate the human character of Scripture.

[14] Brevard S. Childs, *The Struggle to Understand Isaiah as Christian Scripture* (Grand Rapids: Eerdmans, 2004), 296.

[15] See the discussion in the previous chapter and the fourth thesis in Davis and Hays, *The Art of Reading Scripture*, 2–3: "Texts of Scripture do not have a single meaning limited to the intent of the original author. In accord with Jewish and Christian traditions, we affirm that Scripture has multiple complex senses given by God, the author of the whole drama." As we noted in the previous chapter, this does not mean that Scripture

then, both permits and requires us to read Scripture as simultaneously the Word of God and the words of humans.

2. The Catholic (or Universal) Principle

The second principle is that of the unity and universality, or catholicity, of the church and therefore also the catholicity of Scripture. This principle means that although the Scriptures were not written *to* us, they were written *for* us. Paul himself articulates such a principle explicitly (see 1 Corinthians 10:11 and Romans 15:4), and the rest of the biblical writers, who constantly reuse and reinterpret earlier texts and traditions, seem to share that perspective. The principle of catholicity means that all Scripture is written for all God's people in all ages and places.[16] From a theological perspective, Scripture transcends the very contingencies of time and space—as important and helpful for interpretation as they are—that are discovered about the text by historical-critical and social-scientific approaches to it. As Joel Green writes:

> The first question, then, [in the interpretation of the Bible as Scripture] is not what separates us (language, diet, worldview, politics, social graces, and so forth) from the biblical authors, but whether we are ready to embrace the God to whom and the theological vision to which these writers bear witness.[17]

He adds:

> *Historical* judgments about the audience of a biblical text stand in tension with the *theological* affirmation of the oneness of the church that receives this biblical text *as Scripture.* Historical criticism assumes what Christians can never assume—namely, that there is more than one people of God.[18]

This principle both permits and requires the theological interpreter to listen, not only to the scriptural text itself, but also—as much as possible—to the readings of Scripture articulated and performed by God's people in other times, places, and cultures.[19]

---

had or has limitless meanings or that contemporary readings can be incongruent with the sense of the text in its original contexts.

[16]This conviction is *not* meant to minimize the difficulties present in Scripture or to side-step the need for responsible interpretation.

[17]Green, *Seized by Truth,* 18.

[18]Green, *Seized by Truth,* 51 (emphasis his).

[19]See the seventh thesis in Davis and Hays, *The Art of Reading Scripture,* 4: "The saints of the church provide guidance in how to interpret and perform Scripture."

3. The Communal (or Ecclesial) Principle

The third principle is related to the second and refers to the significance of the church (Greek *ekklēsia*), or community of God's people in Christ, for theological interpretation. One way to describe this principle is to say that it expands the concentric circles of contextual analysis beyond even the canonical context and circle (see below) to include the circle of the universal church. The emphasis here, in contrast to the catholic principle, is not on the scope of Scripture's reach but on the proper location for interpretation—within the church itself.

This principle has two major corollaries. One corollary is the recognition that exegesis is not primarily an individual affair but an ecclesial discipline, something that happens in conversation more than in isolation.[20] That conversation may take the form of scholarly theological debate, the reading of ancient interpreters, contextualized Bible study by lay people, and much more.

The other corollary of this principle is an understanding of scriptural interpretation not merely as an academic exercise, but as an ecclesial practice. For theological interpreters, even the most technical and sophisticated academic biblical interpretation has the church as its primary location and ultimate focus. Good theological biblical scholarship is a form of prayer, communion (*koinōnia*), and, most importantly, service to the church.

4. The Canonical Principle

The fourth principle, the canonical principle, means first of all that scriptural texts can and must be heard, not only in their historical and literary contexts, but also in their canonical context. This principle permits and requires the theological interpreter to ask what role a text plays in the canon as a whole, understood theologically not as an arbitrary collection but as a divinely orchestrated whole that unveils the story and the drama of salvation. This principle also permits and requires the theological interpreter to ask questions about the relationship of various parts of the canon to one another (e.g., the imprecatory psalms and the Sermon on the Mount, or the teaching of Paul and the teaching of James)—to put the texts of Scripture in conversation with

---

[20]See the sixth thesis in Davis and Hays, *The Art of Reading Scripture*, 3: "Faithful interpretation of Scripture invites and presupposes participation in the community brought into being by God's redemptive action—the church."

one another. Finally, this principle both permits and requires the theological interpreter to read the two Testaments in light of each other, asking, for instance, how the book of Genesis provides insight into the book of Revelation (and vice versa), and how the use of Isaiah 53 in the New Testament provides insight into Isaiah (and vice versa).

Another way to describe the canonical principle, then, is to say that it expands the concentric circles of contextual analysis beyond the traditional literary framework of immediate context and larger context in a particular writing (see chapter 4) to include the largest literary context—that of the Bible as a single book.[21] Non-theological interpretation does not recognize this context.

5. The Coherence Principle

The principle of coherence follows from the canonical principle and is the theological conviction that, in spite of all its diversity, Scripture is one divinely given book that essentially tells one coherent story of the creator-God's salvation of the world, culminating in Jesus Christ.[22] It is not a collection of mutually competing or contradicting accounts of God and of humanity's experience of God. This principle also has a corollary: that because of the guiding work of the Spirit throughout the history of God's people (see the next principle), those who read Scripture theologically can and should be guided by the basic theological convictions of their reading communities (e.g., the Christian church), which are themselves derived from the Scriptures. These convictions have been set forth in the various Christian creeds, especially those from the earliest centuries of the church—to which most Christians give assent.

In a sense, this principle also widens the context within which Scripture is read to include the confessional expression (sometimes called "the rule of faith") of the reading community named in the previous principle. It means, for instance, that Christian readers will not be satisfied with readings of the text that stand at odds with their most fundamental convictions, such as the good-

---

[21] See the third thesis in Davis and Hays, *The Art of Reading Scripture*, 2: "Faithful interpretation of Scripture requires an engagement with the entire narrative: the New Testament canon cannot be rightly understood apart from the Old, nor can the Old be rightly understood apart from the New."

[22] See the first two theses in Davis and Hays, *The Art of Reading Scripture*, 1–2: "Scripture truthfully tells the story of God's action of creating, judging, and saving the world" and "Scripture is rightly understood in light of the church's rule of faith as a coherent dramatic narrative."

ness of God and of God's creation of the world.[23] This commitment will at times generate tensions between a "plain reading" of the text and the church's theological convictions. This is nothing new; the theological interpreter joins the ranks of generations of faithful Jews and Christians who have participated in the same kinds of struggles.

6. The Charismatic Principle

The sixth principle asserts that theological interpretation is a work of the Spirit of God, the same Spirit who gives the church gifts of grace (Greek *charismata*). The word *charismatic* is not intended, however, to suggest that all interpretation is spontaneous, lacking in control or reason. Indeed, if the gifts of the Spirit include wisdom and understanding, then careful, rational exegetical skill is a charism. But the principle does assert that such exegetical skill needs the grace and guidance of the Spirit to achieve its intended end of greater communion with God and with one another (to return to Fowl's point, rooted in Augustine).[24]

This principle, like the Chalcedonian principle with which we began this discussion, also permits and requires the theological interpreter to be open to new, imaginative readings of Scripture that are appropriate outgrowths of the historical, literary, canonical, and ecclesial contexts.[25] These new readings must not do violence to the text but need to be properly analogous to the sense of the text, as best we can articulate it, in the original historical and literary context. This principle of analogy, or what we may call creative fidelity, is really at the heart of theological interpretation. It is in turn based on the theological conviction that because the Spirit of God, like Christ, is the same yesterday, today, and

---

[23] This perspective is directly at odds with the Enlightenment (and thus also the historical-critical) view that theological convictions should not guide biblical interpretation and that they, in fact, obscure rather than clarify. Many Christian theological interpreters would identify the Nicene Creed as the appropriate framework for interpretation.

[24] See above, p. 147.

[25] See Murray Rae, "Texts in Context: Scripture in the Divine Economy," *Journal of Theological Interpretation* 1 (2007): 23–46. See also the fourth thesis (quoted above) in Davis and Hays, *The Art of Reading Scripture,* as well as their ninth thesis (p. 5): "We live in the tension between the 'already' and the 'not yet' of the kingdom of God; consequently, Scripture calls the church to ongoing discernment, to continually fresh readings of the text in light of the Holy Spirit's ongoing work in the world." I would want to nuance this thesis some, stressing the important dynamic tension between faithfulness and creativity.

tomorrow, the Spirit's *new* work always resembles the Spirit's previous work.

Above all, then, this principle reminds the theological interpreter of Scripture that the Spirit is absolutely necessary to the church if it is to perform Scripture and not merely study it. The Spirit forms in us the mind of Christ so that we may participate appropriately in the dramatic narrative of God's salvation—the story of God's mission to and in the world—that we encounter as we hear or read the words of Scripture. (See further below under "A Missional Hermeneutic.")

7. The Conversion (or Transformative) Principle

The last two principles assert that theological interpretation is more than the linguistic, historical, and even theological analysis of texts. Theological interpretation has a much more ambitious, constructive goal than simply analysis of the text; it is to *form* communities of Christian disciples who can *perform* the Scriptures faithfully and creatively, and to *inform* the theological reflection of such disciples individually and ecclesially.

We may describe this principle of theological interpretation in terms of its function: scriptural interpretation is the primary means by which God effects (in traditional Catholic terms) the church's *ongoing conversion,* that is (in traditional Protestant terms), the church's *continuous reformation,* or (in Orthodox language) the church's increasing participation in the life of the Triune God— its *divinization,* or *theosis.* We may also describe this principle in terms of its *telos:* the ultimate goal of scriptural interpretation is for the individual and especially the community to "perform" the text, to become a living exegesis of the text. We will have more to say about this below.

8. The Constructive Principle

Finally, in addition to the formation of Christian existence, part of the goal of theological interpretation is to contribute in a profound way to the church's constructive task of articulating its convictions and practices faithfully and creatively in ever-changing contexts. Scripture, as the Catholic Church has said, is "the soul" of theology. This constructive process is a two-way street, with Christian theological claims and practices contributing to the task of biblical interpretation even as ecclesially based biblical interpretation seeks to permeate the church's thinking and its public expressions of that thinking.

Ultimately, the constructive principle cannot be separated from the conversion principle, or from any of the other foregoing principles, for the true goal of theological interpretation is the Spirit-inspired formation of communities that think and act like Christ ("the mind of Christ") as they discern their role in what God is doing in the world in faithful and creative response to the divine address they encounter in the Scriptures. And that conclusion leads us to a brief consideration of one additional dimension of theological interpretation.[26]

A Missional Hermeneutic

Another very significant and closely related recent development in the study of theology in general, and more particularly in the study of the church (ecclesiology) and of Scripture (theological hermeneutics), has been a renewed emphasis on *mission* as integral to each of these disciplines. This development is not a move toward a new colonialism in which the more powerful and "Christian" West and North missionizes and colonizes the weaker and "pagan" East and South. Rather, talking its cue from the leading Western theologians of mission (missiologists) from the past half-century, as well as from Christian voices from the two-thirds world, this development takes a decidedly postcolonial approach and, for Western practitioners, a post-Christendom approach to mission and to biblical interpretation.

This new approach is grounded in the theological principle of the *missio Dei,* or mission of God. This term summarizes the conviction that the Scriptures of both Testaments bear witness to a God who, as creator and redeemer of the world, is already on a mission. Indeed, God is by nature a missional God, who is seeking not just to save "souls" to take to heaven some day, but to restore and save the created order: individuals, communities, nations, the environment, the world, the cosmos. This God calls the people of God assembled in the name of Christ—who was the incarnation of the divine mission—to participate in this *missio Dei,* to discern what God is up to in the world, and to join in.

---

[26] For yet another list of similar principles ("marks"), see also Hays, "Reading the Bible with Eyes of Faith," especially 11–15. In addition, John Barton has an essay called "Strategies for Reading Scripture" in the 2006 edition of *The HarperCollins Study Bible* (xxxix–xliii) in which he contrasts a purely "critical" reading with what he calls a "canonical" reading. The latter operates with the presuppositions that Scripture is true (though not necessarily literally so), relevant, important, and self-consistent, and that it should be read in conformity with church teachings.

This way of understanding mission has many implications, only a few of which may be mentioned here briefly:

- Mission is not a *part* of the church's life (represented locally by a small line item in the budget) but the *whole,* the *essence* of the church's existence; mission is *comprehensive.*

- Mission is not the church's initiative but its response, its participation in God's mission; mission is *derivative.*

- Mission is not an extension of Western (or any other) power, culture, and values; rather, it is specifically participation in the coming of the kingdom of God. It is therefore critical of all attempts to coerce Christian mission for implicit or explicit political purposes other than the "politics" of the reign of God—the realities of new life, peace, and justice *(shalom)* promised by the prophets, inaugurated by Jesus, and first spread to the world by the apostles. For Christians in the West, it is crucial that they recognize the failure of Christendom as a positive development, and that they see the church appropriately and biblically as a distinctive subculture within a larger, non-Christian culture. Mission is *theo-* and *Christocentric.*

- Mission is not unidirectional (e.g., West to East) but *reciprocal.*

- Mission must become the governing framework within which all biblical interpretation takes place; mission is *hermeneutical.*

This last claim is obviously the one that is most directly relevant to our concerns in this book. A missional hermeneutic is a type of theological interpretation of Scripture. It acknowledges the Bible as a word from God that bears special witness to the very purposes of God in the world and that therefore invites questions (and responses) appropriate to the subject matter. There are perhaps five key questions that readers operating with a missional hermeneutic will want to ask of the biblical text and themselves:

- What does this text say, implicitly or explicitly, about the *missio Dei* and the missional character of God?

- What does this text reveal about humanity and the world?

- What does this text say about the nature and mission of God's people in the world, that is, about the church understood as an agent of divine mission rather than as an institution, civic organization, or guardian of Christendom?

- How does this text relate to the larger scriptural witness, in both testaments, to the *missio Dei* and the mission of God's people?

- In what concrete ways might we deliberately read this text as God's call to us as the people of God to participate in the *missio Dei* to which it bears witness?

Because for Westerners a missional hermeneutic always has the danger of becoming a revision of the narrow, individualistic, colonizing theology of the not-too-distant past, it may also be helpful to keep in mind some additional critical questions that deal with the need for imagination, transformation, and witness as key components of missional thinking and participation:

- How does this text call us to *imagine and envision the world?*
- What does this text call us to *unlearn and then learn afresh?*
- What *powers* that could deceive, seduce, and harm the world or the church does this text *unveil and challenge*—or call us to unveil and challenge?
- How does this text call us as God's people to be both *different from and involved in the world?*

A brief example of a missional reading of a New Testament text might be helpful. The familiar parable of the Good Samaritan (Luke 10:25–37) is frequently used as an exhortation to Christian compassion, as Jesus tells his audience to "go and do likewise." A missional hermeneutic does not overturn this ethical reading but puts it in a larger theological context. What does the parable tell us about God and the world? God is revealed through the Samaritan as a God of compassion whose heart breaks at the violent world human beings have created—and who is determined to do something about it, as the prophets of Israel had also proclaimed. Those who share this heart of God may not be the religious leaders who study and pray scriptural texts, but the unexpected outsider who is not respected by the leaders yet who empathizes with God and thus with God's creatures in pain. This text indicates the surprising people who can be enlisted in the *missio Dei*. It is also a call to God's people to stand against violence and to take practical, even sacrificial action on behalf of its victims.

Our imagination is enlarged if we consider that "robbers" and "being left half dead" take many forms: physical, to be sure, but also spiritual and emotional. God's mission in the world is to liberate people from all powers that can take away their life and threaten to destroy them: the culture of violence and death; the seductive power of sin; the challenges of daily life in the midst of loneliness, poverty, or terminal illness. The people of God participate in the mission of God when they are present and responsive to those who face such life-robbing powers.

This missional approach to the parable of the Good Samaritan has much in common with the early church's theological reading of the parable as a story of God in Christ, who comes to rescue battered humanity and offers himself and the church (the inn) as the healing balm humanity desperately needs.

As with other forms of theological interpretation, a missional hermeneutic is not committed to any one exegetical method. However, because mission is about discerning God's mission in the world, a missional hermeneutic will naturally pay attention to narratives, since the ways of God and God's people are recounted in them, and it will appreciate synchronic readings of the final form of the text that utilize various forms of narrative analysis. Furthermore, since mission is often about the encounter of different cultures, a missional hermeneutic will naturally make use of methods that pay attention both to the social location of the original readers/hearers of Scripture and to the social location of subsequent interpreters of Scripture. A missional hermeneutic therefore needs to be culturally sensitive, and it benefits from hearing the questions and perspectives on scriptural texts from people of diverse cultures.

I once heard an African pastor, for instance, contrast the traditional Western and the traditional African reading of the story of Joseph in Genesis. The Western reading, he said, was that Joseph's story calls us not to forget God no matter how low we fall. The African reading, he explained, was that Joseph's story calls us not to forget our extended family no matter how high we rise. Both readings are valid (as the pastor himself acknowledged), but each grows out of different social locations, and each will result in a different (though mutually complementary) interpretation of God's mission and the corresponding mission of God's people.

We may summarize the main point of this chapter so far by suggesting that theological interpretation expands the contexts for reading Scripture, as the following graphic illustrates:

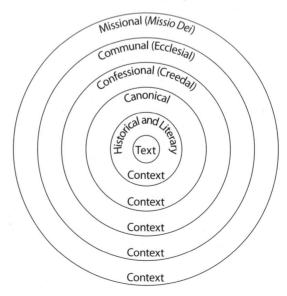

The Two Horizons: Invitation and Cautions

Readers with a hermeneutic of trust, an expanded set of contexts, and a missional framework—theological interpreters—are deliberately reading the Bible with an eye on the "two horizons" mentioned in chapter 1 of this book. They want to know the meaning of the text in its original context as well as the possible significance of the text in their own contemporary context.[27]

Some scholars therefore distinguish between exegesis and reflection, between textual *meaning* and textual (contemporary) *significance*, between "what it meant" and "what it means."[28] For methodological, pedagogical, or organizational purposes, these distinctions may be fine. If we understand exegesis, however, as reading the text in its contexts, there is no inherent reason to bifurcate the reading process so completely—especially if we widen the concentric circles to include the canonical, confessional, and ultimately communal contexts.

To be sure, exegesis is concerned first of all with hearing the voice of the text on its own terms,[29] which means attending as best we can to its *original* contexts. But if a sacred text is worth its salt as *sacred* text, or even as *artistic* text, then (1) it must make some ongoing claims on its contemporary audience, and (2) those claims must have some connection to the claims made on its original audience. Furthermore, admitting that we have an interest in the meaning of the text—since exegesis without presuppositions is impossible—keeps us honest with ourselves and with one another so that we are less likely to engage in *eisegesis* (reading into the text) in the name of objectivity. Theological interpretation of Scripture

---

[27] In a different sense, readers with a hermeneutic of suspicion also read the Bible with an eye on both horizons, often trying to reinterpret texts they perceive to be problematic. One could also argue that a hermeneutic of discernment or appreciation and even of antipathy also involves the two horizons, since readers within these hermeneutical postures may be interested in (or interested in opposing) the text in the contemporary setting. However, readers within these hermeneutical postures differ from those who approach the text with trust/consent or with suspicion by not being part of a community of faith and interpretation that is committed by its very nature to the two horizons.

[28] This distinction was carefully formulated by Krister Stendahl in, for example, "Biblical Theology, Contemporary," in *Interpreter's Dictionary of the Bible* (ed. G. A. Buttrick; 4 vols.; Nashville: Abingdon, 1962), 1:418–32.

[29] I owe this helpful phrase to Joel B. Green.

means that we believe ourselves to be directly addressed by God in and through the words of Scripture. But theological interpretation of Scripture also means that our commitment to the text as divine word spoken to us ought not only guide our approach to the text, but also inhibit our desire to control it, to fashion it in our own image. For this reason, it has sometimes been said that, for theological interpretation, "understanding" Scripture fundamentally means "standing under" Scripture.

Believing that we are addressed by God in Scripture means that we perceive ourselves to be part of the same people of God addressed by the prophets and the apostles many years ago. In other words, we acknowledge the similarities as well as the differences between their ancient situations and our own. (In fact, some contemporary theological interpreters of Scripture have suggested that modern interpretation of the Bible has overemphasized the differences.) The notion of "two horizons" is built on the theory of interpretation that holds that we cannot truly read, interpret, or understand a text until we engage it, until we somehow fuse its "horizon" with our own. According to theorists such as Hans-Georg Gadamer and Paul Ricoeur, the reading or interpretive process is incomplete until or unless that fusion occurs. The process of considering the two horizons is sometimes called "application" (Gadamer) or "appropriation" (Ricoeur).[30] For believers, this application or appropriation can never be merely intellectual or theoretical. The final goal of exegesis is actualization, or embodiment—living the text. The ultimate goal of exegesis is for the individual and community to become a *living exegesis* of the text.

The notion of the "two horizons" is built also on the principle of analogy noted earlier in the discussion of the charismatic principle of theological interpretation. The contemporary reader of the text attempts to discern the message of the text not only in its original setting but also in possible analogous situations today— similar yet different situations, since all analogies have both similarity and difference built into them. Moreover, when the Bible is read as a word from God, readers must always be prepared to have their horizons enlarged and to have new horizons cre-

---

[30]The complex theoretical work of these two philosophers may be found in Hans-Georg Gadamer, *Truth and Method* (trans. Joel Weinsheimer and Donald G. Marshall; 2d rev. ed.; New York: Crossroad, 1989); Paul Ricoeur, *Interpretation Theory: Discourse and the Surplus of Meaning* (Fort Worth, Tex.: Texas Christian University Press, 1976); and idem, *Hermeneutics and the Human Sciences* (ed. John B. Thompson; Cambridge: Cambridge University Press, 1981).

ated.[31] We cannot, therefore, underestimate the importance of imagination—though disciplined and Spirit-guided, rather than freewheeling, imagination—in the interpretation of the Bible for our own contexts.

Some basic hints for reflecting on the text are offered in the next section. But perhaps the most crucial point to remember in this process of reflection is to avoid dullness, which occurs when readers engage in what Anthony Thiselton calls "premature assimilation." Premature assimilation takes place when readers jump into the application of a text without sufficient thought and without respect for the distance between the two horizons, between then and now. The result, says Thiselton, is that "interaction between the two horizons of the texts and readers will . . . appear *uneventful, bland, routine, and entirely unremarkable.*"[32] Furthermore, premature assimilation will result in our controlling or domesticating the text rather than allowing the text to challenge us.

Some Practical Ways to Think about the Two Horizons

We have spent much of this chapter laying the groundwork for theological reflection. To return to the practicalities of the exegetical process, we may rightly ask how to bridge the two horizons.

Once you have carefully reflected on the meaning of the text you are interpreting in its original contexts, you can intelligently think more deliberately about its broader, deeper, or ongoing meaning. First of all, paraphrase the central meaning of the text; that is, put it in your own words. (You should have already begun this process when you prepared a synthesis.)

Have you heard or read this passage before? In what context? What other biblical texts is this passage similar to or different from? Do you know what place this text has had in the life of Jews and/or Christians? In history and culture more generally?

What universal hopes, fears, beliefs, and values do you see expressed in this text? What unique or unusual beliefs and values? What does this text claim about God, human beings, and the relationship between God and people? Specifically, in light of the

---

[31] This is a major thesis of Thiselton, *New Horizons in Hermeneutics*, summarized on 619.

[32] Ibid., 8 (emphasis his).

discussion of theological interpretation above, what does this text affirm about:

- God, including Father/Creator, Son, and Spirit
- the people of God
- sacred, or salvation, history
- the mission of God in the world, the *missio Dei* (see the more specific questions above)
- salvation, or human redemption by God: past, present, and/or future
- the fruits of salvation: the theological virtues of faith, hope, and love
- the love of God: human commitment to God and participation in the divine mission
- the love of neighbor: ethical imperatives
- daily life, worship, and service in community.[33]

How do *you* react to this text? Do you like it? Why or why not? What emotions does it stir up in you? Joy? Wonder? Anger? Frustration? Fear? What response do you have to the image or actions of God implicit in this passage?

Does this text challenge you in any way? Does it open up any new horizons of understanding and insight? Do you feel differently about the passage after careful study than you did on first reading it?

How does your own religious and social location affect your understanding of and reaction to the text? Choose a different context for yourself: imagine yourself part of another century, country, race, socioeconomic group, or religious community. From that new perspective, how do you respond to the text?

Do you see any contemporary issues or situations that seem similar, or analogous, to the issues or situations addressed in the biblical text? How are they similar? dissimilar?

In a word, what claims about God, and about God's claim on us, does the text make? Are these central, marginal, or antithetical to the understanding of God and God's claim on us that you, your religious tradition, or others you know make? If there is conflict between the text and your perspective, how might you resolve that conflict? Will you

---

[33]This list augments a more rhetorically oriented list in Robbins, *Exploring the Texture of Texts*, 120–31.

- ignore the text?

- challenge the text?

- look for a means of reconciliation?

- review and revise your exegesis?

- alter your beliefs and/or behavior?

- consult with others?

These are all possible (and frequently practiced) options.

We should never be surprised when people discern different meanings in the same biblical text; even professional exegetes disagree about the original meaning of the text, so why would we expect anything less in reflecting on its contemporary significance? This does not mean that the text is simply like a ventriloquist's dummy, an instrument to express the capricious desires of the interpreter.[34] What matters for all interpreters is being able to ground reflection in a careful analysis of the text and to engage both the text and others in a spirit of humility.

After thinking through all these things, then, ask yourself, finally, "What might be the significance of this text for today? If readers took the message of this text seriously, how would their lives be different?"

Living Exegesis

To raise this last question—if readers took the message of this text seriously, how would their lives be different?—is to raise the ultimate question of exegesis. It is to accept the text's own invitation to engage the text on its own terms as imagination-transforming and life-transforming word. Readers who decline this invitation are not thereby rendered bad or unwelcome readers, but they have, in some sense, truncated the reading process.

Among persons and communities of faith this invitation is normally taken seriously. It is the question of "embodiment" or "actualization." We may also refer to this final element of exegesis as "living exegesis." The goal of this "method" is for the exegete, whether an individual or a community, in some sense to become the text it reads. This "becoming the text" does not mean the uncritical acceptance and wooden replication of every aspect of every text (e.g., all the cultural values reflected in the text). Rather, it means an

---

[34] This wonderful image is from Schneiders, *The Revelatory Text*, xxxi.

imaginative and discerning engagement with the text from within the particular interpretive posture of the reader(s). In narrative terms, the community or individual as exegete continues the narrative of the text by being part of its ongoing embodiment in the world, a kind of narrative embodiment—"performing" the text of Scripture.[35] This performance will be an act of "creative fidelity," of scriptural and ethical "improvisation"—a unique but recognizably authentic interpretation of the text. This is "not about being clever or original so much as joining in the stream of the action [i.e., the saving action of God in history] in an 'obvious' and 'fitting' way."[36]

This final task of exegesis raises two fundamental questions, two questions that—appropriately—constitute a hermeneutical circle of their own:

- What kind of persons and what kind of community does this text urge its readers to become?

- What kind of community and what kind of individuals are required to hear this text as a divine invitation, and to embody it with "creative fidelity"?

These questions can be asked and answered by any astute readers. For those who hear in the Bible a word from God, however, asking and answering such questions is not merely a possibility but a divine imperative.

On occasion, even faithful religious individuals and communities find texts in the Bible that seem to contradict their fundamental convictions. An example might be Psalm 137, which describes "bashing the Babylonian babies' brains on the boulders," as someone once put it.

When encountering such texts, the faithful have traditionally responded with pragmatic exegetical moves such as allegorical interpretation or reinterpretation in light of later texts and contexts. In so doing, readers create what we might call counter-readings of the text. In these cases, the community then embodies a liv-

---

[35] See, among others, Nicholas Lash, "Performing Scripture," in *Theology on the Way to Emmaus* (London: SCM, 1986), 37–46.

[36] Kevin J. Vanhoozer, "Imprisoned or Free? Text, Status, and Theological Interpretation in the Master/Slave Discourse of Philemon," in *Reading Scripture with the Church* (ed. Adam et al.), 81. Vanhoozer's entire discussion of scriptural interpretation as participation in the great "theodrama" (divine drama) is compelling (73–94). See also Samuel Wells, *Improvisation: The Drama of Christian Ethics* (Grand Rapids: Brazos, 2004).

ing counter-exegesis of the text as its members seek to discern a meaning of the text that is consistent with their most fundamental convictions. For example, Christian readers of Psalm 137 would normally appeal finally to the teaching and example of Jesus regarding enemy-love to provide a fully canonical exegesis (and thus a counter-exegesis) of Psalm 137.

This approach can, of course, be taken to an extreme. It cannot, however, be avoided, at least on occasion. For people of faith, the imperative to read the text as word of God may require a basic posture of trust, but it also requires an openness to difficult questions and new perspectives when problematic texts are taken seriously.

Review & Study

Chapter Summary

- There are five basic interpretive postures or hermeneutics: antipathy, appreciation or noncommitment, discernment or inquiry, suspicion, and consent or trust.

- A hermeneutic of trust is the operative hermeneutic of theological interpretation, which is rooted in certain theological principles that stress such convictions as the divine origin, universality, and unity of Scripture as divine address in human words.

- A theological hermeneutic is also a missional hermeneutic—reading done in order to discern and participate in the mission of God in the world.

- Consideration of the two horizons of past and present—reflection and application or appropriation—is an essential element of a complete reading process, but the application must not be done carelessly or prematurely.

- It is important to ask the right questions of a text when considering its broader, deeper, or ongoing meaning.

- For people of faith, the essential question is, "What claims about God and about God's claims on us does the text make?"

- People of faith seek to perform, embody, or become a living exegesis of the text—to participate in the divine story told by the Scriptures. This is done creatively and faithfully but also sometimes even critically.

Practical Hints

1. Since reflection does not begin at the end of the exegetical process, record preliminary reflections as you work.

2. Use some of the guiding questions in this chapter to reflect on your text.

3. Try to include in your research at least some works with clearly theological or other existential interests.

For Further Insight and Practice

1. Read carefully Psalm 8. State its main point in your own words. What are some contemporary issues to which it might allude? How is the author of this psalm similar to or different from people you know today? What relevance might this psalm have in a technological world?

2. Read the prophetic text in Micah 6:8. Use your imagination to write a short essay on what your church/community or institution might be like if this text were its motto.

3. Read Luke 4:14–30. What intertextual echoes do you hear? Write down your initial thoughts about the explicit and implicit aspects of the mission of Jesus, God, and the people of God/followers of Jesus to which this text bears witness.

4. Choose a religious, social, or ethical issue of concern. Find at least two biblical passages that might be relevant to your issue. Without doing a detailed exegesis of the texts, write down some initial ideas and questions you have about the use of these texts to address the issue you have chosen.

5. Read chapter 11, section 8, pp. 226–32, "Resources for Reflection: Theological Interpretation."

6. Read the sections of the sample exegesis papers entitled "reflection" in Appendix C. How would you describe and respond to their reflections?

CHAPTER NINE

Expansion and Refinement of the Exegesis

> "Do you understand what you are reading?" . . .
> "How can I, unless someone guides me?"
> —*Philip and the Ethiopian eunuch,*
> *Acts 8:30–31 (NRSV)*

What tools are available to expand and refine the exegete's work on the text?

What have biblical scholars said about the passage, and how should their work affect yours?

One of the fundamental assumptions of this book is that exegesis can and must be done by the nonspecialist. The student, teacher, or pastor does not need a Ph.D. in biblical studies in order to do excellent exegesis. This assumption does *not* mean, however, that appropriate tools should be neglected or that the work of expert guides should be ignored. The "tools of the trade" and the field of biblical scholarship can and must inform the student's or preacher's own work if that work is to be responsible. Other colleagues in the investigation, partners in the conversation, and artistic instruments are needed.

Tools

Throughout this book reference has been made to a number of tools that are at the disposal of exegetes. When I was in seminary, one of my biblical professors told us that all we really needed (as long as we had mastered the original languages!) was a concordance, a grammar (of Hebrew, Aramaic, or Greek), and a lexicon (dictionary). There is a lot of truth in those words: a good concordance is a tremendous tool, and certain kinds of dictionaries can be helpful.

Most readers, however, will depend on the opinions of scholars working in the original languages. I, for one, am fearful of exegetes who know very little about Hebrew or Greek but do not refrain from making pronouncements based on their limited knowledge. It is still true that a little bit of knowledge is dangerous.

Thus, listed in chapter 11 of this book are numerous tools for biblical study, as well as other sources to consult for additional tools. The careful exegete will make wise use of certain tools without necessarily becoming an expert in ancient languages. (Of course, the ability to read the original languages greatly enhances the usefulness of many tools as well as one's engagement with the scriptural text itself.)

Biblical Scholarship

The published work of scholars can confirm or correct the disciplined discoveries and conclusions made in the exegetical process as well as resolve unanswered questions that have arisen during the process and generate new questions. Scholars can define unknown terms, show connections to other biblical texts, supply helpful historical information, explain grammatical constructions, and suggest implicit and explicit aspects of the significance of the text.

How many and which scholarly publications should be consulted depends on the nature and purpose of the exegesis. A preacher preparing a Sunday sermon or homily may (or may not) find one or two one-volume commentaries sufficient, whereas a student writing a ten-page exegesis paper will need to consult several detailed commentaries and articles. Some instructors have suggested that a research paper should have about as many items in its working bibliography (the list of works actually cited in the paper) as it has pages of text. That is, for a ten-to twelve-page exegesis paper, one might consult about five to seven commentaries and other books and five to seven articles or chapters in collections of essays. A twenty-page paper might have about twenty items, and so forth. This is only a general guideline, however, and it may not apply to papers shorter than ten pages.

There are some basic starting places that make the search for appropriate resources for an exegesis paper easier.

Commentaries

A good place to begin is with two or three recent major scholarly commentaries that provide a detailed yet holistic interpretation of the passage in its context. Consulting a variety of commentaries will usually give the reader a variety of readings of particular verses as well as of the text as a whole. Scholarly commentaries will also provide references (in the text, footnotes, or bibliographies) that will suggest other relevant commentaries, books, and articles to consult.

Certain commentary series are especially helpful in this regard. For example, the *Word Biblical Commentary, Sacra Pagina,* and *The Anchor Bible* have particularly complete and useful bibliographies for each unit of the text. Other individual commentaries and commentary series also have good bibliographies. At least one of the bibliographies consulted should be less than ten years old; otherwise many of the works listed will be outdated.

Books and Articles

The next resources to check are some of the standard bibliographical tools for articles and other works published in the field of biblical studies. These tools, which are usually quite comprehensive, may list books or articles that shorter or older bibliographies in commentaries do not contain. The most important of these resources are listed in section 9 of chapter 11. If you have access to the CD-ROM or online versions of these tools, you will be able to get a complete list (depending on the specific search you request) of a topic. If not, the most efficient way to use the printed bibliographic sources is to scan the volumes published after the latest relevant entry found in the bibliographies consulted within commentaries. For instance, if one of the commentaries includes articles from as late as 2005, searching through indices and abstracts published in 2005 and later will fill in the bibliographic gaps.

The amount of scholarly material online is growing at a phenomenal rate. Although entering a key word or phrase (e.g., "mark of the beast") into an Internet search engine may yield hundreds if not thousands of links, the value of such links varies significantly. It is much safer to search through some of the academic and other substantive biblical sites listed in Appendix D. For example, textweek.com maintains an excellent bibliography with links to online articles. In addition, online course syllabi often include bibliographies.

One online source that functions as both a search engine for books and a library is Google Book Search, found at http://books.google.com. There you can search for books by (for example) topic, author, or key word. Then, if you wish, you may either preview part of the book or read it in its entirety, depending on how much of the book the publisher has released for online use. As with any search engine, discrimination is needed, but the site is an excellent resource.

Browsing the table of contents of some recent journals (such as those listed in chapter 11, section 6) in the library is also worth doing, especially since printed and electronic indices are never completely up to date. Finding one or two current articles on a topic or passage will usually lead to additional books and articles on the subject of the exegetical paper. (While the success of this effort is largely a matter of serendipity and should therefore not consume a lot of time and energy, it frequently pays off.) References to an older book or article in several recent sources normally indicate the enduring importance of that older work.

One kind of source that too many exegetes avoid is the work of the great exegetes and preachers of the past—Chrysostom, Augustine, Luther, Wesley, and others. Their literary and theological insights are neglected only to our own detriment. These can be very illuminating sources.

Anyone who has ever consulted more than one commentary on a biblical text knows that scholars often disagree on the meaning of a passage. The nonspecialist exegete cannot and should not, therefore, take every sentence from a commentary as "gospel." Rather, each resource must be read carefully and critically, in dialogue with one's own work and with whichever other resources are at hand. One's own work may be just as valid as that of a commentator. A careful interpretation of the text, challenged, informed, and refined by the work of scholars, is the goal of this step in the exegetical process.

Review & Study

Chapter Summary

- People who do good exegesis will consult the tools and resources compiled by experts.
- Pursuing scholarly contributions is made possible through notes and bibliographies in various resources and through several kinds of bibliographical tools.

Practical Hints

1. Professors and advanced students may be able to give guidance about general or particular resources. Students may wish to begin their research with a brief conversation, for example, with their professor. For the most part, however, exegetes should rely on standard bibliographical resources, books, and indices, such as those listed in chapter 11, section 9, to point them in the right direction. When this method produces questions, it is time again to consult with the experts if possible.

2. The wide divergence of opinion in biblical interpretation can be unsettling. The best thing to do is to attempt to organize diversity into various major options and then to weigh for yourself the merits of each option as presented by the proponents of that view. Some articles and commentaries helpfully set out the major interpretations of a particular issue (such as the meaning of a word, the purpose or date of a document, etc.) as well as the strengths and weaknesses of each point of view; these are very valuable pages to find on a controversial issue.

3. As for the amount of information, this too can be overwhelming. Feeling besieged by data is a normal response. The key is to realize that you may be able to gather helpful facts or interpretations from every responsible resource and perspective that you read, even if you disagree with the exegete's overall interpretation. Whatever you read, look for the main pieces of information or perspectives, record them, and begin to evaluate them. Are the arguments valid or questionable? strong or weak? Are the facts and perspectives that are offered *central* to the understanding of the text? *valuable? dubious? extraneous?* Use these questions to decide what matters for the interpretation of the text and to decide what to exclude and include in the writing of your paper.

For Further Insight and Practice

1. Consult at least two scholarly commentaries on Psalm 22. Write up the results of your research and indicate any differences between what you learned and what you thought about the passage based on your previous reading of this psalm.

2. Read at least two scholarly commentaries on Matthew 16:18. List the various major interpretations of this text, your view of the strengths and weaknesses of each, and the reasons for the interpretation that you find most compelling.

3. Recall your earlier analysis of the outline and main point of Romans 8:28–39. Compare this to the comments of at least two scholarly commentaries.

4. Construct a bibliography of articles and essays on Isaiah 6 or John 4:1–42 written in the last ten to fifteen years. What trends in the interpretation of the text do you notice?

5. Review chapter 11, section 9, pp. 231–32, "Bibliographical Resources," and chapter 11 as a whole to familiarize or refamiliarize yourself with the various resources at your disposal.

Part Three

Hints and Resources

CHAPTER TEN

Exegesis and the Exegete
Errors to Avoid, Discoveries to Make

> However a particular epoch or a particular
> community may define a proper mode of attention
> or a licit area of interest, there will always be
> something else and something different to say.
> —*Frank Kermode,* Forms of Attention

You have now worked through the seven elements that make up the process of exegesis—carefully reading and analyzing a biblical text—that is advocated in this book. You are now ready to choose a passage to study and analyze in detail. First, however, some final words of both caution and encouragement.

Two common general errors in using this method of exegesis can easily be avoided if they are known in advance. First, some students become so completely attached to the procedure that they lose any sense of original thinking or creativity. The purpose of the method is not to stifle creativity but to provide a means of *disciplined investigation and imagination.* Students and teachers must always engage in asking new questions of the texts and of themselves. Fear of this creative process is what sometimes drives students simply to collect a series of opinions from scholars, string them together, and call that an exegesis paper. Even when properly documented, a series of quotations does not constitute exegesis; exegesis of a text is *your* reading of the text, albeit a reading informed by scholarship. It is not a hodgepodge—or even an organized collection—of facts, opinions, and possible interpretations.

Second, when writing exegesis papers, some students are prone to be repetitious. The introduction, outline, analysis, synthesis, and even their own reflections sound much the same. This does not need to happen, however, since each part of the exegesis paper has its own particular purpose and focus. There is a difference, for instance, between the discussion of literary context and the discussion of form, structure, and movement, and the two discussions should not be redundant. Moreover, each section of the paper should carry the interpretation of the passage a step further; each part should move the reader's understanding to a new level, not just repeat earlier observations and conclusions.

In addition to these general mistakes to avoid, there are several common mistakes students make at each stage of the exegetical process when writing papers. The following suggestions, each of which echoes one of the practical hints that appears in the appropriate chapter, are offered based on my experience with many, many hundreds of exegetical papers.

The Task

Do not attempt to execute methods that are beyond your ability. Do not attempt, say, to do tradition criticism without the necessary skills, or to discuss the intricacies of Hebrew grammar and vocabulary on the basis of an interlinear Bible. Rather, play to your strengths. Develop and use the skills any careful reader needs to have: observing, questioning, making connections, recognizing patterns, and so on. These will take you a long way.

The Text

Do not choose a passage if you are unwilling to learn about it and from it, even to have your basic presuppositions about its meaning challenged. Avoid, for instance, a passage that is *so* emotionally difficult for you, for whatever reason, that your paper is liable to become more of an exegesis of your psychological state or personal history than of the text itself. Rather, choose a text that is of interest to you and that you will attempt to engage honestly, although not one that is so problematic for you that your work will be an exercise in futility. (This advice may sound unnecessary or even unscholarly. While I certainly do not advocate fear of discovery and challenge, I recognize, from many years of experience, that there are occasions when choosing to do an exegesis paper—with the pressure of academic requirements and evaluation—on a difficult passage is not the best way to reckon with that passage. My concerns are not primarily academic, nor theological or doctrinal, but personal and even pastoral.)

Element 1—Survey (Introduction)

Do not yield to the temptation to provide an extended synopsis of every part of your paper in the introduction; otherwise it will be too long, and the other sections will become repetitious. Rather, use the introduction to hook the reader and provide a succinct overview of the paper, with primary attention to the flow (parts) of the paper and to your thesis (a preview of your synthesis). Remember once again: an exegesis paper without a thesis is not really an exegesis, a reading of the text.

Element 2—Contextual Analysis

Historical Context

Do not think of your paper as a mini-encyclopedia that reports to the reader every imaginable fact about that time period or the community that stands behind, or is addressed in, your text. Rather, provide as much of a general overview as needed, but focus on the particular aspects of the historical, social, and cultural contexts that are directly relevant to your specific text. Details about extratextual items referenced in specific verses are usually best discussed in the detailed analysis.

Literary Context

Do not discuss your passage per se in this section at all. Rather, this is the place to analyze the place of your passage in the larger whole. This may include a discussion of the outline and flow of the book in order to situate your text within the larger work, but do not construct an outline of your particular passage here. Discussion of the structure and movement of the passage itself belongs in the section on formal analysis.

Element 3—Formal Analysis (Form, Structure, and Movement)

Do not turn this section into a discussion of the biblical book in which your text is found. The focus of this section of the paper is on the form, structure, and movement of *your particular passage*, not of the biblical book. Some discussion of the genre of the book may be appropriate, but even here the focus is on how the nature of that genre affects the interpretation of your passage. Do not provide an extended discussion of the characteristics of psalms or gospels or letters in general. Also, do not provide an outline of the book, but rather an outline of the passage itself. If a brief summary and/or outline of the entire book is included in the paper, it should appear in the previous section on literary context, not this section.

Element 4—Detailed Analysis

Do not allow the first sections of your paper to monopolize your space, leaving you insufficient room for truly detailed analysis. Rather, plan your paper carefully so that you devote at least 50 percent of the paper to detailed analysis.

Element 5—Synthesis

Do not try to restate everything you have said in your paper. Rather, restate your thesis, now that you have demonstrated it, creatively pulling together the most important results of all that you have unveiled and argued in the course of the paper. This will indicate to the reader what you take to be the essential significance of the text.

Element 6—Reflection: Theological Interpretation

Do not use this occasion to prepare a sermon on the text, unless specifically asked to do so. Rather, this space provides you the opportunity to be suggestive, even open-ended, in your remarks. The best reflections are often very subtle; they are seldom hammerlike.

Element 7—Expansion and Refinement of the Exegesis

Do *not* make this *a separate part* of the paper as a whole or of each section of the paper. Rather, although this is a separate step in the process, done after your own initial exegesis, the results of your research must be integrated into the paper as a whole. The result is a paper in which your own thesis and interpretation drive the essay, but in which you interact with and gain support from others, who are your conversation partners.

A superior exegesis sheds unique light on a biblical text because the exegesis is the result of one's own personal engagement with the text. Such an exegesis is really an expression of the unique intersection of contexts—those of the author, the original readers, and the interpreter. If you apply yourself to the study of the Bible, always keeping an eye on its various contexts—as well as your own—you may well be surprised at what you discover.

CHAPTER ELEVEN

Resources for Exegesis

> But above all, I beg and entreat your
> clemency earnestly to intercede with the lord
> commissary, that he would deign to allow
> me the use of my Hebrew Bible, Hebrew
> Grammar, and Hebrew Lexicon, and that
> I may employ my time with that study.
> —*William Tyndale, from his prison cell*

> Dictionaries are like watches; the worst
> is better than none, and the best cannot
> be expected to go quite true.
> —*Samuel Johnson*

The following pages contain an annotated bibliography of scholarly resources to help in the process of exegesis. These resources are some of the most important and commonly used tools available especially for the seventh element, expansion and refinement of the exegesis, which is applied to all the other elements. Unlike William Tyndale, however, many contemporary exegetes do not read, or do not remember, Hebrew and Greek. Thus most of the resources listed below do not require a knowledge of the original languages, though in some cases such knowledge helps, and in a few instances it is absolutely necessary (e.g., to use the Greek NT).

This part of the book is divided into nine sections, corresponding to the first nine chapters. The resources for chapter 9 are primarily bibliographical tools and other books that point to additional resources. Some resources defy categorization, and many are useful for a variety of elements of the exegetical process. Commentaries, for example, contain not only detailed exegesis but also information about context, about form and structure, and sometimes about the contemporary significance of a text. I have tried to connect these kinds of multipurpose resources with the element of exegesis for which they are *most* useful.

For a brief list of Internet sources, see Appendix D.

I have made no attempt to be exhaustive, only helpful. Serious exegetes will use these works to pursue other resources as needed. And all readers should use whatever resources they discover with appropriate care and caution; all are beneficial, but none is infallible.

In addition to all of the resources listed below, special attention to the following book is in order:

Alexander, Patrick H., John F. Kutsko, James D. Ernest, Shirley Decker-Lucke, and David L. Petersen, eds. *The SBL Handbook of Style.* Peabody, Mass.: Hendrickson, 1999. This unique book, though designed primarily for biblical scholars preparing works for publication, contains a wealth of useful information for students as well as the conventions for writing in the biblical field. Students will find the correct usage, spelling, and abbreviations of biblical books and other ancient and modern sources; tables for the transliteration of Hebrew, Aramaic, Greek, and other ancient languages; and both rules for and examples of notes and bibliographical entries. This book is the "Turabian" or MLA style manual for biblical studies. The book may also be accessed at http://sbl-site.org/educational/researchtools.aspx.

Section 1. Resources for Understanding the Task

A General Work on Reading

Adler, Mortimer J., and Charles Van Doren. *How to Read a Book: The Classic Guide to Intelligent Reading.* Rev. ed. New York: Simon & Schuster, 1972; Touchstone edition, 1997. A classic on the art of reading and on reading particular kinds of writing.

A General Work on the Bible and Its Interpretation

Gorman, Michael J., ed. *Scripture: An Ecumenical Introduction to the Bible and Its Interpretation.* Peabody, Mass.: Hendrickson, 2005. An overview of the Bible, its formation, and its transmission combined with a survey of the history of its interpretation as well as current critical and theological approaches.

General Works on Exegesis

This list focuses on books that deal primarily with synchronic and diachronic approaches to the text and those that cover the entire range of approaches. Works primarily on theological or other "existential" approaches to the interpretation of the text are listed under section 8 ("Resources for Reflection: Theological Interpretation").

Carson, D. A. *Exegetical Fallacies.* 2d ed. Grand Rapids: Baker Academic, 1996. A helpful guide to avoiding common errors in the study of words, grammar, history, and other aspects of exegesis, most useful to those who read Hebrew and Greek.

Coggins, R. J., and J. L. Houlden. *The SCM Dictionary of Biblical Interpretation.* 2d ed. London: SCM, 2003. A handy, concise, and insightful set of short entries and longer essays on terms, methods, and people.

Gillingham, Susan E. *One Bible, Many Voices: Different Approaches to Biblical Studies.* Grand Rapids: Eerdmans, 1999. An introductory text on the "plurality" involved in both the making and the reading of the Bible, arguing for a theological approach integrated with historical-critical and literary approaches. Illustrated with specific reference to Psalms in general and to Psalm 8 in particular.

Hayes, John H., gen. ed. *Dictionary of Biblical Interpretation.* 2 vols. Nashville: Abingdon, 1999. Contains articles on significant theories of interpretation, approaches, methods, and key practitioners, both past and present.

Hayes, John H., and Carl R. Holladay. *Biblical Exegesis: A Beginner's Handbook.* 3d ed. Louisville: Westminster John Knox, 2007. The newest version of an excellent standard treatment of exegetical methods, largely in the historical-critical tradition but with added attention to literary and other newer approaches, including ideological perspectives (liberationist, postcolonial, etc.) as well as the use of the computer for exegesis; for the beginning and intermediate student. A good next-read.

Kaiser, Otto, and Werner G. Kümmel. *Exegetical Method: A Student's Handbook.* Translated by E. V. N. Goetschius and M. J. O'Connell. Rev. ed. New York: Seabury, 1981. The English translation of a standard German introduction to historical-critical exegesis written for beginning students, with sections on the OT and the NT.

Knight, Douglas A., ed. *Methods of Biblical Interpretation.* Nash-ville: Abingdon, 2004. A small encyclopedia-like book that surveys premodern, modern, and postmodern methods with articles taken from John H. Hayes, gen. ed., *Dictionary of Bibli-cal Interpretation* (see above).

Krentz, Edgar. *The Historical-Critical Method.* Guides to Biblical Scholarship. Philadelphia: Fortress, 1975. Repr., Eugene, Ore.: Wipf & Stock, 2002. A short, classic treatment of the diachronic approach with respect to its origins and uses.

Longman, Tremper, III. *Literary Approaches to Biblical Interpre-tation.* Grand Rapids: Zondervan, 1987. A very good introduc-tion to the theory and application of literary approaches, with a historical survey, evaluations of methods, and sample analy-ses of both prose and poetry in the Bible (especially the ot).

McKenzie, Steven L., and Stephen R. Haynes, eds. *To Each Its Own Meaning: An Introduction to Biblical Criticisms and Their Applications.* Rev. and enl. ed. Louisville: Westminster John Knox, 1999. A superb, very readable collection of essays on vari-ous diachronic, synchronic, literary, and ideological methods under the headings "Traditional Methods of Biblical Criticism," "Expanding the Tradition," and "Overturning the Tradition." Each chapter discusses and illustrates the method and provides a bibliography. An excellent next-read after this book.

Montague, George T. *Understanding the Bible: A Basic Introduc-tion to Biblical Interpretation.* Rev. and enl. ed. New York: Paulist, 2007. A helpful, engaging history of biblical interpre-tation and its various approaches from the ancient church to the end of the twentieth century; from a Catholic perspective but of ecumenical interest.

Robbins, Vernon K. *Exploring the Texture of Texts: A Guide to Socio-Rhetorical Interpretation.* Valley Forge, Pa.: Trinity, 1996. An excellent, detailed introduction to socio-rhetorical criticism as a broad, integrated approach to interpretation that includes analysis of a text's five dimensions or "textures": inner texture, intertexture, social and cultural texture, ideological texture, and sacred (theological) texture. Although the focus of the book is the Gospels, and the examples are drawn largely from them, the principles apply to the exegesis of any text.

Rogerson, John W., and Judith M. Lieu, eds. *Oxford Handbook of Biblical Studies.* New York: Oxford University Press, 2006. A comprehensive, authoritative overview of the discipline of biblical studies, including cognate fields, the biblical text, historical contexts, the nature and growth of biblical materials, scholarly methods of study, interpretation, etc.

Ryken, Leland. ***Words of Delight: A Literary Introduction to the Bible.*** 2d ed. Grand Rapids: Baker, 1992. A superb introduction to traditional literary criticism as applied to the Bible, covering the elements of biblical narrative, poetry, and other forms in both Testaments. Full of short readings of specific texts.

Schertz, Mary H., and Perry B. Yoder. ***Seeing the Text: Exegesis for Students of Greek and Hebrew.*** Nashville: Abingdon, 2001. A useful text for intermediate students of the biblical languages.

Soulen, Richard N. ***Handbook of Biblical Criticism.*** 3d ed. Louisville: Westminster John Knox, 2001. A helpful dictionary-like handbook of terms.

Tate, W. Randolph. ***Biblical Interpretation: An Integrated Approach.*** 3d ed. Peabody, Mass.: Hendrickson, 2008. For intermediate and perhaps some beginning students, an approach that brings together methods of interpreting the "world behind the text," "the world within the text," and "the world in front of the text." Contains helpful vocabularies, summaries, and bibliographies.

———. ***Interpreting the Bible: A Handbook of Terms and Methods.*** Peabody, Mass.: Hendrickson, 2006. An "extended glossary" of approximately fifty methods of biblical interpretation and the technical terminology associated with each.

Tiffany, Frederick C., and Sharon H. Ringe. ***Biblical Interpretation: A Roadmap.*** Nashville: Abingdon, 1996. A basic guide outlining elements of exegesis similar to those proposed in this book, with special emphasis on the effects of social location and the "circular" nature of the process. Contains exegetical examples and a basic bibliography of tools.

Watson, Francis, ed. ***The Open Text: New Directions for Biblical Studies.*** London: SCM, 1993. A collection of essays corporately and individually offering the thesis that the historical-critical method is insufficient and that a plurality of reading strategies, especially those focused on the reader, is needed.

Yarchin, William. ***History of Biblical Interpretation: A Reader.*** Peabody, Mass.: Hendrickson, 2004. A substantive introduction, through primary sources, to the major approaches to biblical interpretation since 150 B.C.E. and to key figures representing each approach.

Old Testament Exegesis

Barton, John. *Reading the Old Testament: Method in Biblical Study.* Rev. and enl. ed. Louisville: Westminster John Knox, 1996. An introduction to and critical analysis of the major criticisms, arguing for a plurality of approaches and for categorizing biblical interpretation as a field in the humanities, not the sciences. For Barton, methods are not rules but descriptive "codifications" of what astute readers have asked and observed about texts. A good next-read for students of the Hebrew Bible/OT.

Brettler, Marc Zvi. *How to Read the Bible.* Philadelphia: Jewish Publication Society, 2005. A Jewish scholar's introduction to reading the Jewish Bible for its unique wisdom by taking a historical-critical approach.

House, Paul R., ed. *Beyond Form Criticism: Essays in Old Testament Literary Criticism.* Sources for Biblical and Theological Study 2. Winona Lake, Ind.: Eisenbrauns, 1992. A collection of important previously published essays, introducing and applying various forms of literary and rhetorical criticism of the OT. For intermediate and advanced students.

Moor, Johannes de, ed. *Synchronic or Diachronic: A Debate on Method in Old Testament Exegesis.* Leiden: Brill, 1995. A collection of essays by Dutch and British scholars on diachronic and synchronic approaches and their potential compatibility. For more advanced students.

Steck, Odil Hannes. *Old Testament Exegesis: A Guide to the Methodology.* Translated by James D. Nogalski. 2d ed. SBL Resources for Biblical Study 39. Atlanta: Scholars, 1998. The English edition of a standard German text (and approach), designed for advanced students. After providing an overview of historical-critical work, it treats the general task, method, results, and bibliography for text criticism, literary criticism, transmission-historical criticism, redaction criticism, form criticism, tradition-historical criticism, and historical-setting criticism. The book is full of brief illustrations and contains a helpful bibliography.

Stuart, Douglas. *Old Testament Exegesis: A Handbook for Students and Pastors.* 3d ed. Louisville: Westminster John Knox, 2001. A basic step-by-step guide that does not require knowledge of Hebrew.

Wilson, Robert R. *Sociological Approaches to the Old Testament.* Guides to Biblical Scholarship. Philadelphia: Fortress, 1984. An early and basic introduction, with application of an "anthropological perspective" to several areas of OT study.

New Testament Exegesis

Black, David A., and David S. Dockery. *Interpreting the New Testament: Essays on Methods and Issues.* Nashville: Broadman & Holman, 2001. A collection of essays for beginning students, from leading evangelical scholars, on interpretive issues and exegetical methods.

Conzelmann, Hans, and Andreas Lindemann. *Interpreting the New Testament: An Introduction to the Principles and Methods of N. T. Exegesis.* Translated by Siegfried S. Schatzmann. Peabody, Mass.: Hendrickson, 1988. A comprehensive handbook, with exercises, to the historical-critical approach to the NT. Also a brief critical introduction to the NT environment and writings. For the advanced student.

Cosby, Michael R. *Portraits of Jesus: An Inductive Approach to the Gospels.* Louisville: Westminster John Knox, 1999. A learning-by-doing approach that has beginning students do close reading of gospel texts to discover literary and theological patterns, themes, and problems.

Egger, Wilhelm. *How to Read the New Testament: An Introduction to Linguistic and Historical-Critical Methodology.* Edited by Hendrikus Boers. Translated by Peter Heinegg. Peabody, Mass.: Hendrickson, 1996. A helpful introduction primarily to the historical-critical approach to the NT.

Elliott, John H. *What Is Social-Scientific Criticism?* Guides to Biblical Scholarship. Minneapolis: Fortress, 1993. A very helpful introduction to the application of the social sciences to NT study, with bibliography.

Erickson, Richard J. *A Beginner's Guide to New Testament Exegesis: Taking the Fear out of Critical Method.* Downers Grove, Ill.: InterVarsity, 2005. A basic but comprehensive and readable guide.

Fee, Gordon D. *New Testament Exegesis: A Handbook for Students and Pastors.* 3d ed. Louisville: Westminster John Knox, 2002. A standard and very helpful detailed guide to exegesis. This book is most useful for those working with the Greek text.

Green, Joel B., ed. *Hearing the New Testament: Strategies for Interpretation.* Grand Rapids: Eerdmans, 1995. Repr., Eugene, Ore.: Wipf & Stock, 2004. A first-rate collection of essays on critical methods and issues of interpretation, for intermediate-level students. An excellent next-read for students of the NT.

Kennedy, George A. *New Testament Interpretation through Rhetorical Criticism.* Chapel Hill, N.C.: University of North Carolina Press, 1984. A standard guide to the use of classical rhetoric to interpret the NT, with applications to specific documents and shorter texts.

Mack, Burton L. *Rhetoric and the New Testament.* Guides to Biblical Scholarship. Minneapolis: Fortress, 1990. A guide to rhetorical criticism that draws on both classical approaches and modern theories, with illustrations of their use on specific texts.

Porter, Stanley E., ed. *Handbook to Exegesis of the New Testament.* Leiden: Brill, 1997. Essays on nearly all the exegetical approaches and methods and on their application to the various parts of the NT.

Schneiders, Sandra M. *The Revelatory Text: Interpreting the New Testament as Sacred Scripture.* 2d ed. Collegeville, Minn.: Liturgical, 1999. A sophisticated defense of the NT as fully human word and as locus of encounter with God, with theoretical consideration of an integrated model of interpretation that looks at the worlds behind, of, and before the text.

Stenger, Werner. *Introduction to New Testament Exegesis.* Edited by John W. Simpson Jr. Translated by Douglas W. Stott. Grand Rapids: Eerdmans, 1993. This translation and adaptation of a standard, hands-on text by a respected Roman Catholic NT scholar devotes a short chapter to each of several broad aspects of the historical-critical method (including textual criticism; structural analysis as a synchronic approach to the text; and the diachronic methods of tradition, source, redaction, and genre criticism). Then follow ten chapters illustrating these methods in practice (eight on gospel texts, one on two hymn texts, and one on the Letter to Philemon). A helpful annotated bibliography is also included. A good next-read for students of the NT.

Weren, Wim (Wilhelmus). *Windows on Jesus: Methods in Gospel Exegesis.* Translated by John Bowden. Harrisburg, Pa.: Trinity, 1999. An excellent, comprehensive, and very accessible handbook to the varieties of contemporary approaches to the gospels, perfect for beginning and intermediate students of the gospels. Knowledge of Greek is not presumed.

Section 2. Resources for Understanding the Text

This section lists resources on the subjects of translations and textual criticism. It also lists editions of the Bible in Hebrew and Greek, multitranslation editions of the Bible, editions of the Bible in parallel format, and electronic versions of the Bible, many of which also contain resources for biblical study. For the issue of defining the limits of a text, consult the books on exegetical method listed in section 1.

Translations

For discussion and analysis of various translations, see the following books:

Dewey, David. *A User's Guide to Bible Translations: Making the Most of Different Versions.* Downer's Grove, Ill.: InterVarsity, 2004. A survey of issues in translation and of English translation from the earliest versions to the many translations since the RSV in the mid-twentieth century.

Fee, Gordon D., and Mark L. Strauss. *How to Choose a Translation for All Its Worth: A Guide to Understanding and Using Bible Versions.* Grand Rapids: Zondervan, 2007. A very helpful analysis, from an evangelical perspective, of various Bible translations by considering various translation issues (idioms, culture, gender, etc.).

Kubo, Sakae, and Walter F. Specht. *So Many Versions? Twentieth-Century English Versions of the Bible.* 2d ed. Grand Rapids: Zondervan, 1983. An overview and evaluation of major English-language translations, with a helpful appendix listing many others.

Lewis, Jack P. *The English Bible, from KJV to NIV: A History and Evaluation.* 2d ed. Grand Rapids: Baker, 1991. A comprehensive, detailed volume devoted to the (generally generous) evaluation of about twenty English translations.

Metzger, Bruce M. *The Bible in Translation: Ancient and English Versions.* Grand Rapids: Baker Academic, 2001. A helpful history and evaluation of Bible translations by one of the greatest biblical scholars of the last hundred years, who chaired the NRSV translation committee.

Sheeley, Steven M., and Robert N. Nash Jr. *The Bible in English Translation: An Essential Guide.* Abingdon: Nashville, 1997. A basic but helpful guide to Bible translation and translations, plus the origins of the Bible and the development of the canon.

Textual Criticism

For discussion of the original text of the Bible, the practice of textual criticism, and the use of modern critical editions of the Hebrew and Greek texts, see:

Aland, Kurt, and Barbara Aland. *The Text of the New Testament.* 2d rev. and enl. ed. Grand Rapids: Eerdmans, 1995. A helpful introduction to textual criticism and to the use of the critical apparatus of textual variants in the Nestle-Aland text of the NT.

Greenlee, J. Harold. *An Introduction to New Testament Textual Criticism.* Rev. ed. Peabody, Mass.: Hendrickson, 1995. A basic text.

McCarter, P. Kyle, Jr. *Textual Criticism: Recovering the Text of the Hebrew Bible.* Philadelphia: Fortress, 1986. A slim but authoritative volume.

Metzger, Bruce M., ed. *A Textual Commentary on the Greek New Testament.* 2d ed. New York: United Bible Societies, 1994. Presents the reasons for the decisions regarding the major text-critical issues of the standard critical text of the NT.

Metzger, Bruce M., and Bart D. Ehrman. *The Text of the New Testament: Its Transmission, Corruption, and Restoration.* 4th ed. New York: Oxford University Press, 2005. A superb introduction to the art and science of textual criticism and to some of the principal NT manuscripts and early versions.

Tov, Emmanuel. *Textual Criticism of the Text of the Hebrew Bible.* 2d rev. ed. Minneapolis: Fortress, 2001. A standard work, now updated.

Wegner, Paul D. *A Student's Guide to Textual Criticism of the Bible: Its History, Methods and Results.* Downers Grove, Ill.: InterVarsity, 2006. An excellent treatment of history and principles, with illustrations of specific texts, guides to using the critical editions, a glossary, and more.

Weingreen, J. *Introduction to the Critical Study of the Text of the Hebrew Bible.* Oxford: Oxford University Press, 1982. A basic introduction to textual criticism for students of the Hebrew Bible.

Würthwein, Ernst. *The Text of the Old Testament: An Introduction to the Biblia Hebraica.* 2d ed. Translated by Erroll F. Rhodes. Grand Rapids: Eerdmans, 1995. A guide to texts, versions, and the use of the critical edition of the Hebrew Bible.

The Bible in Hebrew and Greek

Aland, B., K. Aland, J. Karavidopulos, C. M. Martini, and B. M. Metzger, eds. *The Greek New Testament.* 4th rev. ed. Stuttgart: Deutsche Bibelgesellschaft, 1993. The standard text of the Greek NT, with a critical apparatus of significant textual variants that affect translation, distributed by the United Bible Societies. Abbreviated UBS4.

Biblia Hebraica Quinta (BHQ). Stuttgart: German Bible Society, forthcoming, ca. 2010. A new critical edition of the Hebrew Bible based on the Leningrad Codex, the oldest complete manuscript of the Hebrew Bible, with footnotes referring to, e.g., differences in the biblical texts of the Dead Sea Scrolls. As of 2008 two fascicles have been issued.

Jewish Publication Society. *JPS Hebrew-English Tanakh.* Philadelphia: Jewish Publication Society, 1999. Hebrew and English translation in parallel columns (the preeminent Jewish translation into English).

Kittel, Rudolf, Karl Elliger, Wilhelm Rudolph, Hans P. Rüger, and Gérard E. Weil, eds. *Biblia Hebraica Stuttgartensia.* 5th rev. ed. Stuttgart: Deutsche Bibelgesellschaft, 1968–1977; 1984; 1997. The standard text of the Hebrew Bible. Abbreviated BHS.

Nestle, Eberhard, Erwin Nestle, Barbara Aland, and Kurt Aland, eds. *Novum Testamentum Graece.* 27th ed. Stuttgart: Deutsche Bibelgesellschaft, 1993. The standard text of the Greek NT with the most thorough critical apparatus of textual variants. The text itself is the same as the United Bible Societies' 3d and 4th editions. Available also in an edition with Greek and English on facing pages.

Bible Parallels

Aland, Kurt, ed. *Synopsis of the Four Gospels: Greek-English Edition of the Synopsis Quattuor Evangeliorum.* 10th ed. Stuttgart: United Bible Societies, 1993. This Greek-English synopsis of the Gospels in parallel columns is available also in English-only and in Greek-only *(Synopsis Quattuor Evangeliorum)* editions.

Francis, Fred O., and J. Paul Sampley. *Pauline Parallels.* 2d ed. Philadelphia: Fortress, 1984. A large spiral-bound book that sets out similar passages from the Pauline letters in parallel columns.

Throckmorton, Burton H., Jr., ed. *Gospel Parallels: A Comparison of the Synoptic Gospels.* 5th ed. Nashville: Nelson, 1992. The NRSV text of Matthew, Mark, and Luke in parallel columns.

Additional Texts of the Bible

The Catholic Comparative New Testament. New York: Oxford University Press, 2005. Contains the Douay-Rheims Bible, NAB, RSV, NRSV, JB, NJB, GNB (Good News Bible), and Christian Community Bible.

The Complete Parallel Bible: Containing the Old and New Testaments with the Apocryphal/Deuterocanonical Books. New York: Oxford University Press, 1993. Sets out the NRSV, REB, NAB, and NJB in parallel columns.

Kohlenberger, John R., III, ed. *The Contemporary Parallel New Testament.* New York: Oxford University Press, 1998. Sets out the NT text of eight translations in parallel columns: CEV, KJV, *The Message,* NASB, NCV (New Contemporary Version), NIV, NKJV, and NLT.

Today's Parallel Bible. Grand Rapids: Zondervan, 2000. Contains the KJV, updated NASB, NIV, and NLT.

Bibles on CD-ROM

What follows is only a sample of Bibles available on CD-ROM and a brief introduction to some of those that make various tools available. More and better products will no doubt be produced in the coming years, and the products already on the market are constantly revised and expanded. Some products come as complete systems, while others come in a modular design whereby certain components or bundles of components may be purchased according to the needs of the user. Many of the products offer demonstration videos at their websites, but it is wise to consult the manufacturer, and some actual end users of various products, before making a purchase.

I have divided these Bible packages into three groups: those intended for sophisticated analysis of the texts in their original languages (which also make many translations available), mid-range products with some original-language capacity, and those intended for more general usage.

Sophisticated Original-Language Products

While almost every electronic Bible is capable of rapidly performing simple word searches, and many employ multiple versions augmented by secondary resources of varying quantity and quality, only a handful are capable of applying these resources to the original Greek and Hebrew texts. As the first choice for scholars who are able to read ancient languages (and students who someday hope to acquire such skills), these sophisticated products allow users to search and analyze both lexical (word) and syntactical (words-in-relationship) forms. Although a relatively recent innovation in biblical studies (Gramcord, the granddaddy of the products reviewed here, dates from the midseventies), computerized analysis is increasingly being employed for exegesis, performing complex searches and analyses in mere seconds that used to require many hours of tedious research. These four products are all capable of sophisticated original-language work.

Accordance. OakTree Software, Inc. (Mac; can also be run on a Windows PC using a free emulator.) Presently the only available premier package written natively for Macintosh; packages vary widely. One may pay for the program and receive a small free starter collection of English-language resources, or purchase various collections or à-la-carte packages. All but the starter package include ten to fifteen English translations (e.g., KJV, NASB, NAS95, NET), and there is a Jewish and a Catholic collection (the latter including the NAB, NJB, and NRSV) as well as a basic Spanish package. Scholar's packages also include language tools, some commentaries, and other aids. Significant scholarly exegetical tools, other study aids, and additional translations may be purchased for use with any package. Approx. $39–$2,499. http://www.accordancebible.com

BibleWorks. BibleWorks, LLC. (Windows 98 through Vista; Mac and Linux use via emulator.) Billing itself as "the premier original languages Bible software program for Biblical exegesis and research," this is an incredibly comprehensive package, with various Greek and Hebrew texts, electronic analytical tools, lexicons, and many other first-rate resources. It comes with more than one hundred translations in some 35 languages, including ASV, KJV, NAB, NAS95, NIV, NJB, NKJV, NET, NLT, and NRSV. It is sold as a complete package with all titles unlocked and can be installed directly on a hard drive. Additional modules are available at additional cost. Free postpublication content updates are available. BibleWorks has free customer support and a user forum. Enthusiastic users have created a blog dedicated to BibleWorks. Approx. $350. http://www.bibleworks.com

Gramcord for Windows. The Gramcord Institute. (Windows 3.1 or later; Lite version for Palm and Pocket PC.) Designed especially for scholars and advanced students, these resources, which may be purchased in cost-effective, prepackaged bundles, include editions of the Greek and Hebrew texts, language tools, many translations (NASB, NAS95, NIV, NKJV, NRSV, RSV, etc.), and reference works. Resources are available in Windows and Mac formats. Gramcord's modular format enables the initial purchase of either the Greek or the Hebrew modules with the opportunity to add additional texts and resources at a later time. Approx. $99–$235. http://www.gramcord.org

Logos. Logos Research Systems, Inc. (Windows 98 through Vista; Mac version in development.) The most extensive of all Bible-related and theological CD-ROM collections, the Logos system envisions a full electronic library and has already developed a remarkable collection. Logos makes available numerous translations and resources on several unlockable CD-ROMs, packaged in various bundles, including three "Scholar's" packages. Additional titles can then be purchased and unlocked. More than thirty translations (CEV, ESV, GNB, KJV, LB, *The Message*, NAB, NASB, NAS95, NET, NIV, NJB, NKJV, NLT, NRSV, RSV, etc.) and hundreds of resources—including some of the very best in print, such as *The Anchor Bible Dictionary*—are available in all price ranges. Thousands of books available in Logos's Libronix format can be purchased and added to one's Logos library. Robust additional resources are available online, including extensive online technical support, an official blog, newsgroups for users, tutorial videos and articles, and the option to bid on desired resources. Approx. $150–$1,380. http://www.logos.com

Midrange Products with Some Original-Language Capacity

PC Study Bible (Reference Bible). Biblesoft, Inc. (Windows 98 through Vista.) These five different packages include such translations as the ASV, KJV, LB, NASB, NIV, NKJV, and RSV, each with concordance, plus reference works. Some packages include language helps, which can also be purchased separately. The "Professional" and "Advanced" versions include the standard Hebrew and Greek versions and language aids. Approx. $49.95–$599.95. http://www.biblesoft.com

QuickVerse Deluxe, Deluxe Bible Reference Collection, and *New Bible Reference Collection.* FindEx.com, Inc. (Windows 98 SE through XP; also offers software for Mac, Palm, and Pocket PC.) These packages contain numerous translations (usually including ASV, KJV, NIV, NKJV, NLT, NASB, and NRSV) plus (unfortunately) a lot of generally out-of-date or low-quality reference tools. Most packages do, however, contain Strong's concordance. Approx. $50–$800. http://www.quickverse.com

Products for More General Usage

The Basic Bible Library 6.0 for Windows. Zondervan. This basic package includes the ESV, KJV, *The Message,* NIV, TNIV, and some very basic reference tools. Approx. $29.99. http://www.zondervan.com

The Zondervan Essential Bible Study Suite for Macintosh. Oak-Tree Software, Inc./Zondervan. This basic package includes the KJV, NIV, TNIV, and some resources. Approx. $69.99. http://www.zondervan.com

Section 3. Resources for Surveying the Text

Several kinds of resources are especially helpful for expanding and refining one's initial survey of the text. These are handy reference works that provide a lot of good basic information and study aids in an economy of space and for use within an economy of time. They are particularly helpful for getting the "lay of the land" of a particular book and, later in the exegetical process, for identifying key aspects of the text. Introductions to the Old and New Testaments and one-volume Bible commentaries are included in this section. (Also useful for a brief overview are Bible dictionaries, which are listed in the next section, "Resources for Contextual Analysis.")

Not listed here are any "Bible handbooks." Although some of these works have merit, they generally attempt to be all things to all people, combining historical background information on "biblical times" with introductions to and summaries of biblical books, brief commentary on the text, and graphics. Unfortunately, most Bible handbooks either are not designed for serious students or are of poor quality (or both).

Introductions to the Old and New Testaments

Many introductions to one or the other of the two Testaments are in print. Below are several that are particularly popular and helpful. Each has useful bibliographies, too.

Old Testament/Hebrew Bible

Anderson, Bernhard W., and Katheryn Pfisterer Darr. *Understanding the Old Testament.* 5th ed., abridged and updated. Upper Saddle River, N.J.: Pearson Prentice Hall, 2007. Still at more than six hundred pages, a new version of a balanced, classic introduction.

Bandstra, Barry. *Reading the Old Testament: An Introduction to the Hebrew Bible.* 3d ed. Belmont, Calif.: Wadsworth, 2004. An introductory-level interpretation of the OT writings as historical, literary, and religious documents. Contains an excellent bibliography. A fourth edition is scheduled for 2009.

Birch, Bruce C., Walter Brueggemann, Terence E. Fretheim, and David L. Petersen. *A Theological Introduction to the Old Testament.* 2d ed. Nashville: Abingdon, 2005. A standard historical, canonical, and theological approach to the Christian OT, with new material on socio-theological location in interpretation.

Brettler, Marc Zvi. *How to Read the Jewish Bible.* New York: Oxford University Press, 2007. A basic survey of representative texts and how critical methods illume them.

Brueggemann, Walter. *An Introduction to the Old Testament: The Canon and Christian Imagination.* Louisville: Westminster John Knox, 2003. An introduction that focuses on the "traditioning," or theological replaying, that occurs from book to book in the development of the OT.

Collins, John J. *Introduction to the Hebrew Bible.* Minneapolis: Fortress, 2004. An in-depth survey that deals with the entire OT (including the Apocrypha) and comes with a CD-ROM.

Coogan, Michael D. *The Old Testament: A Historical and Literary Introduction to the Hebrew Scriptures.* New York: Oxford University Press, 2006. A user-friendly text with many tables, figures, and maps, modeled on the similar NT volume from Oxford by Bart Ehrman (see below).

Flanders, Henry J., Robert W. Crapps, and David A. Smith. *People of the Covenant: An Introduction to the Hebrew Bible.* 4th ed. New York: Oxford University Press, 1996. A basic introduction that follows a historical framework but places emphasis on the covenant people's theological interpretations of events and experiences.

Gottwald, Norman K. *The Hebrew Bible: A Socio-literary Introduction.* Philadelphia: Fortress, 1985. An early and now classic approach emphasizing literary features and the political and social functions of the texts; a 2002 edition comes with CD-ROM.

Hill, Andrew E., and J. H. Walton. *A Survey of the Old Testament.* 2d ed. Grand Rapids: Zondervan, 2000. A basic introduction from an evangelical perspective.

Laffey, Alice L. *An Introduction to the Old Testament: A Feminist Perspective.* Philadelphia: Fortress, 1988. A brief introduction to the main divisions of the Hebrew Bible with discussion of themes and texts within each from a feminist perspective.

LaSor, William Sanford, David Allan Hubbard, and Frederic Wm. Bush. With contributions by Leslie C. Allen et al. *Old Testament Survey: The Message, Form, and Background of the Old Testament.* 2d ed. Grand Rapids: Eerdmans, 1996. An excellent basic introduction written from a critical evangelical perspective, with emphasis on literary structure and theological message.

McKenzie, Steven L., and M. Patrick Graham, eds. *The Hebrew Bible Today: An Introduction to Critical Issues.* Louisville: Westminster John Knox, 1998. A survey of the books of the OT or Hebrew Bible with respect to issues such as authorship, structure, sources, and themes.

New Testament

Achtemeier, Paul J., Joel B. Green, and Marianne Meye Thompson. *Introducing the New Testament: Its Literature and Theology.*

Grand Rapids: Eerdmans, 2001. A volume designed to engage the reader with the actual text of the New Testament, rather than merely cover introductory issues.

Barr, David L. *New Testament Story: An Introduction.* 4th ed. Belmont, Calif.: Wadsworth, 2008. An introduction that takes social-scientific and rhetorical approaches seriously while looking at the three "worlds of the text" (behind, within, and in front of).

Brown, Raymond E. *An Introduction to the New Testament.* New York: Doubleday, 1997. A masterful, library-like introduction and mini-commentary, largely in the historical-critical tradition but with appreciation for narrative and other approaches.

Carson, D. A., and Douglas J. Moo. *An Introduction to the New Testament.* 2d ed. Grand Rapids: Zondervan, 2005. A work by two prominent conservative evangelical scholars.

DeSilva, David A. *An Introduction to the New Testament: Contexts, Methods & Ministry Formation.* Downers Grove, Ill.: Inter-Varsity, 2004. A massive introduction with special attention to rhetoric and to bridging the gap to contemporary ministry.

Ehrman, Bart D. *The New Testament: A Historical Introduction to the Early Christian Writings.* 4th ed. New York: Oxford University Press, 2008. A user-friendly, well-written survey that is "historically rather than confessionally oriented," with excellent tables, illustrations, and brief annotated bibliographies.

Gorman, Michael J. *Apostle of the Crucified Lord: A Theological Introduction to Paul and His Letters.* Grand Rapids: Eerdmans, 2004. A work that includes introductions to and brief commentaries on all thirteen of the Pauline letters.

Gundry, Robert H. *A Survey of the New Testament.* 4th ed. Grand Rapids: Zondervan, 2003. A basic, standard introduction from an evangelical perspective.

Johnson, Luke Timothy, with Todd Penner. *The Writings of the New Testament: An Interpretation.* Rev. ed. Minneapolis: Fortress, 1999. A standard, elegantly written introduction with emphasis on the social world and theological message of the text and on early Christian experience.

Matera, Frank J. *New Testament Theology: Exploring Diversity and Unity.* Louisville: Westminster John Knox, 2007. A helpful introduction to the theologies of each NT book or author, with an emphasis on soteriology (theology of salvation) and an attempt at synthesis.

McDonald, Lee Martin, and Stanley Porter. *Early Christianity and Its Sacred Literature.* Peabody, Mass.: Hendrickson, 2000. A comprehensive and well-illustrated introduction to early Christian literature in context, including color photos as well as tables and maps.

Pregeant, Russell. *Engaging the New Testament: An Interdisciplinary Introduction.* Minneapolis: Augsburg Fortress, 1995. A creative introduction that incorporates a wide variety of approaches to reading the NT.

The Entire Bible

Most books that cover the entire Bible do so very superficially; one major exception is the following:

Alter, Robert, and Frank Kermode, eds. *The Literary Guide to the Bible.* Cambridge, Mass.: Belknap Press of Harvard University Press, 1987. A collection of superb essays on the literary genre and features of the various biblical books.

One-Volume Bible Commentaries

A one-volume Bible commentary is a commentary on the entire Bible in one volume (as opposed to a commentary in one volume on one particular book). This kind of reference book is helpful for getting acquainted with a biblical book and passage but is generally not sufficiently in-depth or extensive to be useful for serious research. This is not to say, however, that such a book is unscholarly; indeed, the best ones are written by the best biblical scholars. These scholars cannot, however, fully develop or argue their perspective in such limited space.

The *Eerdmans Commentary on the Bible* (Grand Rapids: Eerdmans, 2003) is a massive volume by an international group of scholars that includes commentaries on the OT (including all the Apocrypha considered canonical by any Christian tradition) and the NT as well as some general articles. The work is edited by James D. G. Dunn and John W. Rogerson. Within its 1,600 pages the reader will find a variety of approaches to exegesis (including recent literary and social-scientific approaches) and thus a variety of results, some outstanding and some less so. What all scholars offer in common is a unit-by-unit (e.g., paragraph-by-paragraph) analysis of the text, often (always, according to the editors) in relatively nontechnical language, but sometimes in dense prose that is not easily accessed or understood. The introductions to each biblical book also vary significantly in length and quality (the former being no guarantor of the latter); bibliographies at the end of each contribution are generally extensive and excellent. Perhaps the greatest strength of this volume is the collection of articles on such topics as the historical development of each Testament, history and analysis of the study of each Testament, and introductions to various parts of the Bible (e.g., Pentateuch, Prophets, Gospels, Letters).

Just as comprehensive, though a bit dated now, is *The New Jerome Biblical Commentary* (Englewood Cliffs, N.J.: Prentice Hall, 1990), edited by the great Roman Catholic scholars Raymond E. Brown, Joseph A. Fitzmyer, and Roland E. Murphy. A revision of *The Jerome Biblical Commentary* (1968) edited by the same scholars, this volume is a library within a book. At nearly 1,500 pages of fine print, it includes scholarly commentary on the entire Bible, including, of course, the deuterocanonical books; introductions (sometimes brief, but sometimes quite lengthy) to and detailed outlines of each book; and, as a bonus, more than twenty-five additional in-depth articles on important topics in biblical studies. These topics include introductions to the various kinds of biblical literature, hermeneutics, biblical geography and archaeology, modern criticism (study) of the Bible, and aspects of the thought (theology) of each Testament and of some of its key writers (e.g., Paul and John). The articles include excellent, extensive bibliographies, as do each of the commentaries proper. Though Roman Catholic in authorship, it is ecumenical in tone. Its only drawback is that the prose is sometimes very technical and dense, making for challenging reading.

Another helpful one-volume commentary is *HarperCollins Bible Commentary* (rev. ed.; San Francisco: HarperSanFrancisco, 2000), edited by James L. Mays and written by members of the Society of Biblical Literature (as in the case of *The HarperCollins Study Bible*). Though less thorough than the *New Jerome*, it is more user-friendly. In addition to introductions to and commentary on each of the biblical books, including the Apocrypha, this resource has several general articles, introductory articles on the main divisions of the Bible, and several dozen short essays within various commentary articles. It also contains a system of cross-references to *Harper's Bible Dictionary*.

A standard for a half-century has been the *New Bible Commentary,* now in the 21st-Century Edition (4th ed.; Downers Grove, Ill.: InterVarsity, 1994), edited by D. A. Carson et al. Evangelical in orientation, the new edition is based on the NIV text. All articles from the last edition (1970) have been revised or replaced. The historically conservative approach of many of the writers for previous editions is still present in some articles but is offered more cautiously and less centrally; the text itself is center stage. A reliable and solid piece of work, this is a good place to begin one's introduction to the biblical texts. The format, however, is less contemporary and visually appealing than some other works.

The Oxford Bible Commentary (Oxford: Oxford University Press, 2001), edited by John Muddiman and John Barton, is a collection of elegantly written scholarly commentaries and essays. Older historical-critical methods are supplemented by more recent literary and social-scientific approaches. The commentary includes the Apocrypha, and it also contains introductory articles, maps, and excellent bibliographies. There are fewer essays than in the *New Jerome* or *Eerdmans,* with most of the volume devoted to commentary per se. But the writers are more diverse than the *New Jerome,* and the quality of commentary more consistent than *Eerdmans.*

A feminist perspective is provided by the *Women's Bible Commentary* (exp. ed., with Apocrypha; Louisville: Westminster John Knox, 1998), edited by Carol A. Newsom and Sharon H. Ringe. This is not a full one-volume commentary but one that comments only on the passages of a book that the commentator judges to be "of particular relevance to women"—especially texts that speak about women or have female characters. Some short articles and brief bibliographies for each book are included. Sometimes offering an unconventional perspective within a hermeneutic of suspicion, these brief articles can be used with other perspectives within the exegetical process.

Similar in focus but more evangelical in approach is the *IVP Women's Bible Commentary* (Downers Grove, Ill.: InterVarsity, 2002), edited by Catherine Clark Kroeger and Mary J. Evans. Treatments of individual books are supplemented by other brief articles, tables, and illustrations.

A unique resource in which very diverse scholars from around the world interpret their assigned biblical book explicitly from their own particular location is the *Global Bible Commentary*

(Nashville: Abingdon, 2004), edited by Daniel Patte. Although not a full-scale one-volume commentary, the readings offered from various economic and cultural contexts are a welcome alternative to strictly Western methods and perspectives.

Similar in focus, but more evangelical in perspective, is the *Africa Bible Commentary: A One-Volume Commentary* (Grand Rapids: Zondervan, 2006), edited by Tokunboh Adeyemo. It has section-by-section exegesis plus extra articles and maps, with all text written in and for Africa, but also for an international audience.

Although covering only the NT, another unique resource is *True to Our Native Land: An African American New Testament Commentary* (Minneapolis: Fortress, 2007), edited by Brian K. Blount and other leading biblical scholars, with commentary plus thematic essays on preaching, slavery, and other significant topics. A companion volume on the Hebrew Scriptures, *Biblia Africana,* is scheduled for publication in 2009.

Bible Dictionaries

Also helpful for the purposes of surveying a passage within its document are the entries on biblical books in Bible dictionaries, which are discussed below under the resources for contextual analysis.

Section 4. Resources for Contextual Analysis

The following resources—Bible dictionaries, studies of the "biblical world," and atlases—assist the exegete especially in analyzing the historical, social, and cultural contexts of the Bible. The articles on particular biblical books (e.g., Exodus) in Bible dictionaries can also be brief but helpful guides to the general literary and rhetorical context of a passage. For more in-depth analysis of literary context, the reader should consult the one-volume commentaries listed in the previous section and especially the full-length commentaries described in section 6.

Bible Dictionaries

A Bible dictionary is an alphabetically arranged encyclopedia of biblical names, places, events, customs, ideas, and books, and of other topics, as well as of (sometimes) technical terms related to the study of the Bible. Bible dictionaries have several uses, such as providing an overview of the historical situation and identifying key figures, events, and customs that appear in a passage. They can serve also as handy sources for surveying the book within which a passage is found.

There are both one-volume and multivolume dictionaries. Of special usefulness and quality are the following:

Achtemeier, Paul J., gen. ed. *HarperCollins Bible Dictionary.* Rev. ed. San Francisco: HarperSanFrancisco, 1996. Contains brief, lucid, up-to-date entries as well as numerous extended essays on selected topics. The entries for biblical books contain detailed outlines.

Bromiley, Geoffrey W., ed. *The International Standard Bible Encyclopedia.* 4 vols. Rev. ed. Grand Rapids: Eerdmans, 1979–1988. The revision of a 1929 conservative classic. Lavishly illustrated with more than three hundred maps, hundreds of illustrations and photos, and several sections of full-color plates. Evangelical in orientation, it contains good bibliographies on many of its topics. Abbreviated *ISBE.*

Douglas, J. D., and N. Hillyer, eds. *The Illustrated Bible Dictionary.* 3 vols. Downers Grove, Ill.: InterVarsity, 1980. Based on the second edition of the *New Bible Dictionary* (see below), this lavishly illustrated mini-encyclopedia welcomes the reader into the world of the text with hundreds of superb colorful photographs, illustrations, and maps to accompany its entries.

Freedman, David Noel, ed. *The Anchor Bible Dictionary.* 6 vols. New York: Doubleday, 1992. This encyclopedia of more than six thousand entries, some the equivalent of small books, is an authoritative guide to scholarly knowledge of and perspectives on every Bible-related topic. Its discussions of specific biblical books are particularly helpful at the survey and contextual analysis stages of exegesis. Available also on CD-ROM. Abbreviated *ABD.*

————, ed. *Eerdmans Dictionary of the Bible.* Grand Rapids: Eerdmans, 2000. This first-rate dictionary has almost five thousand contributions from more than six hundred scholars representing diverse scholarly and theological approaches. It is billed as a "rapid-response reference work."

Mills, Watson, gen. ed. *Mercer Dictionary of the Bible.* Macon, Ga.: Mercer University Press, 1990. Produced under the guidance of Baptist biblical scholars, but ecumenical in tone and substance.

Sakenfeld, Katherine Doob, ed. *New Interpreter's Dictionary of the Bible.* Nashville: Abingdon, 2006–2009. 5 vols. This replacement for the original *Interpreter's Dictionary of the Bible* (abbreviated *IDB*) is a solid reflection of and contribution to biblical scholarship with clear theological interests. Abbreviated *NIDB*.

Wood, D. R. W., et al., eds. *New Bible Dictionary.* 3d ed. Downers Grove, Ill.: InterVarsity, 1996. A very thorough and competent volume in the critical evangelical tradition. Abbreviated *NBD*.

The following series comes from a critical, ecumenical, evangelical perspective. Some of these dictionaries are available, bundled with other InterVarsity reference works, on CD-ROM.

Alexander, T. Desmond, and David W. Baker, eds. *Dictionary of the Old Testament: Pentateuch.* Downers Grove, Ill.: InterVarsity, 2003.

Arnold, Bill T., and Hugh G. M. Williamson. *Dictionary of the Old Testament: Historical Books.* Downers Grove, Ill.: InterVarsity, 2005.

Evans, Craig A., and Stanley E. Porter, eds. *Dictionary of New Testament Background.* Downers Grove, Ill.: InterVarsity, 2000.

Green, Joel B., Scot McKnight, and I. Howard Marshall, eds. *Dictionary of Jesus and the Gospels.* Downers Grove, Ill.: InterVarsity, 1992.

Hawthorne, Gerald F., Ralph P. Martin, and Daniel G. Reid, eds. *Dictionary of Paul and His Letters.* Downers Grove, Ill.: InterVarsity, 1993.

Longman, Tremper, III, and Peter Enns, eds. *Dictionary of the Old Testament: Wisdom, Poetry & Writings.* Downers Grove, Ill.: InterVarsity, 2008.

Martin, Ralph P., and Peter H. Davids, eds. *Dictionary of the Later New Testament & Its Developments.* Downers Grove, Ill.: InterVarsity, 1997.

Reid, Daniel G., ed. *The IVP Dictionary of the New Testament: A One-Volume Compendium of Contemporary Biblical Scholarship.* Downers Grove, Ill.: InterVarsity, 2004. A collection of the most important articles from the four-volume set previously published.

General Books on the "Biblical Worlds"

Chilton, Bruce, et al., eds. *The Cambridge Companion to the Bible.* 2d ed. Cambridge: Cambridge University Press, 2007. An impressive companion/introduction that stresses the sociocultural contexts of the Bible, using text, photos, tables, and maps.

Coogan, Michael D., ed. *The Oxford History of the Biblical World.* New York: Oxford University Press, 1998. Twelve scholars contribute to this elegant volume on the social, economic, political, literary, architectural, and ideological worlds of the Bible. Includes more than two hundred photos (twenty-five in color) as well as drawings and maps, plus annotated bibliographies.

Neusner, Jacob, and William Scott Green, eds. *Dictionary of Judaism in the Biblical Period.* Peabody, Mass.: Hendrickson, 1999. Defines terms, ideas, people, places, and practices of the Jewish people from the time of the formation of the Pentateuch to the Babylonian Talmud.

Books on the Old Testament Historical and Sociopolitical Contexts

Albertz, Rainer. *A History of Israelite Religion in the Old Testament Period.* Translated by John Bowden. 2 vols. The Old Testament Library. Louisville: Westminster John Knox, 1994. A thorough social history of Israel, period by period, in interaction with surrounding cultures and with special emphasis on politics, worship, family life, piety, and community identity.

Clements, Roland E., ed. *The World of Ancient Israel: Sociological, Anthropological, and Political Perspectives.* Cambridge: Cambridge University Press, 1989. A helpful collection of essays on the impact of these perspectives on the understanding of the Bible and the history of its peoples.

Davies, Philip R., and John W. Rogerson. *The Old Testament World.* 2d ed. Louisville: Westminster John Knox, 2006. Contains chapters on the geography, history, religion, life, and literature of ancient Israel.

Soden, Wolfram von. *The Ancient Orient: An Introduction to the Study of the Ancient Near East.* Translated by Donald D. Schley. Grand Rapids: Eerdmans, 1994. A helpful survey of the world within which the ot texts were created.

Sparks, Kenton L. *Ancient Texts for the Study of the Hebrew Bible: A Guide to the Background Literature.* Peabody, Mass.: Hendrickson, 2005. An extensive guide to, and collection of, excerpts from ancient Near Eastern texts of various genres that illuminate the Hebrew Scriptures.

Woude, A. S. van der, ed. *The World of the Old Testament.* Bible Handbook 2. Translated by Sierd Woudstra. Grand Rapids: Eerdmans, 1989. A superb collection of articles in encyclopedia-type format, with excellent bibliographies.

Books on the New Testament Historical and Sociopolitical Contexts

Boring, M. Eugene, Klaus Berger, and Carsten Colpe, eds. *Hellenistic Commentary to the New Testament.* Nashville: Abingdon, 1995. A collection of texts from the Hellenistic world that parallel or illustrate the NT, arranged in order from Matthew to Revelation. Includes cross-references and indexes.

Carter, Warren. *The Roman Empire and the New Testament: An Essential Guide.* Nashville: Abingdon, 2006. A very helpful overview of the politics and economics of life in the empire—and resistance to it.

Cohen, Shaye J. D. *From the Maccabees to the Mishnah.* 2d ed. Louisville: Westminster John Knox, 2006. A clear, concise, and authoritative overview of early Judaism.

Evans, Craig A. *Ancient Texts for New Testament Studies: A Guide to the Background Literature.* Peabody, Mass.: Hendrickson, 2005. An extensive guide to, and collection of excerpts from, noncanonical texts that illuminate the NT writings.

Ferguson, Everett. *Backgrounds of Early Christianity.* 3d ed. Grand Rapids: Eerdmans, 2003. An excellent, readable treatment of politics, religion, and philosophy in the Hellenistic-Roman context.

Jeffers, James S. *The Greco-Roman World of the New Testament Era: Exploring the Background of Early Christianity.* Downer's Grove, Ill.: InterVarsity, 1999. A superb survey of all aspects of life and society in the Greco-Roman era.

Koester, Helmut. *History, Culture, and Religion of the Hellenistic Age. Vol. 1 of Introduction to the New Testament.* Rev. ed. Philadelphia: Fortress, 1995. A thorough, standard study of the world in which the NT was born, with emphasis on the non-Jewish dimensions.

Malina, Bruce J. *The New Testament World: Insights from Cultural Anthropology.* 3d ed. Louisville: Westminster John Knox, 2001. Uses anthropological models to interpret the pivotal values of honor and shame, personality, social status, kinship and marriage, and purity in the first century and in NT texts.

Stambaugh, John E., and David L. Balch. *The New Testament in Its Social Environment.* Library of Early Christianity. Philadelphia: Westminster, 1986. A survey of mobility, economy, society, and urban life.

Atlases

In addition to the printed volumes listed here, many electronic and online atlases now exist. Especially helpful, for example, are the atlas available in the Logos packages, which in some versions is hyperlinked to the biblical text, and the map links at http://ntgateway.com/maps.htm.

Aharoni, Yohanan, and Michael Avi-Yonah, eds. *The Carta Bible Atlas.* Jerusalem: Carta, 2002 (formerly *The Macmillan Bible Atlas*). New York: Macmillan, 1993.

Curtis, Adrian, ed. *Oxford Bible Atlas.* 4th ed. New York: Oxford University Press, 2007.

Lawrence, Paul, et al, eds. *The IVP Atlas of Bible History.* Downers Grove, Ill., 2006.

Pritchard, James B., and L. Michael White, eds. *The HarperCollins Concise Atlas of the Bible.* San Francisco: HarperCollins, 1997.

Section 5. Resources for Formal Analysis

The following resources are useful handbooks for understanding the forms, genres, structures, and other literary aspects of texts identified in the process of exegesis. The general insights of these books may be applied to your specific text. In addition to the books listed below, see Alter and Kermode, *The Literary Guide to the Bible* (section 3 above) for literary genres, and most recent commentaries for discussion of literary and rhetorical structure.

Alter, Robert. *The Art of Biblical Narrative.* New York: Basic Books, 1981. A classic treatment.

———. *The Art of Biblical Poetry.* New York: Basic Books, 1985. Another classic treatment of its subject.

Aune, David. *The New Testament in Its Literary Environment.* Library of Early Christianity. Philadelphia: Westminster, 1987. A superb analysis of the literary genres of the NT writings in context.

Bailey, James L., and Lyle D. Vander Broek. *Literary Forms in the New Testament: A Handbook.* Louisville: Westminster John Knox, 1992. A helpful guide to the specific forms found in the various kinds of NT documents.

Berlin, Adele. *The Dynamics of Biblical Parallelism.* Rev. ed. Grand Rapids: Eerdmans, 2007. An important work on OT parallelism that uses insights from modern linguistics.

Dorsey, David A. *The Literary Structure of the Old Testament: A Commentary on Genesis–Malachi.* Grand Rapids: Baker, 1999. A novel "commentary" that considers the literary structure of each book and how that structure affects interpretation of particular texts.

Fee, Gordon D., and Douglas Stuart. *How to Read the Bible for All Its Worth: A Guide to Understanding the Bible.* 3d ed. Grand Rapids: Zondervan. 2003. A helpful basic introduction to the rules of exegesis and interpretation for the various literary genres (epistles, gospels, parables, law, psalms, etc.) of the Bible, written from an evangelical perspective.

Johnson, Marshall D. *Making Sense of the Bible: Literary Type as an Approach to Understanding.* Grand Rapids: Eerdmans, 2002. An introduction to the importance and interpretation of biblical literary forms.

Lohfink, Gerhard. *The Bible: Now I Get It! A Form-Criticism Handbook.* Translated by Daniel Coogan. Garden City, N.Y.: Doubleday, 1979. A delightful introduction to various literary forms in the Bible, presented in connection with different forms of communication in daily life.

McKenzie, Steven L. *How to Read the Bible: History, Prophecy, Literature—Why Modern Readers Need to Know the Difference, and What It Means for Faith Today.* New York: Oxford University Press, 2005. A treatment of the importance of genre for interpretation, and of five major biblical genres (historiography, prophecy, wisdom, apocalyptic, letters) with respect to their form and purpose.

McKnight, Edgar V. *What Is Form Criticism?* Guides to Biblical Scholarship. Philadelphia: Fortress, 1969. Repr., Eugene, Ore.: Wipf & Stock, 1997. A brief, standard introduction to the origins, practice, and critique of form criticism of the gospels.

Ryken, Leland. *Words of Delight: A Literary Introduction to the Bible.* 2d ed. Grand Rapids: Baker, 1992. A very insightful discussion of biblical narrative, poetry, and smaller literary forms, including encomium, proverb, satire, drama, and the many literary forms found in the gospels (parables, call stories, miracle stories, etc.).

Tucker, Gene M. *Form Criticism of the Old Testament.* Guides to Biblical Scholarship. Philadelphia: Fortress, 1971. A basic guide to the origins and application of form criticism to the ot.

In addition to the works cited above, students of the ot/Hebrew Bible will be interested in a series published by Eerdmans entitled The Forms of the Old Testament Literature, edited by Rolf Knierim and Gene M. Tucker.

Section 6. Resources for Detailed Analysis

There are numerous tools available for detailed analysis of the text. In this section we describe handbooks on detailed analysis, concordances, grammars, dictionaries and similar resources, journals, and commentaries. Those who wish to find such resources on CD-ROM should look at the information on "Bibles on CD-ROM" under section 2, "Resources for Understanding the Text," above.

Handbooks and Other Works on Detailed Textual Analysis

In addition to chapters on such topics as lexical analysis, grammar and syntax, and redaction criticism, which can be found in books on exegetical method (see section 1, "Resources for Understanding the Task"), and in addition to books on the analysis of specific genres (see section 5, "Resources for Formal Analysis"), the following books may be of value in expanding one's theoretical and practical tools for doing detailed analysis from a variety of perspectives.

Barr, James. *The Semantics of Biblical Language.* Oxford: Oxford University Press, 1961. Repr., Eugene, Ore.: Wipf & Stock, 2004. The classic treatment of the abuse and proper use of words, grammar, and other linguistic phenomena in biblical exegesis and theology more generally.

Beale, G. K., and D. A. Carson, eds. *Commentary on the New Testament Use of the Old Testament.* Grand Rapids: Baker Academic, 2007. A book-by-book treatment of scriptural intertextuality by a team of prominent evangelical NT scholars.

Bock, Darrell L. **"New Testament Word Analysis."** Pages 97–113 in *Introducing New Testament Interpretation.* Edited by Scot McKnight. Guides to New Testament Exegesis. Grand Rapids: Baker, 1989. A concise, insightful guide to the practices and pitfalls of word analysis, appropriate for beginning students, especially those using the original languages.

Cotterell, Peter, and Max Turner. *Linguistics and Biblical Interpretation.* Downers Grove, Ill.: InterVarsity, 1989. A superb guide to applying the principles of modern linguistics to the study of the Bible, including words, grammar, sentences, discourses, and nonliteral language. Appropriate for intermediate and advanced readers.

Fewell, Danna N., ed. *Reading between Texts: Intertextuality and the Hebrew Bible.* Louisville: Westminster John Knox, 1992. A collection of articles on the phenomenon of textual borrowing within the Hebrew Bible.

Horrell, David, ed. *Social-Scientific Approaches to New Testament Interpretation.* Edinburgh: T&T Clark, 1999. A collection of classic essays in the field, with bibliographies and an introduction to the social-scientific approach.

Kingsbury, Jack Dean, ed. *Gospel Interpretation: Narrative-Critical & Social-Scientific Approaches.* Harrisburg, Pa.: Trinity, 1997. A collection of articles on each of the four gospels that reveals the methods and insights of recent synchronic approaches to detailed analysis of the gospels. The articles do not focus on the exegesis of short texts but rather on a specific gospel as a whole. Nonetheless, the presentation of the methods in action is extremely useful for beginning to advanced students.

Patte, Daniel. *What Is Structural Exegesis?* Guides to Biblical Scholarship. Philadelphia: Fortress, 1976. An introduction to the theory and practice of structural exegesis applied to the NT.

Perrin, Norman. *What Is Redaction Criticism?* Guides to Biblical Scholarship. Philadelphia: Fortress, 1969. A classic, brief exposition of the origins, practice, and significance of the method, with samples of its use on the gospels.

Porter, Stanley E., ed. *Hearing the Old Testament in the New Testament.* Grand Rapids: Eerdmans, 2006. A collection of essays on scriptural intertextuality in various portions of the NT.

Resseguie, James L. *Narrative Criticism of the New Testament: An Introduction.* Grand Rapids: Baker Academic, 2005. An introduction to principles, with examples.

Silva, Moisés. *Biblical Words and Their Meaning: An Introduction to Lexical Semantics.* Rev. ed. Grand Rapids: Zondervan, 1994. A basic but very helpful introduction to the study of words, informed by modern principles of linguistics.

Concordances

A concordance is an alphabetical listing of the words that occur in a body of literature, with a reference (e.g., 2 Kings 3:4) and usually a brief context line. A "complete" concordance lists every word, but not every occurrence; an "exhaustive" concordance lists every occurrence of every word (though not with context lines for frequent words like "and"); and an "analytical" concordance of an English translation has a system for indicating the occurrences of words according to their equivalents in the original language (e.g., under "love," several kinds of entries appear, corresponding to the various Hebrew and Greek words that are translated "love"). Some concordances provide numbering systems connecting words in the English translation with the words in the original language. Many kinds of concordances are now available electronically, both on CD-ROM and online.

Concordances of the Bible in the Original Languages

Bachmann, H., and W. Slaby. *Computer Concordance to the Novum Testamentum Graece of Nestle-Aland, 26th Edition, and to the Greek New Testament, 3rd Edition.* 3d ed. Berlin: de Gruyter, 1987. The standard Greek NT concordance, computer-generated and printed on large pages with very clear type and formatting.

Clapp, Philip S., Barbara Friberg, and Timothy Friberg, eds. *Analytical Concordance of the Greek New Testament.* 2 vols. Grand

Rapids: Baker, 1991. A concordance to the actual forms and structures of the Greek words in the NT. For students interested in issues of grammar.

Even-Shoshan, Abraham, ed. *A New Concordance of the Bible.* 2d ed. Jerusalem: Kiryat Sefer, 1983. Repr., Grand Rapids: Baker, 1989. A standard concordance to the Hebrew Bible.

Lisowsky, Gerhard, and Hans P. Rüger. *Konkordanz zum hebräischen Alten Testament.* 3d ed. Stuttgart: Deutsche Bibelgesellschaft, 1993. A computer-generated concordance to the Biblia Hebraica. Introductory material in English is included.

Mandelkern, Solomon, et al. *Veteris Testamenti concordantiae hebraicae atque chaldaicae.* Jerusalem: Schocken, 1978. A standard concordance to the OT.

Moulton, William F., Alfred S. Geden, and I. Howard Marshall. *A Concordance to the Greek Testament.* 6th ed. New York: T&T Clark, 2002.

Concordances to Selected English Translations

Goodrick, Edward W., and John R. Kohlenberger III, eds. *NIV Exhaustive Concordance.* Grand Rapids: Zondervan, 1990. A computer-generated concordance with a numbering system to indicate the underlying word in the original language.

———, eds. *The Strongest NIV Exhaustive Concordance.* Grand Rapids: Zondervan, 2004.

Hartdegen, Stephen J., gen. ed. *Nelson's Complete Concordance of the New American Bible.* Nashville: Nelson, 1977. Does not include the NAB update to the NT.

Kohlenberger, John R., III, ed. *The New American Bible Concise Concordance.* New York: Oxford University Press, 2003. Includes the updated NT.

———, ed. *The NRSV Concordance Unabridged, Including the Apocryphal/Deuterocanonical Books.* Grand Rapids: Zondervan, 1991. A computer-generated concordance with an additional "topical index," but no references to the original languages.

Strong, James. *Strong's Exhaustive Concordance.* Various publishers, dates, and formats. Contains a widely used numbering system keyed to the KJV. The Hendrickson edition includes a CD-ROM for Windows, Macintosh, and Palm and Pocket PCs.

Whitaker, Richard E., and James Goehring, eds. *The Eerdmans Analytical Concordance to the Revised Standard Version of the Bible.* Grand Rapids: Eerdmans, 1988. A computer-generated concordance in which every entry is accompanied by the original-language word it translates, which in turn is numbered. The numbers take the reader to an index of all the words from the original languages.

Grammars

Blass, F., and A. Debrunner. *A Greek Grammar of the New Testament and Other Early Christian Literature.* Translated and revised by R. W. Funk. Chicago: University of Chicago Press, 1961. The standard reference grammar for the NT writings. Abbreviated BDF.

Gesenius, W., E. Kautzsch, and Arthur E. Cowley. *Gesenius' Hebrew Grammar.* Mineola, N.Y.: Dover, 2006. An older (orig. 1910) but standard work.

Joüon, Paul. *A Grammar of Biblical Hebrew.* Translated and revised by T. Muraoka. 2 vols. Rome: Pontifical Biblical Institute, 1991. A comprehensive treatment first published in 1923.

Wallace, Daniel B. *Greek Grammar beyond the Basics: An Exegetical Syntax of the New Testament.* Grand Rapids: Zondervan, 1996. A first-rate, user-friendly handbook to the details of Greek grammar and their importance for exegesis, with tables, indexes, and bibliographies.

Waltke, Bruce K., and M. O'Connor. *An Introduction to Biblical Hebrew Syntax.* 9th corrected printing. Winona Lake, Ind.: Eisenbrauns, 2004. A massive intermediate grammar, with copious illustrations from the biblical text.

Dictionaries/Lexicons, Wordbooks, and Encyclopedias

Works That Can Be Used with Minimal or No Knowledge of the Original Language(s)

In addition to the works listed below, see especially *The Anchor Bible Dictionary* listed above in section 4, "Resources for Contextual Analysis."

Brown, Colin, ed. *The New International Dictionary of New Testament Theology.* 4 vols. Grand Rapids: Zondervan, 1975–1978;

1986. Articles on words of theological significance in the NT, arranged alphabetically by English word. Abbreviated *NIDNTT*. Also available on CD-ROM.

VanGemeren, Willem A., ed. *The New International Dictionary of Old Testament Theology and Exegesis.* 5 vols. Grand Rapids: Zondervan, 1997. Articles on words of theological significance in the OT, arranged alphabetically by English word. Abbreviated *NIDOTTE*. Also available on CD-ROM.

Works That Require Facility in the Original Language(s)

Old Testament

Botterweck, G. Johannes, Helmer Ringgren, and Hans-Josef Fabry, eds. *Theological Dictionary of the Old Testament.* Translated by John T. Willis. 10+ vols. Grand Rapids: Eerdmans, 1974– . A "word-study" approach to the key Hebrew and Aramaic terms in the Bible, this set (incomplete as of this writing), like the *TDNT* (see below), makes many contributions but also fosters some misunderstanding as a "wordbook." As an encyclopedia, however, it is a gold mine of information. Abbreviated *TDOT*.

Brown, F., S. R. Driver, and C. A. Briggs, eds. *Hebrew and English Lexicon of the Old Testament.* Boston: Houghton Mifflin, 1906. Repr., Peabody, Mass.: Hendrickson, 2005. A classic Hebrew Bible lexicon. Abbreviated BDB.

Holladay, William L. *A Concise Hebrew and Aramaic Lexicon of the Old Testament.* Grand Rapids: Eerdmans, 1971. A handy basic lexicon for students.

Jenni, Ernst, and Claus Westermann, eds. *Theological Lexicon of the Old Testament.* Translated by M. Biddle. 3 vols. Peabody, Mass.: Hendrickson, 1997. An excellent resource for the theological vocabulary and concepts of the OT.

Koehler, Ludwig, Walter Baumgartner, Mervyn E. J. Richardson, and Johann Jakob Stamm. *The Hebrew and Aramaic Lexicon of the Old Testament.* Translated and edited by M. E. J. Richardson et al. 5 vols. Leiden: Brill, 1994–2000. A thorough, scholarly standard lexicon, also available on CD-ROM. Abbreviated *HALOT*.

New Testament

Bauer, Walter. *A Greek-English Lexicon of the New Testament and Other Early Christian Literature.* Edited and revised by Frederick W. Danker. Translated and adapted by W. F. Arndt, F. W. Gingrich, and Frederick W. Danker. 3d ed. Chicago: University of Chicago Press, 2000. This edition, abbreviated BDAG (Bauer-Danker-Arndt-Gingrich), is a completely revised version of the standard philologically oriented NT lexicon. The 1979 edition, abbreviated BAGD (Bauer-Arndt-Gingrich-Danker), is frequently cited.

Danker, Frederick W., ed. *A Greek-English Lexicon of the New Testament and Other Early Christian Literature.* See "Bauer" above.

Friberg, Timothy, Barbara Friberg, and Neva F. Miller. *Analytical Lexicon of the Greek New Testament.* Victoria, B.C.: Trafford, 2005. An alphabetical presentation of every Greek form found in all the major editions of the Greek NT, providing definitions of all root words and "parsings" (analyses) of all forms.

Kittel, Gerhard, and Gerhard Friedrich, eds. *Theological Dictionary of the New Testament.* Translated and edited by Geoffrey W. Bromiley. 10 vols. Grand Rapids: Eerdmans, 1964–1976. Available also on CD-ROM. An "encyclopaedia of New Testament theology organized alphabetically on the basis of its lexical stock" (Cotterell and Turner, *Linguistics and Biblical Interpretation,* 108). Must be used with some caution because it confuses the sense of words in context and theological concepts/history of ideas. Best used as a resource for the semantic range and usage of words in antiquity. Abbreviated *TDNT.*

Liddell, H. G., and R. Scott. *A Greek-English Lexicon.* Rev. ed. Aug. by H. S. Jones. 9th rev. ed. Oxford: Clarendon, 1996. The standard lexicon of classical Greek. Abbreviated LSJ.

Louw, Johannes P., and Eugene Nida, eds. *Greek-English Lexicon of the New Testament: Based on Semantic Domains.* 2d ed. New York: United Bible Societies, 1989. A dictionary that focuses not on the history of words but on semantic relationships. A good complement to the traditional lexicon. Now available on CD-ROM from a company called iExalt.

Spicq, Ceslas. *Theological Lexicon of the New Testament.* Translated by James Ernest. 3 vols. Peabody, Mass.: Hendrickson, 1994. An excellent resource for the theological vocabulary and concepts of the NT.

Journals

Following is a brief description of some leading journals in the field of biblical studies. They are useful for many topics, but most especially for detailed treatment of texts. Online versions with full articles are noted; other journals may have websites with limited information, including article abstracts.

Biblica—technical articles published in several languages; also online at http://www.bsw.org/index.php?l=71

Biblical Archaeology Review—readable articles on discoveries and scholarly issues (not intended primarily for scholars); partially available online at http://www.bib-arch.org/bar

Biblical Theology Bulletin—despite the title, a journal devoted primarily to social-scientific perspectives; some issues online at http://academic.shu.edu/btb/

Catholic Biblical Quarterly—contributions from an ecumenical group of scholars, largely in the historical-critical tradition

Ex Auditu—exegetical and thematic articles with a strong theological interest; some articles online: http://www.northpark.edu/sem/exauditu/

Expository Times—British publication, international in scope, with brief but helpful articles, reviews, and surveys of current trends in scholarship

Harvard Theological Review—articles in the historical-critical tradition

Horizons in Biblical Theology—articles on methods, issues, and themes in biblical theology

Interpretation—exegetical and thematic articles with a strong theological and homiletical interest; text online for subscribers

Journal for the Study of the New Testament—technical articles from a variety of perspectives and countries, emphasizing literary and theological concerns

Journal for the Study of the Old Testament—technical articles from a variety of perspectives and countries, emphasizing literary and theological concerns

Journal of Biblical Literature—technical articles largely in the historical-critical tradition; some issues and subscription information to the online and print versions are available at http://www.sbl-site.org/publications/journals_jbl_noLogin.aspx

Journal of Hebrew Scriptures—an online journal of OT studies with some issues now in print: http://www.arts.ualberta.ca/JHS/

Journal of Scriptural Reasoning—an online interfaith journal for those reading the Scriptures for religious purposes: http://etext.virginia.edu/journals/ssr/

Journal of Theological Interpretation—a new journal (begun in 2007) dedicated to theological exegesis, the connections between Bible and theology, the history of the interpretation and reception of texts, and related subjects

Journal of Theological Studies—a theological journal with frequent articles related to biblical studies

Neotestamentica—an international NT journal based in South Africa; abstracts and some articles online: http://www.neotestamentica.net/

New Testament Studies—an international journal of technical articles representing various approaches to exegesis; text online for subscribers

Novum Testamentum—an international journal of technical articles representing various approaches to exegesis; text online for subscribers

Review and Expositor—exegetical and thematic articles

Scottish Journal of Theology—a theological journal with strong biblical and hermeneutical interests; text online for subscribers

Semeia—an "experimental" journal focusing on new and recent approaches and methods; ceased publication in 2002, but still a valuable resource

Vetus Testamentum—an international journal of technical articles representing various approaches to exegesis

Word and World—a journal of theology, biblical studies, and Christian life/ministry; some articles at http://www.luthersem.edu/word&world/

In the coming years, an increasing number of journals will no doubt be available online. The American Theological Library Association (ATLA) is in the process of digitizing fifty years' worth of approximately fifty theological periodicals for access by the public. Among these are several devoted to biblical studies, including *Catholic Biblical Quarterly, Interpretation, Journal for the Study of the New Testament, Journal for the Study of the Old Testament, Journal of Biblical Literature, Novum Testamentum,* and *Vetus Testamentum.* Further information is available at the ATLA website: http://www.atla.com. Other journals are or will be available through various personal or library subscription services, including JSTOR, the scholarly journal archive project (http://www.jstor.org/).

Commentaries

Of the making of commentaries there truly is no end. Even the experts who write them complain that there are too many, but the production line is not slowing down. At a professional conference of biblical scholars, a friend asked, "Don't tell me you're writing a commentary on Philippians, too. Everyone I know is!" (Fortunately, I was not.) In this section we consider commentaries that are devoted (generally) to one book of the Bible (or perhaps two or three short books), as opposed to one-volume Bible commentaries, which were discussed in section 3, "Resources for Surveying the Text."

Commentaries are of several types, representing a wide variety of purposes and perspectives. Some are "devotional" or "spiritual" in nature, intended to nourish the religious life of their readers and often (though not always) prepared by authors with little or no scholarly expertise in their subject. Similar to these, but more often written by acknowledged experts, are "homiletical" commentaries, by which I mean either collections of sermons on biblical books or commentary intended primarily to provide responsible insights for preachers. These two kinds of commentaries have their place in the life of faith, in the theological reflection of faith communities, and in the task of exegesis broadly understood as an ongoing conversation that provokes reflection on the text. Indeed, some of the most important commentaries of all time are homiletical, such as the sermons of Augustine, Chrysostom, and Calvin. Unfortunately, most modern exegetes avoid such commentaries, but they do so only to their own detriment. The literary, historical, and especially theological insight of these authors is often profound and provocative.

The following series attempts to capture the exegetical insights of the church fathers on the Bible:

Oden, Thomas C., gen. ed. ***Ancient Christian Commentary on Scripture.*** 27 vols. scheduled. Downers Grove, Ill.: InterVarsity, 1998–. A multivolume set of anthologies of quotations from early Christian writers on each book of the Bible.

Wilken, Robert Louis, series ed. ***The Church's Bible.*** Grand Rapids: Eerdmans, 2003–. A similar series of anthologies of quotations and commentary excerpts from early and medieval Christian writers.

The sermons and commentaries of some of the great theologians and biblical interpreters of the church include those of Augustine, Chrysostom, Martin Luther, John Calvin, John Wesley, and Matthew Henry. These works can be found in various editions. Calvin's complete works, and an extensive collection of Luther's works, are now available on CD-ROM, as are those of the early church fathers.

For the purposes of careful, detailed analysis, contemporary exegetes generally turn first to commentaries prepared by modern biblical scholars. These, too, fall into various categories. Although they are all prepared by scholars working with the Bible in its original languages, the commentaries themselves may be on either the Greek or Hebrew text, a specific translation (such as the NRSV), or the commentator's own translation (as in the case of *The Anchor Bible* series). Exegetes who do not read the original languages can usually still profit from a commentary on the Greek or Hebrew text, but they will often miss nuanced insights, may find the discussion or argument difficult to follow, and may become annoyed at the quantity of Greek or Hebrew in the commentary. For this reason, many commentators choose to base their analysis on a translation and refer to the original languages through the transliteration of terms. When transliteration is used in abundance, however, readers who do not know the original language can easily experience the same problems that they do with commentaries filled with Greek and Hebrew words.

Scholarly commentaries also vary as to their approach and purpose. Some, especially those from the first seventy-five years of the twentieth century, are primarily interested in diachronic exegesis, or the origin and development of the text. These commentaries emphasize source, form, tradition, and redaction criticism as well as historical and literary parallels to the text in the ancient world. Such commentaries are still being produced, using the results of current historical, philological, archaeological, and other scientific research to analyze the text. These commentaries may be referred to as *historical-critical* commentaries.

A recent offshoot of the traditional historically oriented commentary is the *social-science* or *social-scientific* commentary. This kind of commentary emphasizes the importance of understanding the social and cultural dimensions of the text and of the communities by which and in which it was produced. Most recent commentaries, however, even those that stress the sociopolitical context of a writing, are likely to place greater or even exclusive emphasis on the final form of the text rather than on its origins and development. The writers of these commentaries are engaged primarily in synchronic exegesis. They emphasize literary and rhetorical criticism. Indeed, one of the most recent trends has been to combine social-scientific and rhetorical criticisms to produce *socio-rhetorical* commentaries.

Still other commentaries, while benefiting from some or all of the possible approaches to exegesis, emphasize the substantive literary and theological content of the final form of the text. This eclectic approach is likely the one that most beginning exegetes will adopt in some form, simply because they cannot possibly master all the technical critical methods.

A recent development (or the renewal of an ancient approach) in the production of commentaries is the explicitly (and primarily) theological commentary, of which two series began publication in 2005 (Theological Commentary on the Bible, from Brazos, and The Two Horizons Commentary, from Eerdmans), another in 2007 (Paideia: Commentaries on the New Testament, from Baker Academic), and yet another in 2008 (the New Covenant Commentary Series, from Wipf & Stock). More such commentaries are sure to follow, both in series and as stand-alone volumes.

Exegetes can and should benefit from a variety of kinds of commentaries, using the insights of several to correct, refine, and expand their own exegesis of the text.

Commentaries are published either in series, in which generally one volume is dedicated to one biblical book; in multivolume sets, in which several books are treated in each volume of a set; or as stand-alone volumes, or works published independently of a series or set. Following are several of the current series available (many of which are incomplete) and a few of the multivolume sets. Space does not permit discussion of the many fine stand-alone commentaries.

Series

The *Abingdon New Testament Commentaries* series (ANTC; Nashville: Abingdon, 1996–) represents superior scholarship in an accessible format. Each volume has an introduction, unit-by-unit commentary on the text, an annotated bibliography, and a subject index. Commentators are sensitive to literary, historical, and theological dimensions of the text.

The *Abingdon Old Testament Commentaries* series (AOTC; Nashville: Abingdon, 2001–) complements the NT series.

The *Anchor Bible* series (AB; Garden City, N.Y.: Doubleday, 1964–) is an interfaith venture largely in the historical-critical tradition, but originally designed with the "general reader" in mind. All Greek and Hebrew terms appear in transliteration. Each volume provides an extensive introduction followed, for each section of the biblical book, by: the author's own translation of the text; detailed notes on lexical, grammatical, and other interpretive issues; and extended commentary on the text. *The Anchor Bible* series has produced some superb, even classic, volumes but also some disasters (especially early on), which are being replaced. Apart from the few problem volumes, this series is highly respected among scholars. Each volume also includes a superb bibliography.

The *Augsburg Commentary on the New Testament* (Minneapolis: Augsburg, 1980–1990) is an excellent series devoted to literary and theological analysis with students and pastors in mind.

Berit Olam (Collegeville, Minn.: Liturgical, 1996–) is a series that takes a primarily literary approach to exegesis of the OT, with emphasis on the theological message of the text. The NRSV is the main English translation to which the commentators make reference.

Black's New Testament Commentaries (BNTC; orig. New York: Harper, 1957–; now Peabody, Mass.: Hendrickson) is a venerable series, with selected volumes already replaced. The text is explained in blocks, with attention to historical, literary, and theological issues. This series was originally published as *Harper's New Testament Commentaries*.

The *Brazos Theological Commentary on the Bible* (Grand Rapids: Brazos, 2005–) is a unique series being written primarily by prominent theologians (rather than biblical specialists) from an explicitly theological perspective with attention to the tradition of interpretation in the church.

The ***Continental Commentary Series*** (Philadelphia: Fortress, 1984–) is a translation of European (mostly German) works with theological and literary as well as historical-critical interests. So far, more volumes have appeared on the OT than on the NT.

The ***Hermeneia*** series (Philadelphia: Fortress, 1971–) is a classical historical-critical project inspired by German scholarship. (In fact, some of the volumes are translations from German originals.) Its strength is its attention to ancient sources and parallels to the biblical text and, more recently, to ancient rhetorical and literary features of the biblical books.

The ***International Critical Commentary*** series (ICC; Edinburgh: T&T Clark, 1896–) is a highly technical series that was first produced at the turn of the twentieth century and has been in the process of being redone, volume by volume, for several decades. Full of text and footnotes containing intricate discussions of grammar, the history of interpretation, nonbiblical literature, and related topics, these volumes—especially the recent ones—are invaluable for those who work in the original languages and useful even for those who do not.

The ***International Theological Commentary*** series (Grand Rapids: Eerdmans, 1983–) seeks to unpack the religious message of the biblical book in short but insightful commentaries, each centering on a theme identified as central to the particular book under consideration. To date, only volumes on the OT have been issued.

Interpretation (Louisville: Westminster John Knox, 1982–) is an ecumenical series designed for "teaching and preaching." Although the series is somewhat uneven, it has produced a number of very fine commentaries. The goals of the series lead the commentators to focus on the final form of the text and on its significant literary and theological features. Many have notes on the use of their book in the lectionary, and most have specific sections devoted to theological reflection on the text. Available also on CD-ROM.

The ***New Cambridge Bible Commentary*** (NCBC; Cambridge: Cambridge University Press, 2003–) is a scholarly commentary aimed at the nonspecialist that pays particular attention to rhetorical and social-science dimensions of the text, as well as to bridging the ancient and modern horizons.

The *New Covenant Commentary Series* (NCCS; Eugene, Ore.: Wipf & Stock, 2008–) is a new series of relatively brief commentaries on the narrative and rhetorical dimensions of the NT writings that takes the books seriously as the determinative sacred texts of the Christian churches past and present, with special focus on the relationship of the NT to the OT and on fusing the two horizons of past and present contexts (the worlds "in, around, and beyond the text").

The *New International Biblical Commentary* (NIBC; Peabody, Mass.: Hendrickson, 1989–) is a very fine, very affordable paperback series prepared largely, though not exclusively, by well-known evangelical scholars. When quoting the Bible, the commentaries reproduce the NIV in boldface, and the endnotes for each section are especially good at conveying the history of interpretation and the variety of major contemporary interpretations of key aspects of the book. The NT is finished, and the OT is in the process of being completed.

The *New International Commentary on the Old Testament* (NICOT; Grand Rapids: Eerdmans, 1965–) and the *New International Commentary on the New Testament* (NICNT; Grand Rapids: Eerdmans, 1952–) are well-established, scholarly series prepared and edited by many of the major evangelical scholars of the last half-century, with some of the older (and/or lesser) volumes now being replaced. The format is generally translation and notes plus verse-by-verse commentary. Newer volumes have sections on form and structure as well as theological reflection.

The *New International Greek Testament Commentary* (NIGTC; Grand Rapids: Eerdmans, 1978–) is a technical series on the Greek NT. The detailed, lengthy commentaries (several approaching or exceeding one thousand pages) pay close attention to linguistic and historical issues.

The *NIV Application Commentary* (Grand Rapids: Zondervan, 1994–), a series authored for the most part by reputable evangelical scholars, has as its primary goal "bringing an ancient message into a modern context." In addition to an introduction, outline, and bibliography, the commentary itself for each book contains three parts: the "Original Message," a section called "Bridging Contexts," and one called "Contemporary Significance." This approach is ambitious and creative, if at times a bit repetitious. On the whole, however, this series is rich in theological reflection and homiletical insight in the context of

Western culture at the beginning of a new millennium. Available in part on CD-ROM.

The *Old Testament Library* series (OTL; Louisville: Westminster John Knox, 1961–) brought critical German scholarship with literary and theological interests to the English-speaking world and now includes contributions from English-speaking scholars. In addition to commentaries, the series contains monographs on relevant topics. A counterpart for the NT (NTL) is soon to be published with original works in English.

Paideia: Commentaries on the New Testament (Grand Rapids: Baker Academic, 2007–) is a very ecumenical series of NT commentaries that focuses on the narrative and rhetorical features of the final form of the NT writings, with attention to the theological issues they address that are of concern to Christian readers today.

The *Sacra Pagina* series (Collegeville, Minn.: Liturgical, 1991–) is an excellent collection of commentaries on the NT from well-known Roman Catholic biblical scholars. Original-language terms appear in transliteration. The format of each volume includes an introduction and passage-by-passage analysis, each with notes on every verse, a discussion of the passage as a whole, and a fine bibliography. These volumes are very sensitive to contemporary approaches and to theological significance.

The *Smith & Helwys Bible Commentary* series (Macon, Ga.: Smith & Helwys, 2001–) on both Testaments is being prepared largely (though not exclusively) by distinguished Baptist scholars, but with ecumenical sensitivity. Each section of each volume is divided into two parts, "Commentary" and "Connections" (i.e., contemporary reflections), and each commentary comes with a CD-ROM that includes a PDF file of the book plus other features.

The *Two Horizons Commentary* series (Grand Rapids: Eerdmans, 2005–) is designed to bridge the gap between the ancient world and our world through careful literary and historical work leading to theological reflection.

The *Word Biblical Commentary* series (WBC; originally Waco, Tex.: Word; now Nashville: Thomas Nelson, 1983–) is a very thorough, technical, and highly respected series produced by some of the world's top evangelical scholars. Greek and Hebrew are used throughout. The format of each commentary includes an extensive introduction and then, for each passage: a bibliography; a translation with textual notes; an explanation of the "form/structure/setting"; a verse-by-verse "comment"; and an "explanation," which focuses on a synthesis of the meaning and function of the passage in context. Available also on CD-ROM.

Multivolume Sets

Gaebelein, Frank, gen. ed. *The Expositor's Bible Commentary.* 12 vols. Grand Rapids: Zondervan, 1976–1992. This classic set by conservative evangelical scholars based on the NIV is responsible work but somewhat predictable in exegetical and theological perspective. It should therefore be used with some caution and balance from other perspectives. Available also on CD-ROM for both Windows and Mac.

The *New Interpreter's Bible.* 12 vols. plus an index volume. Nashville: Abingdon, 1994–2004. A monumental achievement, this set replaces the old *Interpreter's Bible* (1951–57). The scholarship is ecumenical and first-rate, the format attractive, and the connection between commentary and reflection superb. For each book of the Bible, including the apocryphal/deuterocanonical books, there is a substantial introduction preceding a unit-by-unit commentary and reflection. The entire text of both the NRSV and the NIV (excluding the Apocrypha) is printed, and there are tables and other aids. Many of the volumes contain general articles or articles introducing specific kinds of literature. An invaluable tool, indeed already a classic. Also available on CD-ROM with powerful tools.

Section 7. Resources for Synthesis

Synthesis is an element of exegesis that can be accomplished only after giving careful attention to context, structure, and detail. Moreover, the individual and creative character of this element defies the production of simplistic "how to" manuals for the synthetic dimension of exegesis.

Certain kinds of resources already discussed may, however, prove helpful. One-volume Bible commentaries, for instance, can be helpful in getting to the "punch line" of the text by virtue of their necessary brevity and, therefore, (ideally) succinctness. But perhaps the most helpful resources for synthesis are more thorough commentaries that pay special attention either to the rhetorical features of the text, or to its theological claims, or (preferably) to both.

It is difficult to name particular commentary series that are uniformly useful in this regard, since the volumes in every series vary with respect to quality and insight. The *Interpretation* series is frequently helpful because of its attention to the theological dimensions of the text that can be preached and taught. Also, the *Word Biblical Commentary* and *Sacra Pagina* series, with their frequent attention to form and structure, may be worth consulting for this element of the exegetical process.

Section 8. Resources for Reflection: Theological Interpretation

The following resources provide various frameworks for the actual practice of exegesis. They are books on hermeneutics (generally, the art of interpretation) and theological interpretation. They represent diverse approaches to reading the text for its religious significance. As such, they are best read not in the heat of preparing an exegesis paper or sermon but at other times when more careful reflection on complex issues is possible. Of the many possible books that could be listed here, I have tried to select some that represent important recent trends.

General Works

Adam, A. K. M. *What Is Postmodern Biblical Criticism?* Guides to Biblical Scholarship. Minneapolis: Fortress, 1995. A brief, readable introduction to postmodernism and to deconstruction, political criticism, and related topics.

Ideological Criticism

González, Justo. *Santa Biblia: The Bible through Hispanic Eyes.* Nashville: Abingdon, 1996. Considers five paradigms for biblical interpretation (e.g., marginality, poverty) based on Latino experience.

Gottwald, Norman K., and Richard A. Horsley. *The Bible and Liberation: Political and Social Hermeneutics.* 2d ed. Maryknoll, N.Y.: Orbis, 1993. An impressive collection of more than thirty methodological and interpretive articles by leading proponents of these approaches to exegesis.

Rowland, Christopher, and Mark Corner. *Liberating Exegesis: The Challenge of Liberation Theology to Biblical Studies.* Louisville:

Westminster John Knox, 1989. A provocative discussion of various kinds of biblical study in Latin America and their possible impact on the study of the Bible in the "first world," with illustrations using NT texts.

Schüssler Fiorenza, Elisabeth, ed. *Searching the Scriptures.* Vol. 1. *A Feminist Introduction.* Vol. 2. *A Feminist Commentary.* New York: Crossroad, 1993, 1994. Feminist perspectives on biblical interpretation and texts, with an evaluation of traditional approaches.

Segovia, Fernando F., and Mary Ann Tolbert, eds. *Reading from This Place.* Vol. 1. *Social Location and Biblical Interpretation in the United States.* Vol. 2. *Social Location and Biblical Interpretation in Global Perspective.* Minneapolis: Fortress, 1995. Examples, from a variety of locations, of the importance of the human context in reading the Bible.

Sugirtharajah, R. S., *Postcolonial Criticism and Biblical Interpretation.* New York: Oxford University Press, 2002. A standard work on the relationship between postcolonial criticism and biblical studies by a leading exponent of postcolonial interpretation.

Theological Interpretation, Preaching, and Teaching

In addition to the resources listed below, see also several of the journals and commentary series noted under section 6, above, especially the journals *Ex Auditu, Horizons in Biblical Theology, Interpretation,* and *Journal of Theological Interpretation;* the commentary series *Brazos Theological Commentary on the Bible, Interpretation,* and *The Two Horizons Commentary;* and the multivolume *The New Interpreter's Bible.*

Adam, A. K. M., Stephen E. Fowl, Kevin J. Vanhoozer, and Francis Watson. *Reading Scripture with the Church: Toward a Hermeneutic for Theological Interpretation.* Grand Rapids: Baker Academic, 2006. Four essays and four responses from a quartet of the leading practitioners of theological interpretation, with special emphasis on singularity versus plurality in the interpretation of texts.

Braaten, Carl E., and Robert W. Jenson, eds. *Reclaiming the Bible for the Church.* Grand Rapids: Eerdmans, 1995. A collection of essays by an ecumenical group of biblical scholars and theologians who wish to use the historical approach to the Bible within the hermeneutical contexts of the entire canon and the church's central faith convictions and practices.

Childs, Brevard. **"Toward Recovering Theological Exegesis,"** *Pro Ecclesia* 6 (1997): 16–26. An important essay by one of the leading voices (d. 2007) of canonical criticism and theological interpretation.

Davis, Ellen F., and Richard B. Hays, eds. *The Art of Reading Scripture.* Grand Rapids: Eerdmans, 2003. A very important collection of essays by the editors and twelve other eminent theologians and biblical scholars who participated together in the "Scripture Project," plus sermons by the editors, demonstrating the application of nine theses on the theological interpretation of Scripture.

Fowl, Stephen E. *Engaging Scripture: A Model for Theological Interpretation.* Challenges in Contemporary Theology. Oxford: Blackwell, 1998. A challenging and very significant argument that "Christians must read scripture in the light of their ends as Christians—ever deeper communion with the triune God and with each other," with examples of the model proposed.

————, ed. *The Theological Interpretation of Scripture: Classic and Contemporary Readings.* Oxford: Blackwell, 1997. A collection of significant essays from the past and present.

Fowl, Stephen E., and L. Gregory Jones. *Reading in Communion: Scripture and Ethics in Christian Life.* Grand Rapids: Eerdmans, 1991. Repr., Eugene, Ore.: Wipf & Stock, 1998. A masterful book on the nature of biblical interpretation as a communal practice of embodying Scripture within an ongoing interpretive tradition, with attention to interpreters and to specific texts.

Green, Joel B., and Max Turner, eds. *Between Two Horizons: Spanning New Testament Studies and Systematic Theology.* Grand Rapids: Eerdmans, 2000. A groundbreaking collection of essays on the relationship between Bible and theology in preparation for *The Two Horizons Commentary* series noted above.

Green, Joel B., and Michael Pasquarello III, eds. *Narrative Reading, Narrative Preaching: Reuniting New Testament Interpretation and Proclamation.* Grand Rapids: Baker, 2003. A series of insightful essays displaying the theory and practice of narrative interpretation for various books and genres.

Hall, Christopher A. *Reading Scripture with the Church Fathers.* Downers Grove, Ill.: InterVarsity, 1998. A well-written introduction to the church fathers, their theological methods of exegesis, and especially their insistence on the role of community and character in appropriate biblical interpretation.

Hays, Richard B. **"Reading the Bible with Eyes of Faith: The Practice of Theological Exegesis."** *Journal of Theological Interpretation* 1 (2007): 5–22. A concise, programmatic statement of the marks of theological interpretation of Scripture.

———. **"Salvation by Trust? Reading the Bible Faithfully."** *Christian Century* 114 (February 26, 1997): 218–23. A significant, controversial article arguing for a hermeneutic of trust ("reading receptively and trustingly . . . but not accepting everything in the text at face value") over against a hermeneutic of suspicion. Reprinted in Richard B. Hays, *The Conversion of the Imagination: Paul as Interpreter of Israel's Scripture* (Grand Rapids: Eerdmans, 2005), 190–201.

Lash, Nicholas. **"Performing the Scriptures."** Pages 37–46 in *Theology on the Way to Emmaus.* London: SCM, 1986. A classic essay on biblical interpretation as performance.

Levenson, Jon. *The Hebrew Bible, the Old Testament, and Historical Criticism: Jews and Christians in Biblical Studies.* Louisville: Westminster John Knox, 1993. A significant critique of the historical-critical method from a Jewish and interfaith perspective, with suggestions on more appropriate ways of reading the Bible.

McKim, Donald K., ed. *Dictionary of Major Biblical Interpreters.* Downers Grove, Ill.: InterVarsity, 2007. A collection of more than two hundred articles on key figures and their interpretive strategies.

Peterson, Eugene. *Eat this Book: A Conversation in the Art of Spiritual Reading.* Grand Rapids: Eerdmans, 2006. A pastoral and practical book on the art of *lectio divina* (sacred reading) and on Scripture as script for performance.

Seitz, Christopher, and Kathryn Greene-McCreight, eds. *Theological Exegesis: Essays in Honor of Brevard S. Childs.* Grand Rapids: Eerdmans, 1999. A collection of essays from students, colleagues, and friends dedicated to further reflection on the canonical criticism that Childs espoused.

Stuhlmacher, Peter. *Historical Criticism and Theological Interpretation of Scripture: Toward a Hermeneutics of Consent.* Translated by Roy A. Harrisville. Philadelphia: Fortress, 1977. A brief, classic history and critique of changes in exegetical method since the time of early Christianity that separated faith from exegesis, and a defense of a "hermeneutics of consent" that includes "openness to transcendence."

Thiselton, Anthony C. *New Horizons in Hermeneutics: The Theory and Practice of Transforming Biblical Reading.* Grand Rapids: Zondervan, 1992. A challenging, comprehensive review of hermeneutical approaches and their embodiment in actual biblical interpretation, together with Thiselton's own thesis, drawing upon speech-act theory, about the ways Bible reading can and should transform readers.

Thompson, John L. *Reading the Bible with the Dead: What You Can Learn from the History of Exegesis That You Can't Learn from Exegesis Alone.* Grand Rapids: Eerdmans, 2007. A study of the treatment of nine difficult texts of Scripture by patristic, medieval, and Reformation interpreters.

Treier, Daniel J. *Introducing Theological Interpretation of Scripture: Recovering a Christian Practice.* Grand Rapids: Baker Academic, 2008. A guide to the sources, common themes, and ongoing challenges of the revival in theological interpretation.

Vanhoozer, Kevin J., gen. ed.; Craig G. Bartholomew, Daniel J. Treier, and N. T. Wright, assoc. eds. *Dictionary for Theological Interpretation of the Bible.* Grand Rapids: Baker, 2005. An impressive collection of biblical, theological, and hermeneutical articles one would normally find in a Bible dictionary, a general theological dictionary, and a handbook of biblical interpretation—all in one place and with greater theological purpose and insight than the standard reference books normally demonstrate. This dictionary should become a standard reference work for both new and experienced interpreters of Scripture.

Watson, Francis. *Text, Church, and World: Biblical Interpretation in Theological Perspective.* Grand Rapids: Eerdmans, 1994. Repr., London: T&T Clark, 2004. An important book arguing that "biblical interpretation should concern itself primarily with the theological issues raised by the biblical texts within our contemporary ecclesial, cultural, and socio-political concerns."

Wink, Walter. ***The Bible in Human Transformation: Toward a New Paradigm for Biblical Study.*** Philadelphia: Fortress, 1973. A small classic from the "existentialist" approach to exegesis.

Section 9. Bibliographical Resources

Exegetes have many resources at their disposal beyond those described in this book. Some books devoted to bibliography and some standard indexes to periodical literature are listed below. These may be used to locate books and articles on general or specific topics, and to supplement bibliographies found in or created from other kinds of resources. Searching for course syllabi online and other online sources can also be profitable.

Books

Bauer, David R. ***An Annotated Guide to Biblical Resources for Ministry.*** Peabody, Mass.: Hendrickson, 2003. A list of more than two thousand resources.

Danker, Frederick W. ***Multipurpose Tools for Bible Study.*** Rev. and enl. ed. Minneapolis: Fortress, 2003. The latest edition of a classic first published in 1960, now with a CD-ROM, this book contains a mine of information on the best resources of every type (concordances, editions and translations of the text, dictionaries, commentaries, etc.), advice on how best to use them, and examples of exegesis aided by the tools described. Mandatory repeated reading for serious students of the Bible. Available on CD-ROM powered by Libronix.

Periodicals

Guides to periodicals have been published in three forms: as bound volumes, as CD-ROMs, and as online databases. Among the most important are:

The ATLA Religion Database. Published by the American Theological Library Association (ATLA), this is the premier database of journal articles, collections of essays in book form, and book reviews in the study of religion, including biblical studies (covering all works listed in the old Religion Index One and Religion Index Two, noted below). It is available online by institutional subscription. Publication of the full CD-ROM version will cease after 2008. Subsets of the database on CD-ROM may continue to be available, but only for individuals, in the future.

New Testament Abstracts (NTA) and *Old Testament Abstracts (OTA)*. These two journals, published three times per year by the Catholic Biblical Association *(OTA)* and by Boston College *(NTA)*, provide short summaries of recent scholarly articles, arranged by both topic and book of the Bible. There are also notices of recently published books. By means of joint ventures between ATLA and the two publishers, both journals are also available online through institutional subscription. Publication of the CD-ROM version will cease after 2008 for *OTA* and has already ceased for *NTA*.

Religion Index One: Periodicals. This tool, which has been published annually by ATLA, lists journal articles in all fields of theology and religious studies, including biblical studies. Articles on the Bible can be found arranged by topic, biblical writer, and biblical book. Print publication will cease with the 2009 volume.

Religion Index Two: Multi-Author Works. This ATLA tool, parallel to *Religion Index One* in format, lists articles published in multi-author volumes (collections of essays). Print publication ceased in 1999.

Religious and Theological Abstracts. This handy online resource includes articles on biblical subjects: http://rtabstracts.org/.

Tables of Exegetical Methods
Three Approaches

The following tables attempt to organize and display the various methods employed by practitioners of the synchronic, diachronic, and existential approaches to exegesis. For each method, a table presents the phenomena or problems users of the method observe and seek to address; the goals of the method; and some sample questions that the method might generate.

The tables are not complete, for there are methods and "sub-methods" that could be added, but those included here are the main ones with which all exegetes should be familiar and which are discussed in this book. It should be remembered at all times that there is significant overlap between certain synchronic and diachronic methods and that the existential approach also makes use of methods from the other two approaches.

Synchronic Methods

(synchronic = within time) or Close Reading

Phenomena or Problems: A text is a finished product.

Goals: Analyze the text in its final form.

Literary and Rhetorical Analysis

Method	Phenomena or Problems	Goals	Sample Questions
Literary Criticism (including contextual analysis) Note: "literary criticism" is a rather vague term used in a variety of ways; see also narrative and rhetorical criticism below.	The meaning of texts is dependent on their nearer (or immediate) and larger contexts. Biblical documents exist as various kinds of literary works with corresponding features.	Determine contexts and their significance. Analyze various literary aspects of the text as literature.	What is the literary context of the so-called Suffering Servant hymn (Isaiah 53)? What kinds of figurative language are used in the book of Job? What are the dramatic features of the book of Revelation? Does Psalm 19 or John 1:1–18 have parallelism? inclusio? chiasm?
Genre and Form Analysis (genre = literary type or pattern) *See also* rhetorical criticism below and form criticism under diachronic methods.	Biblical writings contain various kinds of literary types.	Determine the genre or form of the text plus any key variations from normal patterns. Describe the structure and movement of the text (also part of rhetorical and literary criticism).	What type of psalm is Psalm 51? How is it arranged in verses (strophes)? What kind of writing is 1 Corinthians 13? How is 1 Corinthians 13 structured? Are there discernible parts?
Narrative Criticism	Many biblical writings contain, are based on, or are themselves explicit or implicit narratives (stories).	Analyze the text with respect to thematic lines, plot, character development, point of view, or other appropriate features of narratives.	What is the plot, and what are the key points in the sequence of events, in the Joseph cycle (Genesis 37–50)? How does the Gospel of Mark portray the disciples?

Method	Phenomena or Problems	Goals	Sample Questions
Rhetorical Criticism (rhetoric = the art of effective communication)	Texts exist to have an effect on the hearer/reader, and biblical writings exhibit ancient and universal rhetorical devices and forms.	Determine rhetorical strategies used (including tone, style) and their functions. Categorize text in terms of classical rhetorical forms. Describe the rhetorical structure of the text.	What is the rhetorical strategy and effect of God's speeches in Job? Of the kinds of persuasive writing known in antiquity, what kind is Galatians?
Intertextual Analysis	Biblical texts cite, allude to, and echo scriptural and other texts, as well as extratextual cultural realities.	Determine the existence and significance of citations of, allusions to, and echoes of other texts.	To what use does Third Isaiah (Isaiah 56–66) put its allusions to Israel's creation stories? Does Luke echo imperial ideology and, if so, with what theological and rhetorical effects?

Linguistic Analysis

Method	Phenomena or Problems	Goals	Sample Questions
Lexical, Grammatical, and Syntactical Analysis (vocabulary, forms of words, arrangement of words) *See also* historical linguistics below under diachronic methods.	Biblical writings contain significant words, grammatical forms, and syntactical constructions, some of which may be obscure.	Determine the significance of key words, idioms. Determine the significance of key grammatical forms. Determine the significance of key syntactical structures.	Is "Daughter Zion" or "Daughter of Zion" the better translation of the biblical phrase? If the Spirit is a "pledge" or "guarantee" (2 Corinthians 1:22), what did that mean in Paul's day? Does "love of Christ" (2 Corinthians 5:14) mean Christ's love for us or our love for Christ?
Semantic or Discourse Analysis (semantics = study of meaning)	Meaning is found not merely in the words and their forms and arrangements, but also in the contextual relations among them.	Use modern tools of linguistics to analyze the deep structure and other semantic features of discourse units.	How might contemporary understandings of the linguistic function of aphorisms assist in the interpretation of the book of Proverbs? What are the core affirmations in the phrase "[Jesus] was handed over to death for our trespasses and raised for our justification" (Romans 4:25)?

Social-Scientific Criticism

Method	Phenomena or Problems	Goals	Sample Questions
Social Description (general)	Biblical texts were produced in a concrete sociopolitical and cultural situation. Biblical texts refer explicitly or implicitly to political realities and to social customs, classes, conditions, relationships, etc.	Determine and describe the sociopolitical context and cultural conditions of the writer and recipients. Describe the social world of the Israelites or early Christians.	In what changing sociopolitical contexts did Jeremiah preach? What was the situation of the Johannine community? What evidence of patriarchal or elitist values can be found in the book of Proverbs? What was the socioeconomic level of the first followers of Jesus, or of the Corinthian Christians?
Social-Scientific Analysis	Biblical writings may reflect realities that social sciences can explain.	Analyze the text or its community with sociological or anthropological models and methods.	Are there anthropological models or theories that help explain the rise of kingship in ancient Israel? Could belief in Jesus' resurrection be explained by the theory of "cognitive dissonance"?

Diachronic Methods

(diachronic = across time) or Historical-Critical Method

Phenomena or Problems: A text has a history.

Goals: Discern and analyze the text's origin and development (and its final form in light of these).

Method	Phenomena or Problems	Goals	Sample Questions
Textual Criticism	No "autographs" (originals) exist. Manuscripts and other witnesses disagree due to unintentional and intentional changes during the copying and transmission process.	Establish best text, as close to original as possible.	Did the original text say "only begotten God" or "only begotten Son" (John 1:18)? How does Mark's Gospel end? Was the story of the woman caught in adultery originally part of John's Gospel?
Historical Linguistics (vocabulary, forms of words, arrangement of words) *See also* lexical, grammatical, and syntactical analysis above under synchronic methods.	Biblical writings contain significant words, grammatical forms, and syntactical constructions, some of which may be obscure, and these items have an important history.	See goals under Synchronic Methods, Lexical, Grammatical, and Syntactical Analysis, plus . . . Determine the extent to which the historical development of these linguistic items is important for understanding the text.	See sample questions under Synchronic Methods, Lexical, Grammatical, and Syntactical Analysis, plus . . . How do the histories of the words for "assembly" in the Bible develop over time and either reflect or affect writers' understandings of Israel or of the early house church?
Form Criticism (form = consistent pattern) *See also* genre and form analysis under synchronic methods.	Biblical writings contain various preliterary forms or patterns. These include, for example, proverbs, call stories, parables, beatitudes, healing stories, nature miracles, resurrection accounts, hymns, creeds, slogans, benedictions.	Determine the form of the text, plus any forms within it. Analyze any unusual features or changes to the form's normal pattern. Determine the original life setting *(Sitz im Leben)* in general for such a form.	What kind of narrative is the account of Moses and the burning bush (Exodus 3)? What kind of narrative is the story of Jesus' stilling of the storm (Mark 4:35–41)? In what setting(s) of Israel's life or early Christianity would a certain kind of text (such as the two mentioned above) have been created and used, and why?

Method	Phenomena or Problems	Goals	Sample Questions
Tradition Criticism Note: this is a difficult and often speculative venture.	The oral tradition was modified in the transmission process.	Determine how a particular pericope came to be put together through a process of growth by oral transmission.	How was the story of the covenant promise to David (2 Samuel 7) modified as it was transmitted? Is the story of the paralytic man's being lowered and healed (Mark 2:1–12) a single story or a compilation of oral sources?
Source Criticism	Each writer appears to have used various sources to construct the finished product.	Determine the sources used, plus their types and perspectives.	What different sources were used to put together the two creation stories in Genesis 1–3? What was the nature of the material that Matthew and Luke have in common that is absent from Mark?
Redaction Criticism (redaction = editing; cf. also intertextuality [under synchronic methods] = weaving in of other written documents)	Each writer both adopted and adapted sources, resulting in distinct perspectives.	Determine how the writer (or writing) uses (changes, does not change) sources; ask why. Trace tendencies, distinctive features, emphases, etc. in a document.	How has the editor of Exodus combined and edited sources about Moses, and for what purposes? How does Matthew both adopt and adapt Mark's account of Jesus' baptism, and why?
Historical Criticism	Biblical preliterary forms and actual texts were produced in concrete historical situations. Because the oral tradition was modified in the transmission and redaction process, it may be that not every word and deed reflected in the biblical text actually occurred. Other things claimed in the biblical writings may or may not have happened as presented.	Determine the historical contexts reflected in preliterary forms and in the written text. Determine what, if anything, a historical figure actually said and did, and what was modified and/or created by the process of tradition and redaction.	What if anything can be known of the actual experience of the figure Abraham? How does one account for the parting of the Red/Reed Sea in historical and scientific terms? What was the occasion for the writing of Habakkuk? Do the accounts of Jesus' conflict with the Pharisees correspond to his actual conflicts, those of the evangelists' time, or both? Did Jesus predict his own suffering, death, and resurrection, or did the early church put those words on his lips?

Existential Methods

(existential = concerning real life)

Phenomena or Problems: A biblical text makes claims on and speaks to later readers, but there is a wide historical and cultural gap between the time of writing and today.

Goals: Discern the contemporary meaning of the text by using synchronic and diachronic approaches mixed with additional methods, theories, and contexts.

Hermeneutic of Trust or Consent

Method	Phenomena or Problems	Goals	Sample Questions
Canonical Criticism	From the believing community's perspective, biblical texts and documents exist not alone but as part of a larger collection, the canon.	Determine meaning and authority of texts in their relationship with other similar and dissimilar texts.	How do we understand the nature of God portrayed in the books of Hosea and Amos in light of the entire canon? How do Paul's emphasis on justification through faith and James's stress on good works illumine each other?
Theological Exegesis	Ultimately, the Bible is divine address and part of the divine means of revelation and salvation.	Understand the Christian faith in light of the witness of Scripture, and vice versa. Discern the authoritative theological and ethical claims of the text.	What do the images of the book of Revelation say to Christians about God and Christ? To what way of life does the prophet Jeremiah point us?
Missional Hermeneutic	Scripture bears witness to the *missio Dei* and invites the believing community to see itself as an agent of that mission and to discern and participate in it.	Discern and participate in the *missio Dei.*	How might God's promise to bless the nations through Abraham inform the believing community's identity and purpose today? What do the Beatitudes in the Sermon on the Mount (Matthew 5) say about the identity and mission of the church in the world?

Method	Phenomena or Problems	Goals	Sample Questions
Spiritual (or Sacred) Reading (*lectio divina,* or praying Scripture, and "reading in communion")	Ultimately, Scripture, as the word of God, is not something to dissect but to hear and respond to as divine address to individuals and communities.	Discern the specific word of God being addressed to me or us.	How does Psalm 150 express and nurture our life of praise? What does the story of Peter's denial say to us? How might we be denying our Lord?
Embodiment or Actualization (praxis, performance, living exegesis)	Ultimately, Scripture is not something merely to study but to live.	Embody the claims, promises, and imperatives of the text as a faithful person and community.	How are we to identify and treat the "orphan and the widow" in our midst? What are we specifically to do to embody the concern for the marginalized and outcast that Jesus exhibits in Luke?

Hermeneutic of Suspicion

Method	Phenomena or Problems	Goals	Sample Questions
Advocacy and Liberationist Exegesis (includes feminist and other liberationist perspectives)	Biblical writings have been interpreted in ways that offend or oppress (anti-Semitism, slavery, gender discrimination, etc.). Biblical writings may themselves contain things deemed by some to be offensive or oppressive.	Determine how the Bible has been used to oppress, and use specific texts to stress its nonoppressive, liberating meaning. Consider or determine which texts and themes may need to be avoided, and which used, in order to advocate and work for liberation.	How have people used the Bible to justify discrimination against women? Is the Gospel of John so inherently anti-Semitic that its presence in the Christian New Testament is problematic?
Ideological Criticism (includes postcolonial interpretation)	Biblical writings may reflect and support inappropriate expressions of power.	Determine and critique the inappropriate relations of power.	To what appropriate and inappropriate relations of economic power does the wisdom literature bear witness? Do New Testament criticisms of Roman imperial power that transfer imperial titles to God and Jesus help to subvert or to perpetuate later colonial and imperial ideologies?

Practical Guidelines for Writing a Research Exegesis Paper

There are five major phases in the writing of a research exegesis paper: preparation, initial exegesis, research, consolidation, and writing.

I. Preparation

    A. Determine an appropriate text for exegesis: a manageable, relatively self-contained unit with a clear beginning and end (chapter 2).

        1. The length should normally be no less than the equivalent of a paragraph or stanza and no more than the equivalent of a few paragraphs or stanzas (e.g., approximately five to twenty-five verses).

        2. Study Bibles or one-volume commentaries may be helpful in determining units.

        3. Consult with your instructor for advice if necessary.

    B. Obtain the biblical texts with which you plan to work—a study Bible, one or more additional translations, editions with parallel texts (e.g., gospel parallels, if appropriate), and the Greek or Hebrew text (if you read it).

    C. Print out from an electronic text of the Bible, or photocopy from a printed Bible, at least one version of your text for the purpose of marking it up.

        1. Place the text in the center of the page, with wide margins on either side. If possible, import

the text into a word processor and print it out with wide spacing between the lines of text.

2. If possible, also create with the word processor a two-column phrase-by-phrase table of the text for use in the detailed analysis.

II. Initial Exegesis

Note: Work on the text on your own, writing down whatever you discover and whatever questions come to mind, as you follow the main steps of the exegetical process. Mark up your printout or photocopy of the text: underline, circle, make notes, etc. Note any specific questions that you wish to research in the commentaries, books, and articles you will use in the next phase, expansion and refinement of the exegesis. You may wish to organize your observations on note cards or on pieces of paper dedicated to the various elements (with separate cards or sheets for each verse examined in the detailed analysis).

A. Survey: The First Element (chapter 3)

1. Read the text several times and in several translations.

    a. Write down first observations, key differences in the translations, and questions that arise.

    b. Make an initial working translation of the text, if you read the original language.

2. Read or skim the entire book in which the text appears, paying special attention to the text before and after your passage.

3. Consult one or more resources that deal with the book in which the passage is located (introductory text, one-volume commentary, or Bible dictionary).

    a. Take notes on what you discover about the basic historical context—the circumstances of its writing (who, what, when, why, where, etc.).

     b. Take notes on what you discover about the basic literary context—a general outline of the book and the location of the passage in that outline.

  4. Begin to prepare a bibliography by noting any relevant commentaries, books, or articles mentioned in the resources consulted.

  5. Make an educated guess about the meaning of the passage, and use this as a working thesis.

B. Contextual Analysis: The Second Element (chapter 4)

  1. Historical, Social, and Cultural Contexts—Use a Bible dictionary or similar resource to obtain basic information as necessary.

  2. Literary and Rhetorical Context

     a. Find or create a general outline of the book as a whole.

     b. Carefully consider the wider as well as nearer or immediate context.

C. Formal Analysis: The Third Element (chapter 5)
The Form, Structure, and Movement of the Passage

  1. Form—Consider the literary genre of the book and the literary form of the passage.

  2. Structure—Create your own outline of the passage.

  3. Movement—Consider how the text flows from beginning to end.

D. Detailed Analysis: The Fourth Element (chapter 6)
Verse-By-Verse Discussion

  1. Use the two-column, phrase-by-phrase table created during the preparation phase.

  2. Find key actors and actions (subjects, verbs, etc.), qualifying phrases, other key words and images, etc.

  3. Pay special attention to function words (because, for, although, when, if, etc.).

        4. Look for allusions to other texts, especially Scripture, and for evidence of other sources and how they are used.

    E. Synthesis: The Fifth Element (chapter 7)
Formulate the main point of the text.

    F. Reflection—Theological Interpretation: The Sixth Element (chapter 8)
Make observations about the contemporary significance of the text from your perspective.

III. Research: The Seventh Element (chapter 9) Expansion and Refinement of Your Initial Exegesis

    A. Prepare a bibliography.

        1. Whether recording data with pen or keyboard, make sure the information is accurate and complete.

        2. Types of resources: reference books (Bible dictionaries and the like); monographs that discuss your passage; commentaries on the book; periodical articles; chapters in volumes of collected essays.

        3. How to find resources: read bibliographies and notes in textbooks, commentaries, reference books, study Bibles, etc.; use bibliographical tools; browse books in the stacks and current periodicals; search the library's traditional or electronic card catalog; search online bibliographies and relevant sites.

        4. Length of bibliography—rule of thumb: approximately one bibliographical item for each page of text (e.g., a 15-page paper should have about fifteen bibliographical entries).

    B. Take careful notes.

        1. Use commentaries before articles (general to specific).

        2. Look for information, insights, and interpretations that escaped your initial exegesis.

        3. Look to challenge, clarify, and correct your own work.

4. Look for and record evidence of the important aspects of the text.

5. Look for alternative interpretations of important issues and document them.

6. Generally, take notes in your own words; put direct quotes in quotation marks; note all sources. Protect yourself against unintentional plagiarism.

C. Review your notes.

1. Look for any gaps in data or interpretation.

2. Reuse resources or find new resources as necessary.

IV. Consolidation: The Seventh Element (chapter 9) Expansion and Refinement of Your Initial Exegesis (continued)

A. Combine your initial exegesis with the corrections, confirmations, new data and evidence, etc. from other sources.

B. Write down your own conclusions and claims about the context, form/structure/movement, main aspects (including debated points) of the detailed analysis, and synthesis.

C. Develop and record a thesis statement about the main point(s) and function of the passage.

D. Develop an outline of your paper that follows the main steps in the exegetical process.

V. Writing

A. Start with the contexts, then form/structure/movement. Do detailed analysis and synthesis next, and the introduction to the paper last (unless you are to include a section of personal reflection and engagement, which may be written last).

B. Note that "refinement and expansion of the exegesis" is not a separate section of the paper, only a stage in the process.

C. Discuss and evaluate the most important alternative interpretations of the most important issues, but do not create a collage of book reports or a review of research. Constantly keep your thesis in mind, and consistently defend your informed interpretation of the text.

D. Document—in parentheses, endnotes, or footnotes— information (other than common knowledge), insights, and interpretations discovered in your research, thereby giving credit to those whose ideas you have utilized.

E. Follow the form for papers outlined in the standard guide to paper writing used in your institution.

F. Reread, rewrite, reread, rewrite.

Three Sample Exegesis Papers

A Short Exegesis Paper (NT)

The following short exegesis paper was written at about the midway point in a course on the Gospel of John. The author was a part-time student in an M.A. in Theology program and did not read Greek, working instead with the NRSV. The only sources she consulted for the paper were the textbooks for the course and for another class in Christian origins. This fine essay appears unedited except for minor adjustments to its format. The author is now an Episcopal priest.

An Exegesis of John 11:45–53
Annette Chappell

⁴⁵Many of the Jews therefore, who had come with Mary and had seen what Jesus did, believed in him. ⁴⁶But some of them went to the Pharisees and told them what he had done. ⁴⁷So the chief priests and the Pharisees called a meeting of the council, and said, "What are we to do? This man is performing many signs. ⁴⁸If we let him go on like this, everyone will believe in him, and the Romans will come and destroy both our holy place and our nation." ⁴⁹But one of them, Caiaphas, who was high priest that year, said to them, "You know nothing at all! ⁵⁰You do not understand that it is better for you to have one man die for the people than to have the whole nation destroyed." ⁵¹He did not say this on his own, but being high priest that year he prophesied that Jesus was about to die for the nation, ⁵²and not for the nation only, but to gather into one the dispersed children of God. ⁵³So from that day on they planned to put him to death. (NRSV)

John 11:45–53 presents the plotting of the Jewish council in a way that reinforces several Johannine themes, especially the divided responses of the people to Jesus; the increasing hostility of the

Jewish leadership to Jesus; the irony of that hostility in the face of God's unshakable plan; and the divine necessity of the crucifixion as the "completion" of Jesus' career on earth.

Historical Context

In interpreting this pericope it is particularly important to understand the delicate and precarious relationship of the Jewish authorities with their Roman overlords. The deliberations of the Jewish council reveal not only a (perhaps self-serving) concern with preserving the leadership the Romans have permitted them to exercise, but also a probably quite legitimate fear that any activity that upsets the Roman authorities can only result in repression of both the Jewish religion and the Jewish people.

Literary Context

This passage occurs near the end of the first half of the Gospel of John (the "book of signs"), just after the raising of Lazarus from the dead. The raising of Lazarus is the most dramatic, and the most clearly eschatological, of Jesus' signs. That incident is his last "public appearance" before the events we associate with Holy Week (the triumphal entry into Jerusalem and all that follows). John 11:45–53 therefore provides both a bridge between major sections of the narrative and a distillation of the evangelist's understanding of the causes (human and divine so ironically blended) of the trial and crucifixion.

Form, Structure, Movement

This pericope provides both a conclusion to the Lazarus story and a transition to the increasingly tense events of Jesus' final week on earth. Not only does the passage foreshadow the crucifixion in general ("they planned to put him to death," v. 53), but also it hints at the complex manipulations the Jewish authorities will use to persuade their Roman overlords to order and carry out that execution.

The pericope is structured as an extended dialogue, a series of implicit and explicit speeches illustrating the sequence of reactions to Jesus' raising of Lazarus from the dead. The discussion moves from the most public level, where the reaction of bystanders is divided (vv. 45–46), to the inner circles of Jewish leadership, where the event is seen as the latest in a sequence of increasingly objectionable actions by Jesus (vv. 47–50 and vv. 51–52), and where the resolve to eliminate Jesus seems the only appropriate conclusion for the council to reach (v. 53).

Detailed Analysis

In 11:45–46, as on so many occasions in the fourth gospel, the reaction to Jesus' act is decidedly mixed. Raising Lazarus from the dead is the most extraordinary act Jesus has yet performed in this gospel, both because it so far transcends the ordinary laws of nature and because Jesus so explicitly uses the prayer at 11:41–42 as a teaching tool. However, though "many" believe in him as a result, there are "some" who instead go to the Pharisees and bear witness against Jesus. Their witness-bearing is reported, not dramatized as quotation; we can assume, however, that it is not deliberate "false witness" (as in Mark and Matthew), but is nevertheless wrong because those who go to the Pharisees have failed to understand who Jesus is.

The segment 11:47–50 presents a dramatic scene, in which the Jewish authorities articulate the political fears that Jesus' activities evoke. The problem, as it is expressed by the "chief priests and Pharisees" in vv. 47–49, is that Jesus' popularity with the (Jewish) crowds may draw the attention of the Romans to the Jewish nation as a whole. In their estimation, the Romans will assume that Jesus' popularity presages a nationalistic uprising, and in order to forestall such an uprising the Romans will suppress the Jewish religion ("destroy . . . our holy place" in v. 48 may mean physically destroy the temple and certainly means suppress the system of worship that takes place there), which will lead to destruction of the Jewish "nation," since the only national identity the Jews had left under Roman rule was their devotion to temple and Torah.

Commentators note that the fourth evangelist was imprecise in characterizing the members of the council (Kysar 1986, 184), using the term "Pharisees" in a manner appropriate to his own time rather than to Jesus' time. The implication, however, is clear: the council is made up of religious leaders ("chief priests and Pharisees") for whom Jesus poses a threat both to their own status and to their religion and nation.

The high priest, Caiaphas, however, suggests that the solution is quite simple (11:49–50): Jesus must "die for the people" so that the whole nation will not be destroyed. From this clear insight, the plot against Jesus can easily be developed.

The literary focus of the entire pericope is on the layers of irony implicit in Caiaphas's pronouncement. Though there may be historical interest in the question of whether 11:51 indicates a general belief that being high priest conveyed the ability to prophesy (Kysar 1986, 186; Talbert 1992, 177; Meeks 1993, 2037 n.), the main function of vv. 51–52 is to call the reader's attention to the complex irony.

In this passage, at least the following levels of irony are operating all at once: (1) Caiaphas and the rest of the council believe they are opposing Jesus and thwarting his mission, when in fact they are instrumental in precipitating the crucifixion, which is precisely the "completion" toward which Jesus' ministry must move. (2) Caiaphas believes he is smarter than the rest of the council because he alone has discovered how to get rid of Jesus, when in fact he is as oblivious to the truth as the rest of the council. (3) Caiaphas and the council conclude that Jesus' death will save "the whole nation" from the Romans, whereas in fact, his death will save not only the nation of Israel but also "the dispersed children of God," including the Romans and other pagans the council so fears. (4) Caiaphas and the council believe they are protecting the temple and its cultus from destruction at Roman hands, though the evangelist and his readers know that the Romans did destroy the temple in 70 c.e. and with it the social/ecclesiastical/ liturgical structure it supported. (5) Caiaphas and the council are concerned to protect Judaism from pagan Gentiles, the Romans, but since Jesus' death will be "not for the nation only, but to gather together the dispersed children of God," including all those Gentiles, the result will be Christian communities such as John's that exemplify that multiculturalism and make the council's brand of accommodationist Judaism obsolete. (6) The chief servants of YHWH, God's representatives to the people, are convinced that for the sake of the people they need to procure the death of God's prophet, God's Son, God's Logos, God's own self, because they deny that that is who they are condemning. (7) In fact, for God's own purposes, it is necessary that the Son should die; the council unwittingly participates in bringing about that completion of God's plan for the nation of Israel and "the dispersed children of God."

The pericope ends with the council's resolve (11:53) to find a way to put Jesus to death. As we know from ch. 12, they eventually conclude that they will also need to kill Lazarus, who is visibly a beneficiary of Jesus' divine power. The final irony of this passage, then, is that Caiaphas and the council have totally miscalculated the nature of witness. In addition to thinking of Lazarus as no more than an inconvenient piece of evidence, they assume that the people will no longer be witnesses once Jesus is dead. As the evangelist has made increasingly clear in this gospel, however, witness is a result of belief, and once people truly believe in Jesus, they do not cease to witness to him. This passage therefore leads into the second half of John's Gospel, the "book of glory," the story of Jesus' last days on earth and his exaltation as Son of God on the cross.

Synthesis/Conclusion

Through the dramatic little story of the council's discussion after the raising of Lazarus, the fourth evangelist accomplishes several purposes. He creates a transition from the last great sign story, the raising of Lazarus, to the beginning of the story of Jesus' last days. In so doing, he heightens the tension as Jesus is more and more in danger from the authorities. He reminds his audience of the divided response all Jesus' actions evoked from the people, and of the implacable opposition of the Jewish authorities. He uses complex irony to indict the Jewish leadership for their mis-understanding of Jesus, of God, and of God's plan for the world. And he reinforces the sense of inevitability with which his narra-tive builds toward the crucifixion as the moment when Christ is "raised up" as lord and savior.

Reflection

In the context of his own apologetic, the fourth evangelist seems inclined to make the Jewish authorities into deliberately malevo-lent antagonists. After all, for him they "represent" the later syna-gogue authorities who expelled the Johannine Christians from synagogue fellowship and worship. The author's artistry, however, is more generous than he perhaps knew, and his irony in this little scene transcends his antipathy toward the Jewish leaders. Thus, although there is certainly no sweetness in John's treatment of the "chief priests and Pharisees," they do come through as confused but perhaps not evil human beings, caught up in something they could neither understand nor ignore, and addressing a new prob-lem with the wrong old ways of reasoning. Alas, the church today is not immune to that kind of mistake, so it should be a comfort to be reminded that God's gracious irony can make our bumbling errors part of God's great plan.

Works Consulted

Ferguson, Everett. *Backgrounds of Early Christianity.* 2d ed. Grand Rapids: Eerdmans, 1993.

Kysar, Robert. *John.* Augsburg Commentary on the New Testament. Minneapolis: Augsburg, 1986.

Meeks, Wayne, et al., eds. *The HarperCollins Study Bible: New Revised Standard Version, with the Apocryphal/Deuterocanonical Books.* New York: HarperCollins, 1993.

Talbert, Charles H. *Reading John: A Literary and Theological Commentary on the Fourth Gospel and the Johannine Epistles.* New York: Crossroad, 1992.

A Longer Exegesis Paper (NT)

The exegesis paper on the following pages was written toward the end of a course on the Pauline Epistles. The author was a full-time student in an M.Div. program, preparing for priesthood in the Roman Catholic Church. At the time of the course, he was in the beginning of his second of four years in the program. His paper was based largely on the NAB, with reference to the NRSV and some Greek, which he did not know well. This paper was intended to include research in the secondary literature and to include footnotes. This very good essay appears unedited except for minor technical adjustments. The author is now a Catholic priest.

Weakness as an Apostolic Credential: 2 Corinthians 12:1–10
Bryan Lowe

[1]I must boast; not that it is profitable, but I will go on to visions and revelations of the Lord. [2]I know someone in Christ who, fourteen years ago (whether in the body or out of the body I do not know, God knows), was caught up to the third heaven. [3]And I know that this person (whether in the body or out of the body I do not know, God knows) [4]was caught up into Paradise and heard ineffable things, which no one may utter. [5]About this person I will boast, but about myself I will not boast, except about my weaknesses. [6]Although if I should wish to boast, I would not be foolish, for I would be telling the truth. But I refrain, so that no one may think more of me than what he sees in me or hears from me [7]because of the abundance of the

revelations. Therefore, that I might not become too elated, a thorn in the flesh was given to me, an angel of Satan, to beat me, to keep me from being too elated. [8]Three times I begged the Lord about this, that it might leave me, [9]but he said to me, "My grace is sufficient for you, for power is made perfect in weakness." I will rather boast most gladly of my weaknesses, in order that the power of Christ may dwell with me. [10]Therefore, I am content with weaknesses, insults, hardships, persecutions, and constraints, for the sake of Christ; for when I am weak, then I am strong. (NAB)

Paul's Second Letter to the Corinthians is not one of the more well-known Pauline texts. Although there has been much debate about the literary integrity of the letter, there is little doubt that the letter was originally circulated in its present canonical form. The passage to be analyzed, 2 Corinthians 12:1–10, is an interesting one for many reasons. In it we have Paul's firsthand (though narrated in the third person) account of his vision of Paradise. Although by most people's standards this would certainly give Paul something to "brag about," Paul's reason for including it is specifically to show that boasting is not what being an apostle is all about. Paul is providing a polemical argument against so-called "superapostles" in Corinth who seem to be trying to supplement his teaching with a different gospel.

In the larger context of Paul's argument, weakness is a main theme. Paul uses the word often within this passage as well, with "weak" or "weakness" occurring five times. This weakness is a focus for Paul in the apostolic life. In conforming oneself more closely to Christ and living the "cruciform" lifestyle Paul expounds, one will be less self-reliant, and thus God's power can be displayed for all to see.

Paul's argument provides us with more than just a glimpse at what his opponents at Corinth were claiming. This passage gives a clearer understanding of Paul's vision of apostolic ministry in general. Phrases such as "my grace is sufficient for you" and "when I am weak, then I am strong" are well known to most people who have even a limited acquaintance with Scripture. When one analyzes Paul's argument in 2 Corinthians 12:1–10, these statements take on a new, more sophisticated meaning.

Historical and Literary Contexts

Paul was the founder of the Christian community at Corinth. It appears that he initially stayed there for approximately eighteen months. Paul apparently wrote a series of letters to the Corinthians in his ongoing attempt to be an absentee pastor to a community that obviously meant a great deal to him. As Mary Ann Getty describes the situation:

> The letters we call 1 and 2 Corinthians formed a part of a larger collection that originally consisted of several letters Paul wrote to the Corinthian community. Paul's relationship with the Corinthians was complex and tumultuous and it seems as if the Corinthians were a particularly challenging community.[1]

This would seem to be an understatement, to say the least. The issue of allegiance to Paul as opposed to others was apparent in 1 Corinthians, and the same sort of issue is again revisited in 2 Corinthians. The most that I feel can be said with confidence is that Paul had to deal with a number of issues with respect to the Corinthians, among them being his status as an apostle.

There has been a great deal of speculation in regard to the literary integrity of 2 Corinthians, as well as in regard to the date it was written. The biggest source of controversy seems to be 2 Corinthians 10–13. While there are other parts of this letter that are also considered to be insertions (some claim up to five different letters), the focus of this section will be on chs. 10–13. These four chapters are obviously an integral literary unit unto themselves. The disagreement comes in determining whether these chapters were originally part of the letter or were combined with chs. 1–9 by a later redactor. The point of contention comes in the seemingly abrupt change of tone from 9:15 to 10:1. Many commentators (so Martin, Murphy-O'Connor, and Furnish) see this change as so drastic that chs. 10–13 must be a separate letter, or at least a part of a separate letter.

On the other hand, I believe that the themes are so consistent throughout the entirety of 2 Corinthians that the entire letter must be viewed as a whole. Throughout the early parts of the letter Paul refers to problems in the community and to an upcoming visit. This seems to lay the groundwork for chs. 10–13. His discussion of "letters of recommendation" in 3:1 could be seen as a beginning of his discussion that is completed in the later chapters. The discussion of an upcoming visit in ch. 7 is echoed in chs. 10–13. Linda Belleville states that this "visit talk" is what ties chs. 7 to 13 together.[2] Paul's discussion of his ministry in 4:7–18 certainly seems to

---

[1] Mary Ann Getty, "Paul and His Writings," in *The Catholic Study Bible* (ed. Donald Senior; New York: Oxford University Press, 1990), RG [reading guide] 485.

[2] Linda L. Belleville, *2 Corinthians* (IVP New Testament Commentary Series 8; Downers Grove, Ill.: InterVarsity, 1996), 21.

be summed up with "when I am weak, then I am strong" in 12:10b. The continuity of themes expressed between the various parts of the letter are sufficient to convince me that the canonical form of 2 Corinthians was originally sent as an intact letter, but, as Raymond Brown states, "surety is not obtainable."[3]

As far as date written, most commentators choose a date sometime in 55 for ch. 1–9 (or for the entire letter for the minority who agree with my opinion), with chs. 10–13 being written a few months later.[4] The place of composition is generally assumed to be Macedonia. Based on Paul's mention of a third visit, it seems likely that the visit would have been sometime in late 55 or 56.

In the larger literary context, 2 Corinthians 12:1–10 is a part of the unit of chs. 10–13 as discussed above. Paul devotes this entire section to a vigorous defense of his ministry and his apostolic credentials. The unity of this section can be seen particularly in the fact that Paul's "trials-list" occurs midway through the section. "The centrality of this 'trials-list' within chs. 10–13 is also a literal one, since 11:21b–29 occurs exactly in the middle of this last section of the letter."[5] This centrality of Paul's sufferings is key for his argument that apostleship is not about physical appearance. As Jerry Sumney writes:

> Explicit statements in chs. 10–13 show that the *central issue* at Corinth *is the appropriate way of life* for apostles. The opponents contend that true apostles should be impressive individuals. They should be dynamic and persuasive speakers and have a commanding demeanor. This impressive way of life includes the power to rise above troubles.[6]

In the nearer literary context, 2 Corinthians 12:1–10 is a part of the so-called "Fool's Speech" that runs from 11:1 to 12:13.[7] Paul is taking on his opponents by using their own methods, and he begs the Corinthians to "put up with a little foolishness" (11:1) from him.

---

[3] Raymond E. Brown, *An Introduction to the New Testament* (New York: Doubleday, 1997), 551.

[4] See the works by Belleville, Brown, Furnish, Martin, and Murphy-O'Connor for more detailed discussions of the dating of this letter and of Paul's visits to Corinth.

[5] Michael L. Barré, "Qumran and the 'Weakness' of Paul," *Catholic Biblical Quarterly* 42 (1980): 216.

[6] Jerry L. Sumney, *Identifying Paul's Opponents: The Question of Method in 2 Corinthians* (Journal for the Study of the New Testament Supplement Series 40; Sheffield, England: JSOT Press, 1990), 162.

[7] Jerome Murphy-O'Connor, *The Theology of the Second Letter to the Corinthians* (New Testament Theology; Cambridge: Cambridge University Press, 1991), 107.

He is apparently using some of his opponents' arguments against them in the speech, although it is difficult to be certain. The question of who Paul's opponents are in this section also needs to be discussed briefly. Paul's discussion of the two covenants in 2 Corinthians 3 suggests that Paul was dealing with a group of Hellenistic "Judaizers" who valued personal charism in preaching while attempting to supplement Paul's teaching with the Mosaic law.

Form, Structure, and Movement

Paul's Second Letter to the Corinthians is obviously in the form of a letter. When viewed as a whole, the entire structure of canonical 2 Corinthians seems to follow Paul's "typical A-B-A' pattern that influenced so heavily the development of 1 Corinthians": chs. 1–7 are a discussion of difficulties at Corinth (A), chs. 8–9 are a discussion of successes seen at Corinth (B), and chs. 10–13 are a return to difficulties (A').[8] Second Corinthians 12:1–10e is a polemical argument within his larger argument of chs. 10–13 concerning apostolic authority.[9] In this section he addresses his opponents using their own understanding of what constitutes apostolic authority. As Ralph Martin summarizes:

> In 12:1–10, we have a mosaic of literary devices that yields an interesting picture. In this passage Paul is answering a criticism from his opponents, namely, that he boasts little, and even when he boasts, it is only of weakness. Paul's reply is to engage in an *ad hominem* argument. He will presently meet the opponents on their own level and then, in a masterful way, show that it is his ministry, not theirs, that is of God.[10]

For the sake of discussion, this passage can be divided into five separate parts. These divisions, while somewhat arbitrary, are based on thematic changes in the passage as much as on content. The divisions are as follows:

a) Introduction—the need for boasting (v. 1)

b) Paul's "visions and revelations" (vv. 2–4)

c) Return to boasting (vv. 5–7a)

d) Paul's "thorn in the flesh" (vv. 7b–9a)

e) Final boasting of weakness (vv. 9b–10)

---

[8]The quotation and the designation of the various sections come from Getty, "Writings," RG 496.

[9]Ralph P. Martin, *2 Corinthians* (Word Biblical Commentary 40; Waco, Tex.: Word, 1986), 390–91.

[10]Ibid., 390.

Detailed Analysis

Introduction—the need for boasting (v. 1)

Paul begins this section by apparently meeting his opponents on their own terms. His statement "I must boast" (or 'It is necessary to boast' NRSV) seems to be a concession to his opponents that if he is to argue against them he must do so in the same way they have argued against him. However, Paul immediately makes the point that his boasting will not be profitable (or, it will do no good). It seems likely that his opponents must have been making claims of their own ecstatic experiences, and "the value that the early church placed on such experiences can be seen from the fact that Paul in his boasting turns last to *visions and revelations*."[11] Paul has already in 11:17 described his "boastful state" as "foolishness," and he obviously sees no gain in boasting of anything other than his weaknesses, which he previously described in 11:21b–29. Therefore, this final boasting on Paul's part is apparently meant to address the claims that his opponents are making. In the words of Victor Furnish:

> Paul will support his apostleship only by boasting of his weaknesses (11:30; 12:5, 9–10): while he is willing to record this one instance of a private religious experience, he is quite unwilling to claim it as an apostolic credential.[12]

Paul's "visions and revelations" (vv. 2–4)

The structure of Paul's description of his "visions and revelations" is unusual, to say the least. The immediate questions that come to mind are:

a) Why does he use the third person to describe the experience?

b) What is the significance of the date "fourteen years ago"?

c) Why does he use an apparently redundant structure in recounting the experience?

I will address each of these questions individually.

a) Many possibilities have been offered to explain Paul's use of the third person rather than the first person in his account. At first

---

[11] Belleville, *2 Corinthians*, 299.

[12] Victor Paul Furnish, *II Corinthians: Translation, Introduction, Notes and Commentary* (Anchor Bible 32A; New York: Doubleday, 1984), 544.

glance, it seems likely that Paul is simply trying to distance himself from the description since he does not intend to boast about
it. However, on further reflection, I believe that Victor Furnish
offers the most probable reason. He believes that Paul was following in the convention used in other ancient accounts of heavenly
journeys. The use of the third person then becomes a kind of
"self-transcendence" from which to narrate the story.[13] This seems
to make the most sense, because it is clear from the context of the
argument as a whole that Paul is describing something that happened to him personally.

b) The date of "fourteen years ago" seems very important to Paul
in describing his experience. It is probable that tying the ecstatic
experience to an exact date is the only way Paul can validate his
experience. This would be particularly true since he cannot discuss what he heard. It is also likely that the date must have been
significant for Paul personally. "When it comes to such a land-
mark experience he has the exact date well in mind."[14]

c) The structure of Paul's narrative is the most puzzling aspect
of this section because of the way that v. 2 seems to be paralleled
by vv. 3–4. The most common question would be whether Paul is
describing a single journey or two journeys. Once again it seems
unlikely that this is a description of two separate journeys. It is
possible that Paul was using the parallel structure to highlight the
importance of the event, but this does not seem like a technique
that he has employed before. It would then appear to be redundant simply for the sake of being redundant. The most plausible
explanation is offered by James Tabor, and explains the journey
as a single one completed in two stages:

> Paradise is the goal of the journey, and it is the highest goal one could
> claim, something one could call "extraordinary," and over which one
> could easily become elated (2 Cor. 12:7). He reports it in a two stage
> journey, which accounts for the parallel structure. He has been to the
> third heaven, yes, but beyond that, he has entered Paradise. And it is
> there, in Paradise, before God's throne, that he hears things unutter-
> able. This interpretation seems to best fit the structure and content
> of the report.[15]

---

[13] Ibid., 543.

[14] James D. Tabor, *Things Unutterable: Paul's Ascent to Paradise in Its
Greco-Roman, Judaic, and Early Christian Contexts* (Studies in Judaism;
Lanham, Md.: University Press of America, 1986), 115.

[15] Ibid., 119.

In this scenario, the "third heaven" would be the first stage of Paul's journey, which is also a destination his opponents might have been claiming. The second stage of the trip—"Paradise"—would be much more remarkable because it would necessarily entail some kind of direct contact with God. This is where he heard unutterable things. "Significantly, and in striking contrast to other ancient accounts of such journeys, the apostle has nothing to say about what he saw in Paradise."[16] This difference between Paul's report and traditional reports would certainly seem to be intended to place his journey in a higher category than those of his opponents. Paul's statements about not knowing whether his journey was in or out of the body are seemingly of little consequence to his description. They seem merely to be statements of fact that he is not certain how the journey was accomplished, except that he was "caught up." His avoidance of any attempt to understand how this happened could fit well with his desire for his opponents to see this as a factual account and not an interpretation of his journey.

Return to boasting (vv. 5–7a)

Having described his experience in Paradise, Paul returns once again to the subject of boasting. The irony of Paul's account is that an actual encounter with God would seem to be something worth boasting about, but Paul refuses to boast, except about his weaknesses. In this section it becomes apparent that Paul's use of the third person in describing his experience was due to more than just convention. In distancing himself from his ecstatic experience, he is more easily able to point out that this experience is not what he is using as his claim to apostolic credentials. He points out, however, that if he wished to boast about his experience, it would not be foolish because he is "telling the truth" (v. 6). His reason for not boasting is that he believes the only thing an apostle should be judged upon is what his followers see and hear. He does not want the Corinthians to judge his credentials solely on the "abundance of revelations" (v. 7a). This is probably in direct opposition to the claims his opponents are making.

Paul's "thorn in the flesh" (vv. 7b–9a)

Based on the perceived value of his revelations, Paul explains how God has prevented him from becoming too "elated." In the Greek, Paul refers to a *skolops tē sarki*, which has been variously translated

---

[16] Furnish, *II Corinthians*, 545.

as a stake, thorn, or other pointed instrument in his flesh. This could perhaps be equated with our expression "pain in the neck" if it is in fact a reference to his opponents.[17] Other possibilities have been suggested to explain what Paul meant by his "thorn in the flesh," including diseases, debilities, and spiritual torments,[18] but none of these seems to fit into the context from which Paul is speaking in this section. The main problem I see with these other possibilities is that Paul also describes his "thorn" as "an angel (or 'messenger' NRSV) of Satan," which seems to be much too personified to be describing a sickness. In comparing Paul's writing to writings discovered at Qumran, Michael Barré makes a convincing argument for the identification of Paul's distress with his adversaries. His conclusion is that

> the "thorn in the flesh" and the "messenger of Satan" must allude to adversaries of Paul, not to an illness, debility, or any of the other innumerable suggested interpretations of these expressions.[19]

Paul's description of his affliction makes it clear that it has been given to him by the Lord to keep him from becoming too elated. But this is not the only reason. Paul also makes it explicit that his "thorn" is there so that God's power can be made manifest in his weakness. Although Paul "begged the Lord about this" three times in his desire to have the persecution removed, it is likely that in this instance he is describing a different kind of experience from the one described in 12:2–4. As Furnish points out:

> It is surely unwarranted to fuse this account with the preceding report of a heavenly journey, and to suppose that these petitions were addressed to the enthroned Lord as Paul stood before him in Paradise (so R. M. Price 1980:37), for the apostle has already said that what he heard there he was forbidden to repeat (v. 4).[20]

The reason for asking three times has also been variously discussed, but I find that the explanation that makes the most sense to me is found in the footnotes to *The Catholic Study Bible* (NAB) that describe his prayer as "incessant."

Paul does not get the response he desires, that his "thorn" be removed. Instead he is told by the Lord that "my grace is sufficient for you, for power is made perfect in weakness" (v. 9). The impli-

---

[17] Belleville, *2 Corinthians*, 305.
[18] See Furnish, *II Corinthians*, 547–50 for a detailed discussion of the issue.
[19] Barré, "'Weakness,'" 225.
[20] Furnish, *II Corinthians*, 550.

cation seems to be that the Lord will not remove Paul's affliction, but will provide the grace to bear it. Also, it becomes apparent that God's power becomes manifest (perfect) only when the recipient is "weak" or perhaps not self-reliant. Barré seems to offer the most adequate description of this thought process in his translation, "My grace is enough for you; for (my) power is accomplished through (your) weakness/persecution."

Final boasting of weakness (vv. 9b–10)

In the final section of this passage, Paul once again returns to the topic of boasting, but only to boast of his weaknesses. This boasting, however, is different from the kind in which his opponents have been indulging. Rather than boasting solely about his credentials as an apostle, Paul prefers to boast of his weaknesses so that Christ's power will "dwell with" him (v. 9b). It is doubtful that Paul means that weakness is necessary for God's power to be made manifest. Rather, for Paul, personal weakness is the true sign of being an apostle. He is not happy about his weaknesses, but he is "content with" them if they are for "the sake of Christ." Gerald O'Collins summarizes this well:

> "Weakness" constitutes a special mark of apostolic "service." Paul's work of preaching the gospel must not, of course, be interpreted apart from his Christology. The understanding of the crucifixion as the event in which Christ proved radically "weak" forms the background to Paul's whole discussion. In the case of the crucifixion and resurrection, weakness and power constitute an inseparable unity. By raising Christ, God's power was effective and manifested in the face of that ultimate "weakness" which the crucifixion meant. In its turn the apostolic ministry undertaken on Christ's behalf involves participation in this weakness and power of Calvary and Easter. . . . Our passage may be paraphrased as follows: The power which is both effective and manifested in the resurrection of the crucified Christ reaches its fulfillment for the apostle (not in ecstatic experiences but) in diverse "weaknesses." When in this sense the apostle becomes and appears weak, he is in fact strong, effective in his ministry (cf. 10:4).[21]

Synthesis

What is required of the would-be apostle? That is the question that Paul is addressing in this passage. His opponents apparently feel that it is personal charism and rhetorical skill. Paul's

---

[21] Gerald G. O'Collins, "Power Made Perfect in Weakness: 2 Cor 12:9–10," *Catholic Biblical Quarterly* 33 (1971): 532–33.

definition is much simpler—to be an apostle, one must be weak. Paul avoids the temptation to argue for his status as an apostle from his ecstatic experiences. Instead he relies on the Corinthians to recognize that his appearance and deeds are the things upon which he wishes to be judged. Paul's demand is that apostles be those through whom others are able to see the power of God manifested in the world.

Reflection: Second Corinthians 12:1–10 Today

To what areas of our life today can this passage speak? I will suggest three ways. First, it can speak to each of us whenever we are tempted to be too self-reliant. Second, it can speak to the ways each of us manifests apostolic activity in our own particular circumstances. Finally, it can speak to issues of pain and suffering. I will discuss each of these issues in turn.

First, there is often the potential for each of us to become overly self-reliant. Any time we begin to lose sight of the fact that our abilities are free gifts from God, we begin to miss the mark. This seems to have been the situation that Paul was addressing at Corinth. His opponents were boasting about their great accomplishments and belittling Paul's appearance and rhetorical skill. Paul used the irony of his argument to show them that in apparently building themselves up, they were tearing the church down. Paul's message reminds each of us that even if we are able to boast about our abilities, it accomplishes little. Praising our own gifts does nothing to build up Christ's church here on earth. Rather, by using our gifts wisely, we help build up the Christian community, and thus allow the power of the Lord to be seen.

Second, we must each be conscious of how we manifest our own apostolic activity. "My power is made perfect in your weakness" has a great deal of meaning for each of us in our apostolic calling. Is Paul's message that we must actively seek out opportunities to be persecuted, belittled, or injured in order to be faithful to the apostolic mission? Not in the least. But neither does it state that we should avoid those circumstances if they arise. We must each remember that being "weak" means being in conformity to Christ. It is this "cruciformity" that becomes the true sign of apostolic ministry.[22] The church ultimately belongs to

---

[22] I borrow this term from Michael J. Gorman and his forthcoming [now published] book *Cruciformity: Paul's Narrative Spirituality of the Cross* (Grand Rapids: Eerdmans, 2001).

Christ who founded it, not to its members as individuals. Being "weak" can be as simple as seeking counsel from God through prayer, or as complicated as enduring the hardships Paul describes in his letter. This "cruciformity" of lifestyle gives a whole different meaning and emphasis to the idea of living the gospel and spreading it.

Third, and perhaps most importantly, this passage speaks to issues of pain and suffering in our lives. In 2 Corinthians 12:10 Paul states that he is "content with" numerous sufferings that he has had to undergo for the sake of Christ. This is an attitude that can be adopted by any Christian in any life circumstance. Paul is not attempting to understand why he needs to suffer, only to accept that it must happen. Is he happy about it? Apparently not, because he asks God to remove it from him. God's reply is the one that we can each find personally comforting in our time of need—"my grace is sufficient for you." God's promise is not that following his will or that life in general will be easy or free from difficulties. He has always promised, however, to be with us throughout our turmoil. Paul is reminding his readers and his opponents that the power of God is manifested in the difficulties he faces. By uniting our own personal pain and suffering to those of Christ, we are exercising a "cruciform" spirit.

Do we today see examples of the same type of problems Paul faced in Corinth? I would argue that we see them almost daily. Wherever people forget that God is the giver of all of our abilities and gifts, the same attitude that Paul was addressing is alive and well. Any time that persons claim authority because of the gifts they possess instead of as a result of God's power working through them the same is true. People daily suffer hardships while trying to spread the gospel message to others. What must we do? The response Paul would undoubtedly give would be to remember that to be weak in the eyes of the world is to be effective in Christian ministry. Being in conformity with the death and resurrection of Christ is not an easy task, but it is the one sure way to know we are leading a truly Christian life.

Bibliography

Barré, Michael L. "Qumran and the 'Weakness' of Paul." *Catholic Biblical Quarterly* 42 (1980): 216–27.

Belleville, Linda L. *2 Corinthians*. IVP New Testament Commentary Series 8. Downers Grove, Ill.: InterVarsity, 1996.

Brown, Raymond E. *An Introduction to the New Testament.* New York: Doubleday, 1997.

Furnish, Victor Paul. *II Corinthians: Translation, Introduction, Notes and Commentary.* Anchor Bible 32A. New York: Doubleday, 1984.

Getty, Mary Ann. "Paul and His Writings." RG [reading guide] 470–RG 540 in *The Catholic Study Bible.* Edited by Donald Senior. New York: Oxford University Press, 1990.

Gorman, Michael J. *Cruciformity: Paul's Narrative Spirituality of the Cross.* Grand Rapids: Eerdmans, 2001.

Martin, Ralph P. *2 Corinthians.* Word Biblical Commentary 40. Waco, Tex.: Word, 1986.

Murphy-O'Connor, Jerome. *The Theology of the Second Letter to the Corinthians.* New Testament Theology. Cambridge: Cambridge University Press, 1991.

O'Collins, Gerald G. "Power Made Perfect in Weakness: 2 Cor 12:9–10." *Catholic Biblical Quarterly* 33 (1971): 528–37.

Sumney, Jerry L. *Identifying Paul's Opponents: The Question of Method in 2 Corinthians.* Journal for the Study of the New Testament Supplement Series 40. Sheffield, England: JSOT Press, 1990.

Tabor, James D. *Things Unutterable: Paul's Ascent to Paradise in Its Greco-Roman, Judaic, and Early Christian Contexts.* Studies in Judaism. Lanham, Md.: University Press of America, 1986.

A Longer Exegesis Paper (OT)

This exegesis paper was written by a college sophomore majoring in religion and philosophy at Roberts Wesleyan College, in Rochester, New York, for a course on the Psalms and Wisdom Literature taught by Professor J. Richard Middleton. The paper was based largely on the NIV, without the use of Hebrew. It has been edited for length and for some formatting. Because this is an exegesis of a psalm, the less definable issues of historical and literary context are treated only briefly in the introduction, which also considers the psalm's literary form, or genre.

God Is With All Who Walk in His Ways:
An Exegesis of Psalm 84
Amanda Hanselman

PSALM 84[1]

For the director of music. According to gittith. Of the Sons of
Korah. A psalm.

I. Longing to be with the Lord (vv. 1–7)
A. Yearning to be with God in his temple (vv. 1–4)
1. Individual desire to be in God's temple (vv. 1–2)
1 How lovely is your dwelling place,
    O LORD Almighty!
2 My soul yearns, even faints,
    for the courts of the LORD;
my heart and my flesh cry out
    for the living God.

2. All creatures have a place in God's temple (v. 3)
3 Even the sparrow has found a home,
    and the swallow a nest for herself,
    where she may have her young—
a place near your altar,
    O LORD Almighty, my King and my God.

3. All who dwell in God's temple are blessed (v. 4)
4 Blessed are those who dwell in your house;
    they are ever praising you.   *Selah*

B. Journeying to Zion to be with the Lord (vv. 5–7)
5 Blessed are those whose strength is in you,
    who have set their hearts on pilgrimage.
6 As they pass through the Valley of Baca,
    they make it a place of springs;
    the autumn rains also cover it with pools.
7 They go from strength to strength,
    till each appears before God in Zion.

II. Prayer for the king (vv. 8–9)
8 Hear my prayer, O LORD God Almighty;
    listen to me, O God of Jacob.   *Selah*
9 Look upon our shield, O God;
    look with favor on your anointed one.

---

[1]The NIV text has been arranged according to its literary structure,
with heads and subheads added.

III. God is with all who are faithful to him (vv. 10–12)

A. One day with God is greater than an eternity of wickedness (v. 10)

10 Better is one day in your courts
than a thousand elsewhere;
I would rather be a doorkeeper in the house of my God
than dwell in the tents of the wicked.

B. The Lord gives favor and blessing to those who follow him (vv. 11–12)

11 For the Lᴏʀᴅ God is a sun and shield;
the Lᴏʀᴅ bestows favor and honor;
no good thing does he withhold
from those whose walk is blameless.
12 O Lᴏʀᴅ Almighty,
blessed is the man who trusts in you. (ɴɪᴠ)

Introduction to Psalm 84—Genre, Dating, Parallels

Psalm 84 is located in Book III of the Psalter (Psalms 73–89) as a Korahite psalm. The author of Psalm 84 is an unknown Israelite who takes a pilgrimage to Zion for a fall festival (based on the reference to autumn rain in v. 6). This psalm is a song of Zion in that it expresses the psalmist's desire to seek God both in the temple, which was located on Mount Zion in Jerusalem, and on his pilgrimage to Zion. On his journey to the temple, the psalmist discovers that God dwells not only in the temple, but also with those who walk with him, and he blesses those who are obedient. This psalm thus expresses a subtle transition in the psalmist's faith and in his ideas of the presence of God outside the temple.

This psalm is clearly a Zion song according to its topic, but some think it is also in the genre of a hymn. It is not like most hymns, though, because it does not include an explicit call to praise and a reason for praise, but rather it seems that the reason for praise encompasses the entire psalm. According to Sigmund Mowinckel, "Yahweh may also be praised more indirectly, by exalting all that belongs to him."[2]

There is some discussion of the dating of this psalm, but nothing has been conclusive. Artur Weiser, A. F. Kirkpatrick, and Hans-Joachim Kraus all support the dating of this psalm as preexilic,

---

[2]Sigmund Mowinckel, *The Psalms in Israel's Worship* (Grand Rapids: Eerdmans, 2004), 88.

or during the period of the monarchy.[3] However, Erhard S. Gerstenberger supports a postexilic dating of the psalm,[4] and Marvin E. Tate seems to suggest the possibility of a postexilic date as well.[5] Gerstenberger's argument is based on the idea that an individual's relationship with God, as found in this psalm, was not a common theme during the monarchial period, when the community was the focus. Because the dating of this psalm is uncertain, this paper focuses more on literary analysis of Psalm 84.

There are several psalms that are in some way similar to Psalm 84, whether in the feelings they express, the terms and names for God they use, or the way that they speak of Zion. Psalm 46 is similar to Psalm 84 in that it too is a Korahite psalm, a psalm that speaks of the city of God and the place where God dwells (46:4), and it also addresses God using the same name that is found four times in Psalm 84: "Lord of hosts" (46:7, 11). Psalm 48 is also similar; it references Zion specifically three times (vv. 2, 11, 12) and uses the name "Lord of hosts" in v. 8. Psalm 48:9 also specifically mentions the temple.

Psalm 27 is similar to Psalm 84 in its ideas rather than its phraseology. Psalm 27 speaks of a psalmist's desire to be near God, specifically his wanting to "dwell in the house of the Lord" (v. 4), which is the same idea portrayed in Psalm 84. Psalm 42, although in the lament genre, initially speaks of a longing to be with God, and calls God the "living God" in v. 2, as Psalm 84 does in v. 2. Both of these psalms present, in some way, a desire to be near God, using a range of language and techniques to present the basic idea of seeking the Lord.

Literary Structure of the Psalm

Psalm 84 may be broken down into three major sections—two larger units with a smaller transitional section between them. The first major section of the psalm consists of vv. 1–7 and expresses the psalmist's longing to be with God. This section begins by

---

[3] Artur Weiser, *The Psalms* (trans. Herbert Hartwell; Old Testament Library; Philadelphia: Westminster, 1962), 566; A. F. Kirkpatrick, *The Book of Psalms* (1902; repr., Cambridge: Cambridge University Press, 1906), 504; Hans-Joachim Kraus, *Psalms 60–150: A Continental Commentary* (trans. Hilton C. Oswald; Minneapolis: Fortress, 1989), 167.

[4] Erhard S. Gerstenberger, *Psalms, Part 2, and Lamentations* (Forms of Old Testament Literature; Grand Rapids: Eerdmans, 2001), 126.

[5] Marvin E. Tate, *Psalms 51–100* (Word Biblical Commentary 20; Nashville: Thomas Nelson, 1990), 256.

describing the psalmist's yearning to be with God in his temple (vv. 1–4) and concludes with a description of his journey to Zion to be with the Lord (vv. 5–7). The second main section of the psalm is found in vv. 8–9 and consists of a prayer for the king. This section may well deal with the psalmist's entrance into the temple for a festival, where prayers would have been lifted up for the king, the "anointed one" of God (Psalm 84:9). The final main section of Psalm 84 includes vv. 10–12 and develops the theme that God's presence remains with those who are obedient and faithful. Throughout the psalm, there is a constant theme of the presence of God: in the psalmist's yearning for the temple, in his pilgrimage to the temple, and in his awareness of God's blessing on the righteous.

The following overview of the psalm's literary structure is drawn from the presentation of the text at the beginning of this paper:

I. Longing to Be with the Lord (vv. 1–7)
    A. Yearning to be with God in his temple (vv. 1–4)
        1. Individual desire to be in God's temple (vv. 1–2)
        2. All creatures have a place in God's temple (v. 3)
        3. All who dwell in God's temple are blessed (v. 4)
    B. Journeying to Zion to be with the Lord (vv. 5–7)

II. Prayer for the king (vv. 8–9)

III. God is with all who are faithful to him (vv. 10–12)
    A. One day with God is greater than an eternity of wickedness (v. 10)
    B. The Lord gives favor and blessing to those who follow him (vv. 11–12)

Detailed Analysis

Longing to be with the Lord (vv. 1–7)

Yearning to be with God in his temple (vv. 1–4)

Verse 1 begins by speaking of how wonderful God's temple is, here called his "dwelling place." This verse is the first of four times that the name "Lord Almighty" is used, according to the NIV. This name is more literally rendered "Lord of hosts," although it was changed from "Lord of hosts" to "Lord Almighty" by the NIV Committee on Bible Translation. According to the preface of the NIV, because the phrases "the Lord of hosts" and "God of hosts" have little meaning to contemporary readers, the Committee chose to use "Almighty," since it conveys an idea basically equivalent to "he who is sovereign over all the 'hosts' (powers) in heaven and on earth."[6] The term "hosts" is also a term used in the Old Testament to refer to the "cosmic army that fights on God's behalf to ensure an Israelite victory in battle."[7] However we translate this distinctive name for God, it is found four times in Psalm 84, in vv. 1, 3, 8, and 12.

It is important to note that this name of God is typically used in the Old Testament in association with the ark of the covenant. For example, 1 Samuel 4:4 says, "So the people sent to Shiloh, and brought from there the ark of the covenant of the LORD of hosts, who is enthroned on the cherubim" (NRSV). The ark was believed to "represent God's presence . . . and was virtually synonymous with the deity."[8] The Israelites brought the ark with them wherever they moved, and it was believed that God dwelled where the ark was. Naturally, in the times of the tabernacle and the temple, the ark was kept in the holy of holies, or the most holy place, and that is where God was believed to have dwelled. This entire psalm is about God's presence and a longing to be near God, so it is fitting that "LORD of hosts" or "LORD Almighty" is used, since this name suggests God's presence.

In v. 2 of the psalm, the words "soul," "heart," and "flesh" are all used, "marking the whole man, with every faculty and affection."[9] The psalmist is longing for God not with just one part of himself, but with the entirety of his being. The term "living God" is used only twice in the book of Psalms, although it is used throughout the rest of the Bible rather commonly. It is found in the Psalms in this verse, 84:2, and also in Psalm 42:2. In v. 2 of our psalm we also see the transition in the psalmist's thought: first, he desires the courts of the Lord, presumably in the temple, and in the second part of the verse he desires the living God, without making reference to where God might be. This is the beginning of the psalmist's shift in his understanding of the presence of God, which is developed more fully during later verses of the psalm.

---

[6] The Committee on Bible Translation, "Preface to the NIV Bible," n.p. [cited 2 December 2007]. Online: http://www.hissheep.org/kjv/preface_to_the_niv_bible.html.

[7] Susan Ackerman, "Ark of the Covenant," *Eerdmans Dictionary of the Bible* (ed. David Noel Freedman; Grand Rapids: Eerdmans, 2000), 103.

[8] Ackerman, "Ark," 102.

[9] J. J. Stewart Perowne, *The Book of Psalms* (2 vols.; 1878; repr., Grand Rapids: Zondervan, 1966), 2:117.

Verse 3 no longer speaks of the psalmist's desires as an individual to be with God as vv. 1 and 2 do, but rather speaks of the other creatures who find their place in the house of God. This beautiful figurative language is used to suggest a feeling of safety that the birds have in building nests to protect their young near the altars of the Lord. Artur Weiser states that the "seeking soul of the psalmist has found a home and rest where he knows himself to be safe under God's protection like the bird in the nest."[10] Joseph Addison Alexander portrays the language slightly differently, suggesting that the psalmist, on his journey, will have no place to rest, and that the "sparrow and the swallow [are] emblems of the worshipper himself" and that the psalmist longs for "a resting-place, a home" for himself in the same way that the birds have found a place to rest in the temple.[11] Either way, the verse seems to depict an understanding by the psalmist that if even some of the smallest of creatures (the birds) can find a resting place in the temple, then surely there will be room for him to rest in God's house as well.

In v. 3, the intensity of the personal relationship the psalmist seems to have with God is portrayed through the use of specific possessive pronouns. The use of the word "my" twice in this verse represents the idea that the psalmist has an intimate relationship with God; it is not only a communal relationship, suggesting that this is just the God that all people worship, but that this is *his* God, whom he knows and longs to know in a greater way with every moment. In v. 4, the characters then change again, and the psalmist references those who "dwell in [God's] house," that is, the priests of the temple.[12] The psalmist believes that the priests are truly blessed, because they are able to spend every moment praising God, as he wishes to do.

Journeying to Zion to be with the Lord (vv. 5–7)

Verses 5–7 describe the psalmist's pilgrimage to the temple. The psalmist seems to long for the "devout experience of a pilgrimage,"[13] hoping that he might be called blessed along with all of the others who find strength in God when they "set their hearts on pilgrimage" (v. 5). Verse 6 presents a few specific details of the journey, noting that those on pilgrimage "pass through the Valley of Baca,"

---

[10] Weiser, *The Psalms*, 567.
[11] Joseph Addison Alexander, *The Psalms: Translated and Explained* (Grand Rapids: Baker, 1977), 355–56.
[12] Kirkpatrick, *The Book of Psalms*, 506.
[13] Weiser, *The Psalms*, 567.

where the autumn rains cover the ground. The "Valley of Baca" is a greatly disputed name. Many interpret it to be a fictional place, or a metaphor, saying that it should be translated as a "valley of weeping."[14] If it is interpreted this way, then whatever the region they are traveling through, it is one of great strife, and one that does not bring joy. However, another way of interpreting it suggests that the word "Baca" is the name for a type of balsam tree, which would grow in a dry area.[15] This would make sense with the rest of the verse, where the rain makes the land a "place of springs"; if it had been dry before, the rain would have been a blessing. The rain can be considered a symbol for the blessings that God provides along the difficult road.[16] The rains are also given a specific season, being labeled "autumn rains" in this same verse, which helps to explain the timing of the pilgrimage. If the rains came in the autumn, then the psalmist was probably on his way to a fall festival. The fall festival cycle contained festivals that would celebrate God as the divine king[17] and also petition for the earthly king (as is found in vv. 8 and 9).

In v. 7, the phrase "strength to strength" is not an easily understood one, because the Hebrew in this verse is "vague,"[18] but it is usually understood as suggesting that the psalmist gains strength from God on his journey to the temple,[19] taking in all the blessings that he receives along the way. One translation suggests that the phrase might even be interpreted as denoting "geographical locations, like forts along the highway,"[20] but this is highly unlikely considering that there are other possible metaphorical ideas in the psalm, such as the birds in v. 3 and the Valley of Baca in v. 6. This phrase can thus be considered as referring merely to the strength which the psalmist gains from God on his journey, giving him the energy to carry on until he is renewed again. It is in this section, vv. 5–7, that further transition in the psalmist's way of thinking is evident. If the idea of rain is metaphorical, suggesting blessings from God, and the meaning of "strength to strength" is that God renews the strength of the travelers on their journey, then the psalmist understands that God is with them when they

---

[14] Tate, *Psalms 51–100,* 359.

[15] Kirkpatrick, *The Book of Psalms,* 507.

[16] Tate, *Psalms 51–100,* 359–60.

[17] Bernard W. Anderson, with Stephen Bishop, *Out of the Depths* (3d ed.; Louisville: Westminster John Knox, 2000), 157–58.

[18] Schaefer, *Psalms,* 207.

[19] Weiser, *The Psalms,* 568.

[20] Schaefer, *Psalms,* 207.

travel as well, rather than just being in the temple. However, the psalmist does maintain his belief that God dwells in the temple, because v. 7 states, "till each appears before God in Zion."

Prayer for the king (vv. 8–9)

Verses 8 and 9 contain a petition for the king. Because the festival probably celebrated God as king (see v. 3), it makes sense that there would be prayer for the earthly king, who was considered the "extended arm of Yahweh" on earth.[21] The earthly king is considered the "anointed one" of God (v. 9). The king is called the "shield" in this passage, which is a common metaphor for both God and the king. The king is called the "shield" also in Psalm 89:18, which says, "Indeed, our shield belongs to the LORD, our king to the Holy One of Israel" (NIV). The basis for this term applied to the king is that he is the earthly "protector" of the Israelites, and of the temple. It is, therefore, proper that the people offer a petition on his behalf in this section of the psalm.[22]

God is with all who are faithful to him (vv. 10–12)

One day with God is greater than an eternity of wickedness (v. 10)

Verse 10 is a comparison of a life in God's presence and a life of wickedness. With the exaggerated suggestion that *one day* with God is better than *one thousand days* elsewhere, the psalmist is showing just how important his relationship with God is: even a moment in God's presence is better than great lengths of time anywhere else. This statement is continued in the second half of the verse with the opposed ideas of living in humility and living a comfortable life. One commentary says that the psalmist is basically saying, "I had rather perform the humblest service at the temple of Him who tolerates no evil than be entertained as a guest where wickedness makes its home."[23] The psalmist would rather stand on the doorstep, not even *inside* the temple, just to be anywhere near his Lord, than live comfortably in a life of wickedness. This verse is an extremely powerful statement of faith.

The Lord gives favor and blessing to those who follow him (vv. 11–12)

In the final verses of this psalm, the psalmist speaks of his new understanding of God's presence. The psalmist finally comes to the

---

[21] Tate, *Psalms 51–100*, 360.

[22] Schaefer, *Psalms*, 208.

[23] Kirkpatrick, *The Book of Psalms*, 509.

understanding that God blesses those who are obedient and walk with him, even when they are not in the temple. Verse 11 names God as a "sun and shield." God is a shield because he is the king, as the psalmist names him in v. 3; he is the ultimate protector of his people. God is frequently referred to as a shield in the book of Psalms, for example, 3:3, 18:2, and 28:7. However, God as a "sun" is not a common metaphor in the Bible. Malachi 4:2 says, "But for you who revere my name, the sun of righteousness will rise with healing in its wings." This is the only other reference to God as a "sun."[24] It is generally taken to mean that God provides light and guidance for his people. Konrad Schaefer claims that God envisioned as a combination of the "sun and shield" (v. 11) "bespeaks glorious light and reliable protection."[25] God is elsewhere referred to as a "light" for his people, as in Psalm 27:1, which says, "The LORD is my light and my salvation—whom shall I fear?"[26] The idea of God as a sun or a light could suggest that he provides guidance, as though on a dark path, while the psalmist is on pilgrimage. The ideas of God as light and protector (sun and shield) are simply more ways for the psalmist to name and praise God whom he has experienced on the journey.

The psalmist continues in v. 11 by claiming that God does not keep anything "from those whose walk is blameless," that the Lord "bestows favor and honor" upon them. Marvin Tate claims that the idea of *walking* is a "positive double entendre," speaking about those who travel on pilgrimage and those who live "with obedience and faith in the way of Yahweh."[27] This idea that God blesses both those who walk on pilgrimage and those who "walk" in his ways is a positive one that finalizes the psalmist's understanding of God and how he works. For all those who obey—whether or not they are in the temple—God provides blessing, favor, and honor; therefore, according to v. 12, "blessed is the man who trusts in" this God.

Synthesis

The psalmist in Psalm 84 begins with great longing to be with God where he dwells, in his temple, and completes the psalm with a new understanding that God provides for and remains with all who walk in his ways. The psalmist, who has an intimate relationship with and fierce love for God in the beginning of the psalm,

---

[24] Tate, *Psalms 51–100*, 361.
[25] Shaefer, *Psalms*, 207.
[26] Alexander, *The Psalms*, 358.
[27] Tate, *Psalms 51–100*, 360–61.

gains great insight and truly matures in his knowledge of the Lord. It is through a difficult pilgrimage to a festival celebrating God as king that this psalmist grows in his faith, showing that each obedient step taken in following God's path will bring greater understanding of life, and the presence of the Lord of hosts himself.

Reflection

The psalmist has traveled on a great and possibly dangerous journey to arrive at the temple, in order that he might spend just one day with his Lord and King. Along his journey, the psalmist discovers that his God remains with him all the time, rather than dwelling only in the temple. This is the understanding that present-day Christians also maintain: those who trust in God can be assured of his presence with them in every place, every situation, and every moment of life. Believers in Old Testament times sometimes held to the belief that God dwelt only in the temple. The psalmist in Psalm 84, therefore, was ahead of his time in his understanding of God's presence. Many Christians today, however, confess with their lips that God is "always there," but still live as if special times of prayer and worship (equivalent to sacrifice in the temple) somehow bring us nearer to God's face than the daily walk of obedience and faithfulness. Christians today should therefore take v. 10 to heart: "Better is one day in your courts than a thousand elsewhere; I would rather be a doorkeeper in the house of my God than dwell in the tents of the wicked." The contrast is not between being with God in some "sacred" place and life in the so-called secular world. Rather, the contrast is between faithfulness—which is accompanied by God's presence—and wickedness. Believers thus need to heed v. 10 and live with the same longing and desire to know God that the author of Psalm 84 had.

Works Cited

Ackerman, Susan. "Ark of the Covenant." Pages 102–3 in *Eerdmans Dictionary of the Bible*. Edited by David Noel Freedman. Grand Rapids: Eerdmans, 2000.

Alexander, Joseph Addison. *The Psalms: Translated and Explained*. Grand Rapids: Baker, 1977.

Anderson, Bernhard W., with Stephen Bishop. *Out of the Depths: The Psalms Speak for Us Today*. 3d ed. Louisville: Westminster John Knox, 2000.

Committee on Bible Translation. "Preface to the NIV Bible." No pages. Cited 2 December 2007. Online: http://www.hissheep. org/kjv/preface_to_the_niv_bible.html.

Gerstenberger, Erhard S. *Psalms, Part 2, and Lamentations.* Forms of Old Testament Literature. Grand Rapids: Eerdmans, 2001.

Kirkpatrick, A. F. *The Book of Psalms.* 1902. Repr., Cambridge: Cambridge University Press, 1906.

Kraus, Hans-Joachim. *Psalms 60–150: A Continental Commentary.* Translated by Hilton C. Oswald. Minneapolis: Fortress, 1989.

Mowinckel, Sigmund. *The Psalms in Israel's Worship.* Grand Rapids: Eerdmans, 2004.

Perowne, J. J. Stewart. *The Book of Psalms.* Vol. 2. 1878; repr., Grand Rapids: Zondervan, 1966.

Schaefer, Konrad. *Psalms.* Berit Olam. Collegeville: Liturgical, 2001.

Tate, Marvin E. *Psalms 51–100.* Word Biblical Commentary 20. Nashville: Thomas Nelson, 1990.

Weiser, Artur. *The Psalms: A Commentary.* Translated by Herbert Hartwell. Old Testament Library. Philadelphia: Westminster, 1962.

Selected Internet Resources for Biblical Studies

The technology of the day has affected the reading, study, and distribution of the Bible since the time of its writing. In our own era the advent of the Internet has made many resources for biblical study available online. As in every other field of study, the quality of those online resources varies considerably even as the quantity seems to grow exponentially. Listed below are a few Internet sites that seem to have established themselves as reliable, multipurpose online resources by virtue of their being produced or hosted by educational or other scholarly institutions, recognized scholars working independently, or reputable religious bodies. The focus here is on sites where the biblical text is available and on "gateways," or sites with links to other resources.[1]

The Bible Online

Many searchable versions of the Bible (KJV, NIV, NASB, NLT, TNIV, and more, including other languages) may be found at http://www.biblegateway.com.

The GNB, KJV, NASB, NIV, NLT, NRSV, RSV, and others may be found at this useful, though not scholarly, site: http://www.crosswalk.com.

Biola University runs a site with the KJV, NASB, NRSV, Greek NT, Hebrew text, and more (including versions in many languages), displaying up to four versions in parallel columns: http://unbound.biola.edu.

The NAB may be found at http://www.nccbuscc.org/nab/bible.

---

[1]All sites were verified and the list updated in August 2008.

Free software for Bible study on PCs, Macs, Pocket PCs, and Palm systems is available for the KJV, ASV, and other translations, as well as *Strong's Concordance,* and more from the Online Bible: http://www.onlinebible.net.

The NRSV is available at http://bible.oremus.org and http://www .devotions.net/bible/00bible.htm, and the KJV may also be found at the former.

The NET Bible, including extensive translation notes, is available at http://www.bible.org/netbible/index.htm.

The Divinity School at Vanderbilt has constructed a site containing the NRSV texts for all Sundays of the three-year common lectionary: http://divinity.library.vanderbilt.edu/lectionary.

Books Online

Many Internet users have already discovered that Amazon.com and other vendors have part or all of the text of some of their books online. But the premier site for books online is Google Book Search, found at http://books.google.com. It is both a powerful search engine and a collection of books at one place.

Gateways to Resources

A gateway is an Internet site with links to other sites. Among the most important of these for biblical studies are the following.

The "All-in-One Biblical Resources Search," produced by Professor Mark Goodacre of Duke University, includes excellent links to Bible texts and resources, most of which can be searched from Goodacre's site: http://www.ntgateway.com/multibib.

The New Testament Gateway, and the Greek New Testament Gateway, also produced by Professor Mark Goodacre of Duke University, provide regularly updated, annotated links to many good academic NT web resources: http://www.ntgateway.com and http://www.ntgateway.com/greek.

The Old Testament Gateway, an academic site based at Tabor College, Victoria, Australia, is modeled on Professor Mark Goodacre's NT site: http://www.otgateway.com.

Tyndale House in Cambridge, England, maintains a blogsite on electronic resources for biblical studies that includes a sidebar with several gateway-type links to "Online Resources": http://tabs-online.com/Tyndale/TTech/index.htm.

Professor Torrey Seland, of the School of Mission and Theology in Stavanger, Norway, operates a site that focuses on the early Christian writings and their social world, with many links to texts, electronically published scholarly work, and more: http://www.torreys.org/bible.

Professor Felix Just, Director of Biblical Education at Loyola Institute for Spirituality, maintains a helpful site that, despite its address, is not just for Catholics: http://catholic-resources.org; the most relevant part of the site is "E.N.T.E.R.," or "Electronic New Testament Educational Resources": http://catholic-resources.org/Bible/index.html.

The Faculty of Religious Studies at McGill University in Canada also has a page of links for "Bibles and Biblical Studies": www.mcgill.ca/religiousstudies/online-resources/subject/bibles.

A site mentioned above includes not only versions of the Bible but also links to other resources: http://www.biblegateway.com/resources.

The Society of Biblical Literature has a section of its site devoted to electronic resources for biblical studies: http://sbl-site.org/educational/researchtools.aspx.

The Wabash Center annotated Internet Guide to Religion, at Wabash College, including links to sites on Bible and archaeology, may be found at: http://www.wabashcenter.wabash.edu/resources/guide_headings.aspx.

The Text this Week, run by Jenee Woodard since 1998, is an excellent gateway for resources related to exegesis and preaching, including scholarly articles, sermons, art work, and more; in her words, "a virtual study desk for students, teachers and preachers": http://www.textweek.com.

The unofficial webpage of the Catholic Biblical Association's Computer Committee contains links to scholarly societies, websites maintained by biblical scholars, Bible software companies, and resources for biblical studies: http://www.cbacomputercommittee .org.

The Perseus Project at Tufts University permits access to searchable ancient Greek and Latin texts and to the Liddell-Scott-Jones lexicon of classical Greek: http://www.perseus.tufts. edu/cache/perscoll_Greco-Roman.html. LSJ lexicon: http://www .perseus.tufts.edu/cgi-bin/resolveform.

The Yale University Divinity School library hosts the Bible Reference Tools Tutorial, a site about finding and using tools for exegesis: http://library.yale.edu/div/tutframe.htm.

Journals

Some journals that are available in print versions are, or will be, available also online, either by subscription or at no charge. In addition, a growing number of electronic journals can be expected.

The following pages provide links to online journals:

http://www.atla.com/products/titles/titles_atlas.html

http://www.ntgateway.com/journals.htm

http://www.torreys.org/bible/biblia02.html#journals

Some of the biblical journals with full articles online include:

Biblica, the electronic version of the journal of the same name: http://www.bsw.org/project/biblica

The Journal for the Study of Rhetorical Criticism of the New Testament: http://www.rhetjournal.net

The Journal of Biblical Literature: http://www.sbl-site.org/publications/ journals_jbl_noLogin.aspx

The Journal of Biblical Studies: http://www.journalofbiblicalstudies .org

Word and World: Theology for Christian Ministry: http://www.luthersem
.edu/word&world

The *Review of Biblical Literature,* an online journal of book reviews published by the Society of Biblical Literature, offers free
subscriptions: http://bookreviews.org

Popular articles by scholars from the print magazine *Bible Review* may be found at http://members.bib-arch.org/publication
.asp?PubID=BSBR, and from its sister publication, *Biblical Archaeology Review,* at http://www.bib-arch.org/bar/

See also the list of journals in chapter 11, section 6, "Resources
for Detailed Analysis."

Websites and Blogs

One relatively new, and perhaps unexpected, resource for serious biblical study and research is the growing body of individual
scholars' websites and especially blogs. Websites sometimes contain links to articles or podcasts of a scholar's lectures or other
presentations. One especially popular site is the (unofficial but
very well done) website of the Anglican bishop and biblical theologian N. T. Wright: http://ntwrightpage.com.

Blogs by graduate students and professional biblical scholars provide some of their most current thinking on topics, often reveal-
ing the major points of a scholar's forthcoming article or book
and giving opportunity for immediate reaction by others. Such
blogs also often summarize scholarly conferences, announce new
books or electronic resources, and generally furnish helpful, up-
to-date information for students and scholars.

The best way to find such sites is to begin with one and follow the
links (sometimes called the "blogroll") to other sites. Among the
many scholarly blogs, one of the most useful—because it regularly has comments about and links to many others—is NT Gateway Weblog, the blogsite of Duke's Professor Mark Goodacre (see
above under gateways to resources): http://ntgateway.com/weblog.

Index